Deconstructing Derrida

Deconstructing Derrida

Tasks for the New Humanities

Edited by
Peter Pericles Trifonas and Michael A. Peters

DECONSTRUCTING DERRIDA

First published in 2005 by
PALGRAVE MACMILLAN™
175 Fifth Avenue, New York, N.Y. 10010 and
Houndmills, Basingstoke, Hampshire, England RG21 6XS
Companies and representatives throughout the world.

PALGRAVE MACMILLAN is the global academic imprint of the Palgrave Macmillan division of St. Martin's Press, LLC and of Palgrave Macmillan Ltd. Macmillan® is a registered trademark in the United States, United Kingdom and other countries. Palgrave is a registered trademark in the European Union and other countries.

ISBN 0–312–29609–6 (hardcover)
ISBN 0–312–29611–8 (paperback)

Library of Congress Cataloging-in-Publication Data

    Deconstructing Derrida : tasks for the new humanities / edited by Peter Pericles Trifonas and Michael A. Peters.
      p. cm.
    Includes bibliographical references and index.
    ISBN 0–312–29609–6 (hardcover)—ISBN 0–312–29611–8 (pbk.)
    1. Derrida, Jacques. 2. Humanities. I. Trifonas, Peter Pericles, 1960– II. Peters, Michael A.

B2430.D484D38 2005
194—dc22   2004060111

A catalogue record for this book is available from the British Library.

Design by Newgen Imaging Systems (P) Ltd., Chennai, India.

First edition: November 2005

10 9 8 7 6 5 4 3 2 1

Printed in the United States of America.

CONTENTS

INTRODUCTION

The Humanities in Deconstruction

MICHAEL A. PETERS AND
PETER PERICLES TRIFONAS

To the discovery of the outward world the Renaissance added a still greater achievement, by first discerning and bringing to light the full, whole nature of man. This period . . . first gave the highest development to individuality, and then led the individual to the most zealous and thorough study of himself in all forms and under all conditions. Indeed, the development of personality is essentially involved in the recognition of it in oneself and in others. Between these two great processes our narrative has placed the influence of ancient literature because the mode of conceiving and representing both the individual and human nature in general was defined and colored by that influence. But the power of conception and representation lay in the age and in the people.

Jacob Burckhardt, *The Civilization of the Renaissance in Italy*

Burckhardt's extraordinary essay published in an edition of 1,000 copies was hard to sell and he received no royalties. Nietzsche, who joined Burckhardt at the University of Basel in 1868, greatly admired the work, although they were never friends. It was one of the few *modern* books Nietzsche recommended. Burckhardt, a conservative antimodernist, emphasized the individual person as the starting point of historical study. For Burckhardt history provided the means to study the relation of contemporary culture to the cultures of the past, and in *The Civilization of the Renaissance in Italy* he registers the different ways in which the Renaissance first gave the highest value to individuality. He believed that the early signs of "the modern European Spirit" could be seen in Florence. It was a historical vantage point for him to observe the declining fate of the individual who had become increasingly domesticated and commodified in modern society, thus dimming the creative energies that had first come to fruition in ancient Greece and were rediscovered and extended during the Renaissance. He saw the rise of capitalism, self-interest, and national wars and warned of the coming struggle between freedom and the all-powerful State. Yet though a humanist in the old sense of the word, he was not an idealist in his descriptions of Greek civilization, demonstrating how Athenians were victims of their democracy.

Burckhardt strongly influenced Nietzsche demonstrating a philosophy of history that portrayed "man" as a historical construction, even though he came to praise humanism through his historical excavations. They shared a similar interpretation of classical Greek culture and Burckhardt also anticipated important themes in Nietzsche's work, including the concept of the overman who realized his own unique individuality. Nietzsche, inspired by Burckhardt's method, and his concept of the State as a work of art, applied his insights to the genealogy of values, of philosophy, knowledge, and man in a way that radically called into question the premises of the modern age, including its free-floating Cartesian–Kantian rationally autonomous sovereign subject.

In the essay "Expeditions of an untimely man" (*Twilight of the Idols*), Nietzsche writes a section titled "Criticism of modernity," beginning with the words:

> Our institutions are no longer fit for anything: Everyone is unanimous about that. But the fault lies not with them but in *us*. Having lost all instincts out of which institutions grow, we are losing the institutions themselves, because *we* are no longer fit for them. . . . For institutions to exist there must exist the kind of will, instinct, imperative which is anti-liberal to the point of malice: The will to tradition, to authority, to centuries-long responsibility, to *solidarity* between succeeding generations backwards and forwards *in infinitum* . . . The entire West has lost those instincts out of which institutions grow, out of which the future grows: Perhaps nothing goes so much against the grain of its "modern" spirit as this. One lives for today, one lives very fast—one lives very irresponsibly: It is precisely this one calls "freedom" (1968, orig. 1888, pp. 93–94).

In passages like the one presented here in *Twilight of the Idols*, and in *Beyond Good and Evil* and *The Will to Power*, Nietzsche identifies the break with tradition as the defining feature of modernity, and underscores its accompanying recognition that the sources of its values can no longer be based upon appeals to the authority of the past. Modernity, understood as a break with the past—an aesthetic, political, and epistemological break, encourages a self-consciousness of the present and an orientation to the future based on notions of change, progress, experiment, innovation, and newness. Most importantly modernity involves the myth it constructs about itself—that it is somehow able to create its own values and normative orientations out of its own historical force, movement, and trajectory. Nietzsche rejects any simple-minded opposition and refuses to embrace one option or the other unreservedly; rather, we might see him contemplating how and why "we moderns" want to draw up the historical stakes in terms of such an exhaustive dichotomy.

Heidegger takes up Nietzsche's legacy and his critique of modernity in various ways. The Italian philosopher Ernesto Grassi (1983: p. 9), who was the first to publish Heidegger's *Letter on Humanism* in 1947,[1] defines Humanism as "that philosophical movement which characterized thought in Italy from the second half of the fourteenth century to the final third of the fifteenth century." In his view it was Ficino's translation of Plato at the end of the fifteenth century, which led to a speculative Platonism and Neo-Platonism, that broke with the Humanist approach to philosophy. As he also suggests:

> From the beginning of the study of Humanism a century ago, with Burckhardt and Voigt, to Cassirer, Gentile, and Garin, scholars have seen the essence of Humanism in the rediscovery of man and his immanent values (Grassi, 1983, p. 17).

It was this notion of Humanism as a naive anthropomorphism, as Grassi points out, that Martin Heidegger was at pains to expose, especially the traditional interpretation of Humanism, "either as a new affirmation of man and, therefore, as an anthropology involving particular epistemological problems [Ernst Cassirer], or as a renewal of Platonism or Neo-Platonism and so of Western metaphysics [Paul Oskar Kristeller]" (p. 31).[2]

Heidegger's famous essay responds to all forms of humanism—the first humanism, which he christens as Roman, and both forms of Renaissance and Enlightenment humanisms, though he does not make this distinction. As he famously argues,

> Every humanism is either grounded in metaphysics or is itself made to be the ground of one. Every determination of the essence of man that already presupposes an interpretation of beings without asking

about the truth of Being, whether knowingly or not, is metaphysical (Heidegger, 1996, pp. 225–226).

Heidegger's *Letter* is a necessary preliminary to understanding Jacques Derrida's "humanism"—his engagement with and deconstruction of the humanist subject—and his recasting of the "new humanities" without a naive anthropology at the center. Derrida is, perhaps, the foremost philosopher of the humanities and of its place in the university. Over the long period of his career he has been concerned with the fate, status, place, and contribution of the humanities. Through his deconstructive readings and writings he has done much not only to reinvent the Western tradition by attending closely to the texts that constitute it, but has also redefined its procedures and protocols, questioning and commenting upon the relationship between commentary and interpretation, the practice of quotation, the delimitation of a work and its singularity, its signature, and its context—the whole form of life of literary culture, together with textual practices and conventions that shape it. From his very early work on he has occupied a marginal in-between space—simultaneously, textual, literary, philosophical, and political—one that permitted him freedom to question, to speculate, and to draw new limits to *humanitas*. In a way that few before him have done, with, perhaps, the exception of Heidegger, Derrida has demonstrated his power to reconceptualize and reimagine the humanities in the space of the contemporary university.

Mindful of Nietzsche's critique of modernity, post-Nietzschean philosophy of the university developed along two interrelated lines. The first, pursued by Weber and continued by Heidegger, Jaspers, Lyotard, and Bourdieu, emphasized the dangers of economic interest vested in the university through the dominance of *technical* reason. The second, initiated by members of the Frankfurt School and developed differently by Foucault, traces the imprint and controlling influence of the state in the academy through the apparatus of *administrative* reason. Jacques Derrida, in novel and unexpected ways, has contributed to both lines of inquiry. He has done something different by engaging in a deconstructive analysis that is both affirmative and utopian. He has pointed toward the university to come and the future of the professions within a place of resistance, and has yet maintained the historical link to the two ideas that mediate and condition both the humanities and the performative structure of acts of profession: Human rights and crimes against humanity. Derrida maintains that the "modern university should be unconditional," by which he means that it should have the "freedom" to assert, to question, to profess, and to "say everything" in the manner of a literary fiction.

Yet this play, these deconstructive moves within the language game, needs to be understanding within Derrida's broader vision.

How does one represent Derrida and his writing? The linguistic notion of representation is central to Derrida's work and to his critique of Western metaphysics. He is suspicious of the view that language represents the world, at least in any straightforward sense. But "representation" is also important to him as a political principle indicating the ethical and political stakes in presenting an argument or characterizing a people, a text, an image, or (one's relation to) another thinker—the so-called politics of representation. Not least, the word representation captures his concerns for the genres of autobiography and confession, philosophy as a certain kind of writing, the "personal voice," and the signature. Derrida is also careful of journalists and tends to refuse most invitations for interviews, especially by the popular press. Paradoxically *Points . . . Interviews, 1974–1994*, a collection consisting of 23 interviews given over the course of the last two decades, provides a good introduction to Derrida (see especially his "The work of intellectuals and the press").

Jacques Derrida, a Frenchman of Jewish extraction who was born and grew up in Algeria, was undoubtedly one of the world's most distinguished contemporary philosophers of both the humanities and *humanitas*. As the Stanford University website (http://prelectur.stanford.edu/lecturers/derrida/) indicates his work has been the subject, in whole or part of, some 400 books and "In the areas of philosophy and literary criticism alone, Derrida has been cited more than 14,000 times in journal articles over the past 17 years." This proves that his work is well cited though not necessarily universally acclaimed or appreciated. Both conservatives and members of the radical left have fiercely attacked his work. The former deny he is a philosopher and the latter dismiss his work as frivolous and apolitical.

Perhaps more than any philosopher before him, and from his earliest beginnings, Jacques Derrida has called attention to the *form* of "philosophical discourse"—its "modes of composition, its rhetoric, its metaphors, its language, its fictions," as he says—not in order to assimilate philosophy to literature but rather to recognize the complex links between the two, and to investigate the ways in which the institutional authority of academic philosophy, and the autonomy it claims, rests upon a "disavowal with relation to its own language." (His doctoral thesis investigated "The ideality of the literary object.") The question of philosophical styles, he maintains, is itself a philosophical question.

"Deconstruction," the term most famously associated with Derrida, is a practice of reading and writing, a mode of analysis and criticism, which depends deeply on an interpretation of the question of style. Here Derrida follows a Nietzschean–Heideggerian line of thought, which repudiates Platonism as the source of all metaphysics in the West. Where Heidegger still sees in Nietzsche the last strands of an inverted Platonism, tied to the metaphysics of the *will to power*, and pictures himself as the first genuinely *post*-metaphysical thinker, Derrida, in his turn, while acknowledging his debt, detects in Heidegger's notion of Being a residual and nostalgic vestige of metaphysics. He agrees with Heidegger that the most important philosophical task is to break free from the "logocentrism" of Western philosophy—the self-presence, immediacy, and univocity—which clouds our view and manifests its nihilistic impulses in Western culture. And yet "breaking free" does not mean overcoming metaphysics. Deconstruction substitutes a critical practice focused upon texts for the ineffable or the inexpressible. It does so not by trying to escape the metaphysical character of language but by exposing and undermining it. Heidegger's strategy for getting beyond man will not do the trick: Derrida suggests that "a change of style" is needed, one that will "speak several languages and produce several texts at once," as he says in an early essay titled "The ends of man" (Derrida, 1982).

Toward the end of his essay "The future of the profession or the unconditional university (thanks to the 'Humanities,' What *Could* Take Place Tomorrow)," delivered during conferences at Stanford and Auckland Universities in 2000 and included as the opening essay in this collection, Jacques Derrida outlines seven programmatic theses or what he calls "seven professions of faith" for the new Humanities. Six of these theses, on the whole, are "reminders" or "recapitulations" whereas the seventh attempts to take a step beyond the others "toward the dimension of the *event*." Derrida (2000) suggests "The Humanities of tomorrow, in all their departments, will have to study their history, the history of the concepts that, by constructing them, instituted the disciplines and were coextensive with them" and he provides the list of his seven programmatic propositions.

This collection, spearheaded by Derrida's essay, engages the ethical ground of the Humanities and the pedagogy of its disciplines. It addresses the question of the future horizons of its disciplinarity after the closure of Western metaphysics and the subsequent destabilization of the fixed grounding of truth. It seeks to begin a discussion, after Jacques Derrida, about whether or not it is possible to expose or create within the university a location that still occupies the colonized space of the archive of Western knowledge we call "the Humanities" and is at the same time alterior to it.[3] The inside and outside borders of an Occidental psychography open up the material locations within which theory and praxis are

renewed through the syncretic nature of a mondialized subjectivity, as the product of a cosmopolitical, philosophical point of view. The ethics of deconstruction and its incursion into the conceptual ground of the Humanities focuses attention on the question of human rights and education to rethink the certainty of where and how[4] such a thinking "ought" to take place, as a philosophical project of genealogical excavation. Deconstruction is always already implicated in the perennial question of democracy and discipline, of pedagogy and the responsibility to acknowledge the difference of the Other. For Derrida the right to education and the question of the Humanities is articulated as the problem of protecting the right to a free expression of subjectivity and the alterity of human being. What constitutes the question of the epistemological archive of the Humanities is a question of privilege and social justice. Engaging the connections between culture and knowledge extends the problem of how rights are tied to the responsibilities and principles of education as the instauration of cultural capital relating to the formation and formativity subjectivity within academic institutions.

This collection is an expression of the desire to rethink the future of thinking within the Human Sciences. It is an invitation to work toward a genealogy of the cultural archive we call "the Humanities" by questioning the reason of their institutional ground with respect to the formation of subjectivity. Epistemological discourses engender a reason for founding institutions like the university. Since the eighteenth century, the idea of the modern university has promoted the ideal of a natural universalism of thought and action, uniting thinking and subjectivity in the image of the enlightened, global citizen. Human rights and difference are linked within the conception of the university as a "cosmopolitical institution" that levels alterity through a common epistemological archive.

The modern university immediately comes to mind as a "difference reduction machine" because of its constitutional commitments and formal configurations of the disciplines via "an assignable philosophical history"[5] that "impl[ies] sharing a culture and a philosophical language."[6] Insofar as "no experience in the present allows for an adequate grasp of that present, presentable totality of doctrine, of teachable theory," Derrida has read these idealist presuppositions of the conditions that spawn the university and the straining interrelations of the disciplines elsewhere before: "An institution—this is not merely a few walls or some outer structure surrounding, protecting, guaranteeing or restricting the freedom of our work; it is also and already the structure of our interpretation." The ethics of the foundation of that edifice of the university is what is being questioned here along with the responsibility to be taken for it, and who this "our"

does or *can* refer to exactly. This is not to aver, as Kant would have it, that philosophy—the faculty from which the "Great Model of the University" acquires the academic legitimacy of its ideal autonomy—is completely "outside" and "above" any hierachization of knowledge due to a "higher" responsibility it claims to answer for/to Reason and Truth. There is another side to it.[7] Concurrently philosophy (unlike other disciplines) would also need to be "inside" and "below" the structure of the institution, filling-out the reason of the lower ground on which its being stands. But what of the originary violence of a *faculty of Right*? Is the "mystical foundation of its authority" as a legislator of "Reason" and "Truth" for the university assuaged by an inverted mirroring of its stature? Could it be? And what would that mean for the Humanities?

Even if we choose to believe Kant, there is a minimal security, if any at all, to the tautological notion of "the essence of knowledge as knowledge of knowledge":[8] The stolid (meta-philosophical) ground of university autonomy has to have a responsibility to humanity. This ignorance has been "justified [Derrida stresses] by the axiom stating that scholars alone can judge other scholars."[9] But this still says nothing of academic responsibility to the human science. And by this we do not mean the obligation of the institution, a mere husk or shell, a clever figment of a living entity. It goes deeper. The responsibility we are speaking of is that of the teaching body (*le corps enseignant*), the soul of the university. There is no ambivalence about the threat resistance deconstruction poses to the reason of the university and its vision of a universal, epistemological subjectivity wrought from the metanarrative of its disciplinary archives and genealogy of exclusion. For some the analytical situation Derrida annotates, we could say "of deconstruction," is an equivocatory nonsense of self-cancellations, a being-on-both-sides of the issue, thereby betraying a lack of ethical or political resolve; for others its complexity consigns the "*coups nouveau*" of a *post*modern responsivity to an ineffectual rejection of the totality of what has come before in the hopes of improving what will come after. Few concerned will have no appraisement to offer. The gamut of judgments arising from within the general distinctions of perspective I have made begs the question of the "Other of Reason" within the construction of the Humanities depicted as "irrationality" without classifiably reducing the content or the *mal*content of arguments under the qualitative dichotomy of a "good" versus "bad" opposition. That is because deconstruction calls for an open obligation, an academic responsibility without conditions, of unlimited and unforeseen possibility: Deconstruction is of the order of rationality, but not of the metaphysical standards of

"critique." The immanent force of a deconstructive questioning succeeds in collapsing the oppositional logics of metaphysical self-substantiation, which excludes, *sui generis*, the relative independence of the subalterned voice of an overlooked middle. And this is where the politics and the ethics of the Humanities lies, within ontology and "first philosophy," in a philosophy of being. Submitting the university and the Humanities to the hermeneutical conundrum of their own logic *in-itself* and *for-itself* is a start toward interrogating the ground of their meaning, their historicity, possibilities, goals, and limits. Derrida reminds us that such a critique yields tensions commanding neither an obeyance to unforgiving precepts nor a rejection of them:

> The time of reflection is also the chance for turning back on the very conditions of reflection, in all the sense of that word, as if with the help of a new optical device one could finally see sight, could not only view the natural landscape, the city, the bridge and the abyss, but could view viewing. As if through an acoustical device one could hear hearing, in other words, seize the inaudible in a sort of poetic telephony. The time of reflection is also another time, it is heterogeneous with what it reflects and perhaps gives time for what calls for and is called thought.[10]

Notes

The epigraph to this chapter is drawn from Jacob Burckhardt (1945 orig. 1860), *The Civilization of the Renaissance in Italy* (Oxford and London: Phaidon Press), p. 184. An electronic version can be found at: http://www.boisestate.edu/courses/hy309/docs/burckhardt/burckhardt.html

1. See Grassi's (1983) comment on p. 49.
2. Grassi (1983: p. 29) argues, "Historically, we should note that Heidegger's definitions of Western thought—as rational deductive metaphysics which arise and unfolds exclusively from the problem of the relationship between beings and thought, i.e., in the framework of the question of logical truth—does not hold. In the Humanist tradition, there was always a central concern for the problem of the primacy of unhiddenness, openness, that in which historical 'being-there' can first appear."
3. Jacques Derrida (1994). "Of the humanities and the philosophical discipline: The right to philosophy and the cosmopolitical point of view." *Surfaces*, 4, 1.
4. Ibid., 1.
5. Ibid., 2.
6. Ibid., 2.
7. Ibid., 6.
8. Derrida, "Mochlos," 5.
9. Ibid., 5.
10. Ibid., 19.

References

Derrida, J. (1982). "The ends of man," in A. Bass (trans.), *Margins of Philosophy* (Chicago: University of Chicago Press), pp. 109–136.

Derrida, J. (1983a). "The principle of reason: The university in the eyes of its pupils." *Diacritics*, Fall, 3–20.

Derrida, J. (1983b). "The time of the thesis: Punctuations," in Alan Montefiore (ed.), *Philosophy in France Today* (Cambridge: Cambridge University Press), pp. 34–50.

Derrida, J. (1994). "Of the humanities and the philosophical discipline: The right to philosophy from the cosmopolitical point of view." *Surfaces*, 4, at http://tornade.ere.umontreal.ca/~guedon/Surfaces/vol4/derrida.html

Grassi, E. (1983). *Heidegger and the Question of Renaissance Humanism: Four Studies* (New York, Binghamton: Center for Medieval and Early Renaissance Studies).

Heidegger, M. (1996). "Letter on humanism," in David Farrell Krell (ed.), *Basic Writings* (London: Routledge), pp. 225–226.

Nietzsche, F. (1968 orig. 1888). *Twilight of the Idols; and, The Anti-Christ.* Translated, with an introduction and commentary, by R. J. Hollingdale (Harmondsworth: Penguin).

Roundtable Discussion: Jacques Derrida's "Of the Humanities and Philosophical Disciplines: The Right to Philosophy from the Cosmopolitical Point of View (the Example of an International Institution)." *Surfaces*, 4, at http://tornade.ere.umontreal.ca/~guedon/Surfaces/vol4/ derrida.html

CHAPTER ONE

The Future of the Profession or the Unconditional University (Thanks to the "Humanities," What Could Take Place Tomorrow)

JACQUES DERRIDA
(Translated by Peggy Kamuf)

This will no doubt be *like* a profession of faith: the profession of faith of a professor who will act as *if* he were nevertheless asking your permission to be unfaithful or a traitor to his habitual practice.

So here is the thesis, in direct and broadly simple terms, that I will submit for your discussion. In truth, it will be less a thesis, or even an hypothesis, than a declarative engagement, an appeal in the form of a profession of faith: faith in the university and, within the university, faith in the Humanities of tomorrow.

The long title proposed for this lecture signifies first that the modem university *should* be without condition. By "modem university," I mean the one whose European model, after a rich and complex medieval history, has become prevalent, which is to say "classic," over the last two centuries in states of a democratic type. This university claims and ought to be granted in principle, besides what is called academic freedom, an *unconditional* freedom to question and to assert, or even the right to say publicly all that is required by research, knowledge, and thought concerning the *truth*. However enigmatic it may be, the reference to truth remains fundamental enough to be found, along with light (*lux*), on the

symbolic insignias of more than one university. The university professes
the truth, and that is its profession. It declares and promises an unlimited
commitment to the truth. No doubt the status of and the changes to the
value of truth can be discussed *ad infinitum* (truth as adequation or truth
as revelation, truth as the object of theoretico-constative discourses or as
poetico-performative events, and so forth). But these are discussed, precisely, in the university and in departments that belong to the
Humanities. These immense questions of truth and of light, of the
Enlightenment—*Aufklärung, Luminares, Illuminisimo*—have always been
linked to the question of man, to a concept of that which is proper to
man, on which concept were founded both Humanism and the historical
idea of the Humanities. Today the renewed and re-elaborated declaration
of "human rights" (1948) of as we say in French, "*des Droits de l'homme,*"
the rights of man, and the institution of the juridical concept of "crime
against humanity" (1945) form the horizon of *mondialisation*, and of the
international law that is supposed to keep watch over it. (I am keeping
the French word "mondialisation" in preference to "globalization" so as
to maintain a reference to the world—monde, Welt, mundus—which is
neither the globe nor the cosmos.) The concept of man, of what is proper
to man, of human rights, of crimes against the humanity of man, organises
as we know such a mondialisation or worldwide-isation. This worldwide-
isation wishes to be a humanisation. If this concept of man seems both
indispensable and always problematic, well—and this will be one of the
motifs of my thesis, one of my theses in the form of a profession of
faith—it can be discussed or re-elaborated, as such and without conditions,
without presuppositions, only within the space of the new Humanities.
But Whether these discussions are critical or deconstructive, everything
that concerns the question and the history of truth, in its relation to the
question of man, of what is proper to man, of human rights, of crimes
against humanity and so forth, all of this must in principle find its space
of discussion without condition and without presupposition, its legitimate space of research and re-elaboration, in the university and within
the university, above all in the Humanities. Not so that it may enclose
itself there, but on the contrary so as to find the best access to a new public space transformed by new techniques of communication, information, archivisation, and knowledge production. (Although I must leave
this aside, one of the most serious questions that is posed, and posed here,
between the university and the politico-economic outside of its public
space is the question of the marketplace in publishing and the role it plays
in archivisation, evaluation, and legitimation of academic research.)
The horizon of truth or of what is proper to man is certainly not a very

determinable limit. But neither is that of the university and of, the Humanities. The university without condition does not, in fact, exist, as we know only too well. Nevertheless, in principle and in conformity with its declared vocation, its professed essence, it should remain an ultimate place of critical resistance—and more than critical—to all the powers of dogmatic and unjust appropriation. When I say "more than critical," I have in mind "deconstructive" (so why not just say it directly and without wasting time?). I am referring to the right to deconstruction as an unconditional right to ask critical questions not only to the history of the concept of man, but to the history even of the notion of critique, to the form and the authority of the question, to the interrogative form of thought. For this implies the right to do it performatively, that is by producing events, for example by writing, and by giving rise to singular oeuvres (which up until now has not been the purview of either the classical or the modem Humanities). With the event of thought constituted by such oeuvres, it would be a matter of causing something to happen, without necessarily betraying it, to this concept of truth or of humanity that forms the charter and the profession of faith of all universities. This principle of unconditional resistance is a right that the university itself should at the same time reflect, invent and pose, whether it does so through its law faculties or in the new Humanities capable of working on these questions of right and of law—in other words, and again why not say it without detour—the Humanities capable of taking on the tasks of deconstruction, beginning with the deconstruction of their own history and their own axioms.

Such an unconditional resistance could oppose the university to a great number of powers: to State powers (and thus to the power of the nation-state and to its phantasm of indivisible sovereignty, which indicates how the university might be in advance not just cosmopolitan, but universal, extending beyond worldwide citizenship and the nation-state in general), to economic powers (to corporations and to national and international capital), to the powers of the media, ideological, religious and cultural powers, and so forth—in short, to all the powers that limit democracy to come. The university should thus also be the place in which nothing is beyond question, not even the current and determined figure of democracy, and not even the traditional idea of critique, meaning theoretical critique, and not even the authority of the "question" form, of thinking as "questioning." That is why I spoke without delay and without disguise of deconstruction.

Here then is what I will call the university without condition: the principal right to say everything, whether it be under the heading of fiction and the experimentation of knowledge, and the right to say it publicly, to publish it. This reference to public space will remain the link that affiliates the new Humanities to the age of Enlightenment. It distinguishes the university institution from other institutions founded on the right or the duty to say everything, for example religious confession, and even psychoanalytic free association. But it is also what fundamentally links the university, and above all the Humanities, to what is called literature, in the European and modern sense of the term, as the right to say everything publicly, or to keep it secret, if only in the form of fiction. I allude to confession, which is very close` to the profession of faith, because I would like to connect my remarks to the analysis of what is happening today, on the worldwide scene, that resembles a universal process of confession, avowal, repentance, expiation, and asked-for forgiveness. One could cite innumerable examples, day after day. But whether we are talking about very ancient crimes or yesterday's crimes, about slavery, the Shoah, Apartheid, or even the acts of violence of the Inquisition (concerning which the Pope just announced that they ought to give rise to an examination of conscience), repentance is always enacted with reference to this very recent juridical concept of "crime against humanity."

By reason of this abstract and hyperbolic invincibility, by reason of its very impossibility, this unconditionality exposes as well the weakness or the vulnerability of the university. It exhibits the fragility of its defences against all the powers that besiege it, and attempt to appropriate it. Because it is a stranger to power, because it is heterogeneous to the principle of power, the university is also without any power of its own. That is why I speak of the *university without condition.* I say "the university" because I am distinguishing here, *stricto sensu,* the university from all research institutions that are in the service of economic goals and interests of all sorts, without being granted in principle the independence of the university; I also say "unconditional" or "without condition" to let one hear the connotation of "without power" and "without defence." Because it is absolutely independent, the university is also an exposed, tendered citadel, to be taken, often destined to capitulate without condition, to surrender unconditionally. It gives itself up, it sometimes puts itself up for sale, it risks being simply something to occupy, take over, even buy; it risks becoming a branch office of conglomerates and corporations. This is today, in the United States and throughout the world, a major political stake: to what extent does the Organisation of research and teaching have to be supported, that is directly or indirectly controlled, let us say euphemistically "sponsored," by commercial and industrial interests?

By this logic, as we know, the Humanities are often held hostage to departments of pure or applied science in which are concentrated the supposedly profitable investments of capital foreign to the academic world. A question must then be asked and it is not merely economic, juridical, ethical, or political: can the university (and if so, how?) affirm an unconditional independence, can it claim a sort of *sovereignty*, without ever risking the worst—namely, by reason of the impossible abstraction of this sovereign independence, being forced to give up and capitulate without condition, to let itself be taken over and bought at any price? What is needed then is not only a principle of resistance, but a force of resistance—and of dissidence. The deconstruction of the concept of unconditional sovereignty is doubtless necessary and underway, for this is the heritage of a barely secularised theology. In the most visible case of the supposed sovereignty of nation-states, but also elsewhere, the value of sovereignty is today in thorough decomposition. But one must beware that this necessary deconstruction does not compromise, too much, the university's claim to independence, that is, to a certain very particular form of sovereignty that I will try to specify later. This would be what is at stake in political decisions and strategies. This stake will remain on the horizon of the hypotheses or professions of faith that I submit to your reflection—how to deconstruct the history (and first of all the academic history) of the principle of indivisible sovereignty, even as one claims the unconditional right to say everything and to pose all the deconstructive questions that are called for on the subject of man, of sovereignty, of the right to say everything, therefore of literature and democracy, of the world-wide-isation underway, of its techno-economic and confessional aspects, and so forth?

I will not claim that, in the torment threatening the university today and within it some disciplines more than others, this force of resistance, this assumed freedom to say everything in the public space, has its unique or privileged place in what is called the Humanities—a concept whose definition it will be advisable to refine, deconstruct and adjust, beyond a tradition that must also be cultivated. However, this principle of unconditionality *presents itself*, originally and above all, in the Humanities. It has an originary and privileged place of *presentation*, of manifestation, of safekeeping in the Humanities. It has there its space of discussion as well, and of re-elaboration. All this passes as much by way of literature and languages (that is, the sciences called the sciences of man and culture) as by way of the non-discursive arts, by way of law and philosophy, by way of critique, questioning and, beyond the philosophy of critique and questioning, by way of deconstruction—there where it is a matter of nothing less than rethinking the concept of man, the figure of humanity in general, and singularly the one presupposed by what we call, in the university, for the last few centuries, the Humanities.

From this point of view at least, deconstruction (and I am not at all embarrassed to say so and even to claim) has its privileged place in the university and in the Humanities as the place of Irredentist resistance or even, analogically, as a sort of principle of civil disobedience, even of dissidence in the name of a superior law and a justice of thought. Let us call here *thought* that which at times commands, according to a law above all laws, the justice of this resistance or this dissidence. It is also what puts deconstruction to work or inspires it as justice. This right must be without limit, if I may say so, to authorise the deconstruction of all the determined figures that this sovereign unconditionality may have assumed through history. For this, we have to enlarge and re-elaborate the concept of the Humanities. To my mind, it is no longer a matter simply of the conservative and humanist concept with which most often the Humanities and their ancient canons are associated—canons which I believe ought to be protected at any price. This new concept of the Humanities, even as it remains faithful to its tradition, should include law, "legal studies," as well as what is called in the United States, where this formation originated, "theory" (an original articulation of literary theory, philosophy, linguistics, psychoanalysis, and so forth), but also, of course, in all these places, deconstructive practices. And we will have to distinguish carefully here between, on the one hand, the principle of freedom, autonomy, resistance, disobedience or dissidence, the principle that is coextensive with the whole field of academic knowledge and, on the other hand, its privileged place of *presentation*, of re-elaboration, and of thematic discussion, which in my opinion would more properly belong to the Humanities, but to the transformed Humanities. If I insist on linking all of this not only to the question of literatures, to a certain democratic institution that is called literature or literary fiction, to a certain simulacrum and a certain "as if," but also to the question of the profession and of its future, it is because throughout a history of *travail* (usually translated as "work" or "labor" but I will leave it in French for the moment) which is not only trade or craft, then a history of trade or craft, which is not always profession, then a history of the profession, which is not always that of professor, I would like to connect this problematic of the university without condition to a pledge, a commitment, a promise, an act of faith, a declaration of faith, a profession of faith that in an original way ties faith to knowledge in the university, and above all in that place of self- presentation of unconditionality that will go by the name Humanities. To link in a certain way faith to knowledge, faith in knowledge, is to articulate movements that could be called performative with constative, descriptive, or theoretical movements. A profession of faith, a commitment, a promise, an assumed responsibility, all that calls not upon discourses of knowledge but upon performative discourses that produce the event they speak of. One will therefore have to ask oneself what "professing" means. What is one doing when, performatively, one professes but also when one exorcises a profession and singularly the profession of professor? I will thus rely often and at length on Austin's now classic distinction between performative speech acts and constative speech acts. This distinction will have been a great event in this century—and it will first have been an academic event. It will have taken place *in* the university and in a certain way, it is the Humanities that explored its resources. Even while recognising the power, the legitimacy, and the necessity of this distinction between constative and performative, I have often had occasion, after a certain point, not to put it back in question but to analyse its presuppositions and to complicate them. I will do so once again today, but this time from another point of view and I will end up designating a place where this distinction fails and must fail. This place will be precisely what happens, what comes to pass, that at which one arrives or that which happens to us, arrives to us, the event, the place of the taking-place—and which cares as little about the performative as the constative. And this can happen, this can arrive in and by the Humanities.

Now I am going to begin, at once by the end and by the beginning. For I began with the end *as if* it were the beginning.

As if the end of work were at the origin of the world.

Yes, "as if," I indeed said "as if .."

At the same time as a reflection on the history of work, that is *travail*, it is also no doubt a meditation on the "as if" and the "as such" that I will propose to you, and perhaps on a politics *of the* virtual. Not a virtual politics but a politics of the virtual in the cyberspace or cyberworld of worldwide-isation. One of the mutations that affect the place and the nature of university *travail* is today a certain delocalising virtualisation of the space of communication, discussion, publication, archivisation. It is not the virtualisation that is absolutely novel in its structure. As soon as there is trace there is some virtualisation and this is the abc of deconstruction. What is new is the acceleration of the rhythm, the extent and powers of capitalisation of such a virtuality. Hence the necessity to rethink the concepts of the possible and the impossible. This new technical "stage" of virtualisation (computerisation, digitalisation, virtually immediate worldwide-isation of readability, tele-work, and so forth) destabilises, as we well know, the university habitat. It upsets the university's topology, worries everything that organises the places defining it, namely, the territory of its fields and its disciplinary frontiers as well as its places of discussion, its field of battle, its *Kampfplatz*, its theoretical battlefield—and the communitary structure of its "campus." Where is to be found the communitary *place* and the social bond of a "campus" in the cyberspatial age of the computer, of tele-work, and of the World Wide Web? Where does the exercise of democracy, be it a university democracy, have its *place* in what is often called "CyberDemocracy?" One has the clear sense that, more radically, what has been upset in this way is the topology of the event, the experience of the singular taking-place. What then are we doing when we say "as if"? Notice that I have not yet said "it is as if the end of work were at the origin of the world." I left suspended, I abandoned to its interruption a strange subordinate clause ("as if the end of work were at the origin of the world"), as if I wanted to let an example of the "as if" work on its own, outside any context to attract your attention. What are we doing when we say "as if"? What does an "if" do?

One of the tasks to come of the Humanities would be, *ad infinitum*, to know and to think their own history, at least in the directions that can be seen to open up (the act of professing, the theology and the history of work, of knowledge and of the faith in knowledge, the question of man, of the world, of fiction, of the performative and the "as if," of literature and of *oeuvre*, etc., and then all the concepts that can be articulated with them). This deconstructive task of the Humanities to come will not let itself be contained within the traditional limits of the departments that today belong, by their very status, to the Humanities. These Humanities to come will cross disciplinary borders without dissolving the specificity of each discipline into what is called, often in a very confused way, inter-disciplinarity or into what is lumped with another good-for-everything concept, "cultural studies." But I can very well imagine that departments of genetics, natural science, medicine and even mathematics will take seriously, in their work itself, the questions that I have just evoked. This is especially true, besides medicine, of law schools and departments of theology or religion.

I must now hasten my conclusion, I will do so in a dry and telegraphic manner with seven theses, seven propositions, or seven professions of faith. They remain altogether programmatic. Six of them will have only a formalising value of serving as reminders, of reassembling or recapitulating. The seventh, which will not be sabbatical, will attempt a step beyond the six others toward a dimension of the *event* and of the *taking-place* that I have yet to speak of. Between the first six theses—or professions of faith—and the last, we will get our foothold in preparation for a leap that would carry us beyond the power of the performative "as if," beyond even the distinction between constative and performative on which we have up until now pretended to rely.

The Humanities of tomorrow, in all their departments, will have to study their history, the history of the concepts that, by constructing them, instituted the disciplines and were coextensive with them. There are many signs that this work has already begun, of course. Like all acts of institution, those that we must analyse will have had a performative force and will have put to work a certain "as if." I just said that one must "study" or "analyse." Is it necessary to make clear that such "studies," such "analyses," for the reasons already indicated, would not be purely "theoretical" and neutral? They would lead toward practical and performative transformations and would not forbid the production of singular oeuvres. To these fields I will give therefore six, and then seven thematic and programmatic titles, without excluding, obviously, cross-fertilisations and reciprocal interpellations.

1. These new Humanities would treat the history of man, the idea, the figure, and the notion of "what is proper to man" (and a non-finite series of oppositions by which man is determined, in particular the traditional opposition of the life-fonn called human and of the life-form called animal). I will dare to claim, without being able to demonstrate it here, that none of these traditional concepts of "what is proper to man" and thus of what is opposed to it can resist a consistent scientific and deconstructive analysis.

The most urgent guiding thread here would be the problematisation (which does not mean the disqualification) of these powerful juridical performatives that have given shape to the modem history of this humanity of man. I am thinking, for example, of the rich history of at least two of these juridical performatives: *on the one hand*, the Declarations of the Rights of *Man*—and of the woman (for the question of sexual differences is not secondary or accidental here and we know that these Declarations of the Rights of Man were being constantly transformed and enriched from 1789 to 1948 and beyond: the figure of man, a promising animal, an animal capable of promising, as Nietzsche said, remains still to come) and, *on the other hand*, the concept of "crime against humanity," which since the end of the Second World War has modified the geopolitical field of international law and will continue to do so more and more, commanding in particular the scene of worldwide confession and of the relation to the historical past in general. The new Humanities will thus treat these perfonnative productions of law or right (rights of man, human rights, the concept of crime against humanity) there, where they always imply the promise and the conventionality of the "as if."

2. These new Humanities would treat, in the same style, the history of democracy and the idea of sovereignty, that is to say as well, of course, the conditions or rather the unconditionality on which the university and within it the Humanities are supposed (once again the "as if") to live. The deconstruction of this concept of sovereignty would touch not only on international law, the limits of the nation-state, and of its supposed sovereignty, but also on the use made of them in juridico-political discourses concerning the relations between what is called man and woman. This concept of sovereignty has been recently at the centre of very poorly thought-out and poorly conducted debates, in my country, on the subject of man-woman "parity" in access to political offices.

3. These new Humanities would treat, in the same style, the history of "professing," of the "profession," and of the professoriat, a history articulated with that of the premises or presuppositions (notably Abrahamic, biblical, and above all Christian) of work and of the worldwide-ised confession, there where it goes beyond the sovereignty of the head of State, of the nation-state, or even of the "people" in a democracy. An immense problem: how to dissociate democracy from citizenship, from the nation-state, and from the theological idea of sovereignty, even the sovereignty of the people? How to dissociate sovereignty and unconditionality, that is, the power of sovereignty and the powerlessness of unconditionality? That is a difficult border to draw but a necessary one and here again, whether it is a question of profession or confession, it is the performative structure of the "as if" that would be at the centre of the work.

4. These new Humanities would treat, in the same style, the history of literature. Not only what is commonly called history of literatures or literature themselves, with the great question of its canons (traditional and indisputable objects of the classical Humanities), but the history of the concept of literature, of the modern institution named literature, of its links with fiction and the performative force of the "as if," of its *concept of oeuvre*, author, signature, national language, of its link with the right to say or not to say everything that founds both democracy and the idea of the unconditional sovereignty claimed by the university and within it by what is called, inside and outside departments, the Humanities.

5. These new Humanities would treat, in the same style, the history of profession, the profession of faith, professionalisation, and the professoriat. The guiding thread could be, today, what is happening when the profession of faith, the profession of faith of the professor, gives rise to

singular *oeuvres*, to other strategies of the "as if" that are events and that
affect the very limits of the academic field or of the Humanities. We are
indeed witnessing the end of a certain figure of the professor and of his
or her supposed authority, but I believe, as should now be obvious, in a
certain necessity of the professoriat.

6. These new Humanities would thus finally treat, in the same style,
but in the course of a formidable reflexive reversal, both critical and
deconstructive, the history of the "as if" and especially the history of this
precious distinction between performative acts and constative acts that
seems to have been indispensable for us lip until now. It will surely be
necessary (things have already begun) to study the history and the limits
of such a decisive distinction, and to which I have made reference as if
I believed in it without reservation up until now, as if I held it to be
absolutely reliable. This deconstructive work would not concern only the
original and brilliant *oeuvre* of Austin but also his rich and fascinating
inheritance, over the last half-century, in particular in the Humanities.

7. To the seventh point, which is not the seventh day, I arrive finally
now. Or rather I *let perhaps* arrive at the end, now, the very thing that, by
arriving, by taking place or having place, revolutionises, overturns, and
puts to rout the very authority that is attached, in the university, in the
Humanities:

    i. to knowledge (or at least to its model of constative language);
    ii. to the profession or to the profession of faith (or at least to its
       model of performative language);
    iii. to the *mise en oeuvre*, the putting to work, at least to the perfor-
       mative putting to work of the "as if."

That which happens, takes place, comes about in general, that which is
called an event, "what is it?" Can one ask with regard to it: "What is it?"
It must not only surprise the constative and propositional mode of the
language of knowledge (S is P) but also no longer even let itself be
commanded by the performative speech act of a subject. As long as I can
produce and determine an event by a performative act guaranteed, like
any performative, by conventions, that is by legitimate fictions, and a certain "as if," then to be sure I will not say that nothing happens or comes
about, but what takes place, arrives, happens, or happens *to me* remains
still controllable and programmable within a horizon of anticipation or
precomprehension, within a horizon period. It is of the order of the mas-
terable possible, it is the unfolding of what is already possible. It is of the
order of power, of the "I can" or "I may" which is implicit in the performative. No surprise, thus no event in the strong sense. Which is as much

as to say that, to this extent at least, it does not happen, it does not come about, or as I would say in French: *cela n'arrive pas*, it does not arrive. For if there is any, if there is such a thing, the pure singular eventness of *what* arrives or of *who* arrives and arrives *to me* (which is what I call in French the *arrivant*), it would suppose an *irruption* that punctures the horizon, *interrupting* any performative Organisation, any convention, or any context that can be or could be dominated by a conventionality. Which is to say that this event takes place only there where it does not allow itself to be domesticated by any "as if," or at least by any "as if" that can already be read, decoded, or articulated as such. This small word, the "as" of the "as if" as well as the "gas" of the "as such"—whose authority founds and justifies every ontology, as well as every phenomenology, every philosophy and science of knowledge—this small word "as" is then everywhere the name of the very issue, not to say the target, of deconstruction. It is often said that the performative produces the event of which it speaks. One must also realise that, inversely, there where there is a performative, an event worthy of the name cannot arrive. To the extent that there is a performative this event is limited as event, it doesn't happen, there is no surprise, no unpredictability. If what arrives belongs to the horizon of the possible, or even of a possible performative—of its power, its "I can" or "I may"—it does not arrive, it does not happen, in the full sense of the word. As I have often tried to demonstrate, only the impossible can arrive. By frequently pointing out about deconstruction that it is impossible or the impossible, and that it is not a method, a doctrine, a speculative metaphilosophy, but *what arrives, what comes about*, I was relying on the same thought. The examples with which I have attempted to accede to this thought (invention, the gift, forgiveness, hospitality, justice, friendship, and so forth) all confirmed this thinking of the impossible possible, of the possible as impossible, of an impossible-possible that can no longer be determined by the metaphysical interpretation of possibility or virtuality. I will not say that this thought of the impossible possible, this other thinking of the possible is a thinking of necessity but rather, as I have also tried to demonstrate elsewhere, a thinking of the "perhaps," of that dangerous modality of the "perhaps" that Nietzsche speaks of and that philosophy has always tried to subjugate. There is no future and no relation to the coming of the event without experience of the "perhaps." What takes place does not have to announce itself as possible or necessary; if it did, its irruption as event would be in advance neutralised. The event belongs to a *perhaps* that is in keeping not with the possible but the impossible. And its force is therefore irreducible to the force of a performative, even if it gives to the performative, to what is called the force of the performative, its chance and its effectiveness. The force of the event is always stronger than the force of a performative. In the face of what arrives to me, happens to Me and even in what I decide (which, as I tried to show in *Politics of Friendship*, must involve a certain passivity, my decision being always the decision of the other), in the face of the other who arrives and arrives to me, all performative force is overrun, exceeded, exposed.

This force in keeping with an experience of the perhaps keeps an affinity or a complicity with the "if" of the "as if." And thus with a certain grammar of the conditional: what *if* this arrived, what *if* this happened? This, that is altogether other, *could well* arrive, this *would* happen. To think perhaps is to think "if," "what if" But you see quite clearly that this "if," this "what if," this "as if" is no longer reducible to all the "as ifs" that we have been talking about up until now. And if it is declined according to the verbal mode of the conditional, this is also to announce the unconditional, the eventual, or the possible event of the impossible unconditional, the altogether other which we should from now on (and this is something else I have not yet said or done today) dissociate from the theological idea of sovereignty. Basically, this would perhaps be my hypothesis: it would be necessary to dissociate a certain unconditional independence of thought, of deconstruction, of justice, of the Humanities, of the university, and so forth from any phantasm of sovereign mastery. Well, it is once again in the Humanities that one would have to make arrive, make happen the thinking of this other mode of the "if," this more than difficult, impossible thing, the exceeding of the performative and of the opposition constative/performative. By thinking, in the Humanities, this limit of mastery and of performative conventionality, this limit of performative authority, what is one doing? One is acceding to that place where the always necessary context of the performative operation (a context that is, like every convention, an institutional context) can no longer be saturated, delimited, fully determined. The brilliant invention of the constative/performative distinction would basically still have sought, in the university, to reassure the university as to the sovereign mastery of its interior, as to its proper power, the power of its own. One thus touches on the very limit, *between the inside and the outside*, notably the border of the university itself, and within it, of the Humanities. One thinks in the Humanities the irreducibility of their outside and of their future. One thinks in the Humanities that one cannot and must not let oneself be enclosed within the inside of the Humanities. But for this thinking to be strong and consistent requires the Humanities. To think this is not an academic, speculative or theoretical operation, nor a neutral utopia. No more than saying it is a simple enunciation. It is on this always divisible limit, it is at this limit that what arrives arrives. It is this limit that is affected by the arriving and that changes. This limit of the impossible, the "perhaps," and the "if," this is the place where the university is exposed to reality, to the forces from without (be they cultural, ideological, political, economic, or other). It is there that the university is in the world that it is attempting to think. On this border, it must therefore negotiate and organise its resistance and take its responsibilities. Not in order to enclose itself and reconstitute the abstract phantasm of sovereignty whose theological or humanist heritage it will perhaps have begun to deconstruct, if at least it has begun to do so. But in order to resist effectively, by allying itself with extra-academic forces, in order to organise an inventive resistance, through its oeuvres, its works, to all attempts at reappropriation (political, juridical, economic, and so forth), to all the other figures of sovereignty.

I do not have time to justify any further my profession of faith. I do not know if what I am saying here is intelligible, if it makes sense. I especially do not know what status, genre, or legitimacy the discourse has that I have just addressed to you. Is it academic? Is. it a discourse of knowledge in the Humanities or on the subject of the Humanities? Is it knowledge only? Only a performative profession of faith? Does it belong to the inside of the university? Is it philosophy or literature or theatre? Is it a work, *une oeuvre*, or a course, or a kind of seminar? I have numerous hypotheses on this subject, but finally it will be up to you now, it will be up to others to decide this. The signatories are also the addressees. For if this impossible that I'm talking about were to arrive perhaps one day, I leave you to imagine the consequences. Take your time but be quick about it because you do not know what awaits you.

CHAPTER TWO

Sovereignty Death Literature
Unconditionality Democracy University

J. HILLIS MILLER

*C'est aussi pour annoncer l'inconditionnel, l'éventuel ou le possible événe-
ment de l'inconditionnel impossible, le tout autre—que nous devrions
désormais . . . dissocier de l'idée théologique de souveraineté.*

(It is also in order to announce the unconditional, the eventuality,
or the possible event of the impossible unconditional, the wholly
other—which we must henceforth . . . dissociate from the theological idea of sovereignty.)

Derrida, *L'Université sans condition*

My title is a series of six nouns set side by side without any verb or other
ligature. How can they all be related? Perhaps it is impossible. That is my
question here. Before trying to answer that question, let me begin by saying that it is difficult these days to talk dispassionately about sovereignty
and death. We are now living in the United States in the midst of an
unparalleled example of usurped or illegitimate sovereignty wantonly
exercised. We have a president who was not elected and who is with his
executive branch pursuing a policy of preemptive strikes, rejection of
international treaties or international law, destruction of the environment, bankrupting the nation by running up gigantic deficits in order to
benefit the rich, establishment of a permanent state of emergency
justifying the suspension of constitutional civil liberties, and infliction of
a constant state of terror on our citizens through the mass media and
daily lies, such as the lies about Saddam Hussein's "weapons of mass

destruction" and his ties with Al-Qaeda. The United States is being run in the same way that the administration's friends at Enron, Ken Lay, and the rest ran their companies, that is, by lying to the shareholders (read, U.S. citizens, voters), running up huge debts, and bilking the company to satisfy their own limitless greed, as, for example, in the abrogation of EPA regulations concerning factory emission cleanups when plants are renovated, or the attempt to develop the oil in the Arctic North Shore Wild Life Refuge with huge government subsidies to the developers. Meanwhile, though we are already armed to the teeth with weapons of mass destruction and have a larger military budget than those of all our "allies" combined, the administration is quietly going about developing and testing new nuclear weapons.

And talk about death! I mean the death of all those we killed and are killing in Iraq. I also mean the Americans being killed there every day in the exercise of the president's sovereignty over the life and death of U.S. citizens. This is exemplified in the power of the commander in chief to declare war and send troops into combat or into occupation duty. The so-called ambassador Paul Bremer, actually the imposed dictator of occupied Iraq and viceroy of George W. Bush, who is vicar of God, in a PBS interview on the Lehrer News Hour asserted repeatedly that "we," meaning the United States, masquerading as a "coalition of the willing," are "sovereign" in Iraq. He appealed to international law for the claim that a sovereign occupying power has a responsibility to feed and shelter the conquered, to give them medical treatment and basic service. Bremer has no doubt been reading Carl Schmitt or Leo Strauss. The latter is the unacknowledged ideologue of the present administration, as embodied, for example, in Paul Wolfowitz. Two days later (September 26, 2003), again on Lehrer News Hour, a member of the Iraqi "Governing Council," which was of course handpicked by our government, said that Iraq is still a sovereign nation. Either he or Paul Bremer must be wrong. In this case, as in most others, surely might makes right. The true sovereign in Iraq is George W. Bush. In speaking of the connection between sovereignty and death in the United States today, I also mean those who will be killed by uncontrolled factory pollutant emissions, or by unchecked global warming, or by tax breaks offered to those who buy monster SUVs. The United States is the only first-world country that still has the death penalty. George W. Bush was famous as governor of Texas for the number of executions he authorized. As far as I know he has never, either as governor or as president, exercised his sovereign right to pardon. As I say it is difficult these days to think dispassionately about the abstract question of the relation of sovereignty to death or to any of the other concepts named in my title. Nevertheless I shall try to do so.

It is impossible, for me at least, to think about sovereignty without having in mind Jacques Derrida's treatment of sovereignty in *L'amitié*, in *Echographies*, and in a whole series of recent seminars on sovereignty and the death penalty, and on "The beast and the sovereign." The current seminars under the latter rubric juxtapose Defoe's *Robinson Crusoe* and Heidegger's theory of animality in *The Fundamental Concepts of Metaphysics*. As Derrida has patiently shown, through discussions of concepts about sovereignty from Aristotle and Plato on down to Hobbes, Rousseau, Beccaria, Schmitt, Heidegger, and many others, the essence of sovereignty lies in three features. The first is the idea that the king, emperor, or chief executive is above the law, just as the animal, the supposedly ferocious lion or wolf or tiger, is. Such animals are outside the law because they are below the human, outside the human.

The second feature is the way the concept of sovereignty is theological through and through. It cannot be detached from its theological roots. This is true even in democratic nations where the people are supposed to be sovereign or where one speaks of the "sovereign individual." The revised version of our pledge of allegiance, now widely used, says we are "one nation, under God, with liberty and justice for all." The addition of "under God" is not only contrary to our constitutional separation of church and state, it also has a quite different meaning from Abraham Lincoln's appeal, in the Gettysburg Address, to "government of the people, by the people, and for the people." To say the concept of sovereignty is theological is to say, as the new version of the pledge of allegiance does, that all earthly sovereigns, even democratically elected ones, are representatives of the deity, vicars of God. They act in the name of God's divine omnipotent authority. This means that they are not so much lawmakers as above any law that may have been made. The abrogation of the law in sovereign acts of pardon is a clear example of this. Though George W. Bush is not conspicuously given to acts of pardoning "evildoers," it is highly significant and, to me at least, deeply disquieting to know that he is, though this is kept rather quiet, a born-again Christian. He probably believes in the Armageddon and apparently believes that he has been chosen by God to carry on the deity's work of preparing for the Last Days. This may explain the administration's refusal to accept the evidence of global warming. They may look at the inundation of our coasts, the vanishing of most of Florida, and the transformation of California into a sterile desert as the judgment of God on a wicked people, leaving Bush, Cheney, Rumsfield, Rice, and a few corporate friends standing on a mountaintop as the Saving Remnant, while the streets run in blood below.

The third feature of sovereignty is the way it cannot be dissociated, in the Western tradition, from the notion of the nation-state. All recent

wars, for example, in Kosovo or Rwanda, not to speak of our occupation
of Iraq, have been carried out in the name of a given national sovereignty, established or to come. This ideal nation-state is made of a single
ethnically pure people and, usually, is organized around a single national
religion. Arabic terrorism differs from this in being not in the name of a
single-nation but in the name of a Pan-Arabic Muslim regime. As everyone
knows globalization is rapidly erasing the separate hegemony of nation-
states and even the nation-states themselves, as, for example, the European
Union gradually replacing in power and authority the countries within
it. When something so politically important as the concept of the
sovereign nation-state is on the way out, it is likely to be reaffirmed
hyperbolically in its death-throes. We are witnessing that, to our sorrow,
in the United States today. The reluctance of certain nations, Turkey, the
People's Republic of China, and the United States, to give up the death
penalty is probably not so much a belief that the death penalty is a
deterrent as it is an unwillingness to give up something historically
essential to state sovereignty. To give up the death penalty is to give up
the God-sanctioned right of life and death over the citizens of that state.
The abolishment of the death penalty in the European Union is a sign
of the weakening of state sovereignty among its member nations.

What is laughably absurd but also profoundly disquieting about the
way each nation-state thinks it has God's mandate for imperialist wars is
exposed in a passage in E. M. Forster's *Howards End*. Margaret and Helen
Schlegel, the chief protagonists of that novel, are half English, half
German:

> It was a unique education for the little girls. The haughty nephew
> [a German relative] would be at Wickham Place one day, bringing
> with him an even haughtier wife, both convinced that Germany
> was appointed by God to govern the world. Aunt Juley [an English
> relative] would come the next day, convinced that Great Britain had
> been appointed to the same post by the same authority. Were both
> these loud-voiced parties right? On one occasion they had met, and
> Margaret with clasped hands had implored them to argue the sub-
> ject out in her presence. Whereat they blushed and began to talk
> about the weather. "Papa," she cried—she was a most offensive
> child—"why will they not discuss this most clear question?" Her
> father, surveying the parties grimly, replied that he did not know.
> Putting her head on one side, Margaret then remarked: "To me one
> of two things is very clear; either God does not know his own mind
> about England and Germany, or else these do not know the mind

of God." A hateful little girl, but at thirteen she had grasped a dilemma that most people travel through life without perceiving (1989, pp. 30–31).

George W. Bush has evidently traveled so far through his life without grasping this dilemma. If he had, he might be more hesitant about declaring nations that "harbor terrorists" no more than evildoers. They clearly think God in the person of Allah is on their side and has appointed them to dominate the world. In a similar way Paul Bremer and the Iraqi Governing Council disagree about who is sovereign in Iraq. It is hard to imagine George W. Bush, though he had the advantage of a Yale education, sitting down an evening to read *Howards End*. We were all invited to sing "God Bless America" after 9/11, in order to reassure ourselves that God is on our side or to pray that he may be. The Al-Qaeda members no doubt praised Allah as they flew into the Trade Center towers. The theological basis of sovereignty has caused and will continue to cause much mischief and grief.

If one takes seriously the implications of what Forster, with such delicious irony, says, namely that the divine support of sovereignty and therefore sovereignty itself is, as Derrida repeatedly calls it, a "phantasm," and if sovereignty is always above the law, it would follow that assertions of sovereignty, such as our current self-proclaimed sovereignty in Iraq, but also including acts of pardon, such as those recently declared by the governor of Illinois, are baseless. They are no more than groundless and unjustified performative assertions: "I declare that we are sovereign, under God."

Derrida does not say that theologically based sovereignty is a falsehood, or a lie, or an ideological aberration. He says, precisely, that it is an "abstract phantasm" (Derrida, 2001a, p. 78). What is a phantasm? *The American Heritage Dictionary* defines a phantasm as "(1) Something seen but having no physical reality; a phantom. (2) An illusory mental image. (3) In Platonic philosophy, objective reality as perceived and distorted by the five senses." The word comes from Middle English and Old French "from Latin *phantasma*, apparition, specter, from Greek, from *phantazein*, to make visible, from *phainein*, to show." A phantasm is a ghost, something seen with the eyes, something that shows forth but is not there. In Derrida's usage phastasm is more to be associated with Freud than with Carl Schmitt. Sovereignty is a ghost in broad daylight. It is there and also not there. It is to be associated with uncanny apparitions, as Freud interprets them in "*Das Unheimliche.*" Sovereignty is something that has come back, that is strange in the sense of alien, and yet strangely familiar. This ghost cannot easily be laid by any act demystifying or deconstructing ideology. The phantom of God-based sovereignty always comes back, keeps coming back, as a revenant. It is almost impossible to exorcise such a ghost.

I have related sovereignty and death easily enough, and have even related the two to democracy, but what about the other concepts in my title? They seem another kettle of fish. Here I appeal once more to Jacques Derrida as my sovereign authority. His *L'Université sans condition*, originally a president's lecture at Stanford, and a related essay, the speech he gave on receiving an honorary degree from the University of Pantion in Athens in 1999, entitled *"Inconditionnalité ou souveraineté: L'Université aux frontiers de l'Europe,"* are based on a fundamental distinction between sovereignty and what he calls (the word is a neologism in English) "unconditionality." What is the difference? Sovereignty is a theologically based phantasm. Unconditionality has, apparently, no such basis. Derrida associates it with the weakness (in the might makes right sense) of the research university's historical claim to be free of all external conditions and constraints and to have the right to put everything in question, even to have the right to put in question the right to put everything in question. Derrida recognizes as well as anyone else that the university has never actually been free of external conditions and constraints. Perhaps the university in the West has never been so conditioned as it is today by its obligations to corporate and government funding sources. Nevertheless the horizon for the university is an unconditional freedom to question everything; Derrida associates this freedom especially with the humanities and within the humanities especially with literary studies as the place where engagement with a certain *"comme si"* or "as if" is institutionalized. That engagement with the virtual is inherently dissident. It is inherently difficult to recuperate within instrumental concepts of the university. An example of such a concept is the one asserted several years ago by the then president of the nine campus University of California. He said that the goal of the university is "to make California competitive in the global economy." Studying Shakespeare or Dickens or Mallarmé or Maurice Blanchot's "Literature and the right to death" is not easily defensible as helping to achieve that goal.

Blanchot sees literature as having a special relation to death, but not death conceived of as a sovereign act that is the obliteration of an evildoer by gunfire, precision bombing, or lethal injection. The argumentation of Blanchot's essay is subtle, complex, and by no means easy to understand or summarize. The essay might be defined as a virtually endless series of formulations, which attempt once and for all to express the relation between literature and the right to death, but which never quite succeeds in getting it right. They must therefore eternally begin again with another formulation, like literature itself in Blanchot's conception of it. Blanchot's notion of literature depends on a strange notion of "death as the impossibility of dying" (Blanchot, 1981, p. 55). Death for him is not obliteration but an endless empty wakefulness without content. Literary uses of language for Blanchot have a unique relation to death conceived of in this way. "When I speak," says Blanchot, "death speaks in me" (p. 43), or rather, in a characteristic Blanchotian reversal, speech silences the "infinite disquiet, formless and nameless vigilance," (p. 45) which is death as what precedes the language of literature and persists after it stops. "The language of literature," says Blanchot, "is a search for this moment which precedes literature" (p. 46). Literature for Blanchot, one can see, both speaks death and silences death. "In speech," he says, "what dies is what gives life to speech; speech is the life of that death, it is 'the life that endures death and maintains itself in it' " (p. 46).

I have now succeeded by way of Blanchot in relating literature to death, but to a radically different conception of death from that implicit in most ideas of state sovereignty as unwilling to abandon the death penalty. Derrida's concept of literature, however, appears to be quite different from Blanchot's. My final task will be to try to relate them to one another and to Derrida's idea of unconditionality as the basis of the university. I have said that Derrida defines the university's unconditionality as the privilege without penalty to put everything in question, even put in question the right to put everything in question. In the interview with Derek Attridge, which forms the first essay in the volume of Derrida's essays on literature that Attridge gathered and called *Acts of Literature*, Derrida defines literature in much the same way as he defines the university in more recent speeches. Literature is dependent in its modern form on the rise of constitutional democracies in the West from the seventeenth century on and on the radical democratic freedom to say anything, that is, precisely, to put everything in question. Such a democracy is of course never wholly established in fact. It is always "to come":

"What is literature?"; literature as historical institution with its conventions, rules, etc., but also this institution of fiction which gives *in principle* the power to say everything, to break free of the rules, to displace them, and thereby to institute, to invent and even to suspect the traditional difference between nature and institution, nature and conventional law, nature and history. Here we should ask juridical and political questions. The institution of literature in the West, in its relatively modern form, is linked to the authorization to

say everything, and doubtless too to the coming about of the
modern idea of democracy. Not that it depends on a democracy in
place, but it seems inseparable to me from what calls forth a democracy, in the most open (and doubtless itself to come) sense of
democracy (Derrida, 1992, p. 37).

Such a definition of literature allows us to understand better the role of
the *comme si* or as if in *L'Université sans conditon*. Literature, or what
Derrida here calls "fiction," can always respond (or refuse to respond) by
saying that was not I speaking as myself, but as an imaginary personage
speaking in a work of fiction, by way of a *comme si*. You cannot hold me
responsible for my "as ifs." Derrida says just this in passages that follow
the one quoted earlier:

> What we call literature (not belles-lettres or poetry) implies that
> license is given to the writer to say everything he wants or every-
> thing he can, while remaining shielded, safe from all censorship, be
> it religious or political. . . . This duty of irresponsibility, of refusing
> to reply for one's thought or writing to constituted powers, is per-
> haps the highest form of responsibility. To whom, to what? That's
> the whole question of the future or the event promised by or to
> such an experience, what I was just calling the democracy to come.
> Not the democracy of tomorrow, not a future democracy which
> will be present tomorrow but one whose concept is linked to the
> to-come [*à-venir*, cf. *avenir*, future], to the experience of a promise
> engaged, that is always an endless promise (1992, pp. 37, 38).

Crucial in the passage just cited is the "To whom, to what?" How can a
refusal to take responsibility, a refusal addressed to sovereign state powers,
be defined as "perhaps the highest form of responsibility?" To whom or
to what else can it have a higher obligation? Derrida's answer to this
question goes by way of the new concept of performative language that
he proposes in "*Psyché: l'invention de l'autre*" and again as the climax of
L'Université sans condition. It might seem that literature, conceived by
Derrida as an as if, a free, unconditioned fiction, would correspond to a
concept of literature as unconditioned performative speech acts, speech
acts not based on previously existing institutionalized sanctions. The title
of the honorary degree lecture in Athens is "*Inconditionalité ou souveraineté*"
and *L'Université sans condition* distinguishes sharply between the phantasm
of theologically based state sovereignty and the unfettered, "unconditioned" liberty to put everything in question in the ideal university—the

university without condition. Such a university like a truly democratic state is always to come. Derrida seems to pledge allegiance to, or, to use his own expression, make a "profession of faith in," a stark either/or. Either always illegitimate sovereignty or unconditional freedom. This unconditionality, it might seem, is especially manifested in literary study, since literature, as institutionalized in the West in the last three centuries, is, according to Derrida, itself unconditioned, irresponsible, free to say anything. Literature is an extreme expression of the right to free speech. Literature conceived of in this way seems, however, to have little or nothing to do with death, at least with the kind of death that is for Blanchot fundamentally expressed and at the same time covered over by all literary uses of language.

Matters are, however, not quite so simple. In the last section of *L'Université sans condition*, in the seventh summarizing proposition, Derrida makes one further move, which undoes all he has said so far about the university's unconditionality. He poses a "hypothesis," which he admits may not be "intelligible" (Derrida, 2001a, p. 79) to his Stanford audience. (This audience may have included Condoleezza Rice, the then provost of that university. Would that she had listened, understood, and given her allegiance.) Derrida admits, in a quite unusual confession, that what he asserts is not easy to understand. It is "*extrêmement difficile et presque im-probable, inaccessible a une preuve*" (p. 76). What he says is based on a hypothesis that is extremely difficult, almost improbable, prima facie highly unlikely, and almost impossible to prove. What he proposes, that is, is contrary to a true scientific hypothesis. A bona fide hypothesis can be proved to be false, if it is false.

What is this strange hypothesis? It is the presupposition that the unconditional independence of thinking in the university depends on a strange and anomalous speech act that brings about what Derrida calls an "event" or "the eventful (*l'éventuel*)" (p. 76). Such a speech act is anomalous both because it does not depend on preexisting rules, authorities, and contexts, as a felicitous Austinian speech act does, and because it does not posit freely, autonomously, lawlessly, outside all such preexisting contexts, as, for example, de Manian speech acts seem to do, or as judges do in Austin's surprising and even scandalous formula, "As official acts, the judge's ruling makes law" (Austin, 1980, p. 154).

No, the performative speech act Derrida has in mind is a response to the call of what Derrida names "*le tout autre*," the wholly other. Such a response is to some degree passive or submissive. It obeys a call or command. Only such a speech act constitutes a genuine event, which breaks the predetermined course of history. Such an event is "impossible." It is always an uncertain matter of what, Derrida recalls, Nietzsche calls "this dangerous perhaps" (Derrida, 2001a, p. 75). Nevertheless, says Derrida, "*seul l'impossible peut arriver*" (p. 74). That is why Derrida, in the passage I have cited as my epigraph, speaks of "*le possible événement de l'inconditionnel impossible, le tout autre*" (p. 76). He is playing here on the root sense of event as something that comes, that arrives. It appears of its own accord and in its own good time. We can only say, "yes" or, perhaps, "no" to it. We cannot call it. It calls us.

What is "the wholly other?" Derrida works out in detail, in "*Psyché, ou l'invention de l'autre*," what he means by "invention" as discovery, uncovering, rather than making up, and by the wholly other. For my purposes here, however, the crucial text is *Donner la mort*, translated in part as *The Gift of Death*. Here Derrida makes spectacular readings of the story of Abraham and Isaac in Genesis, of Kierkegaard's *Fear and Trembling*, and of Melville's *Bartleby the Scrivener*. In extended sections of this book he defines the wholly other in ways that identify it with a certain conception of God, as "absent, hidden and silent, separate, secret" (Derrida, 1995, p. 57), with the secret in general, and with death, the gift of death, as always my own solitary death, and as wholly other to my knowledge. "Without knowing from whence the thing comes," says Derrida, "and what awaits us, we are given over to absolute solitude. No one can speak with us and no one can speak for us; we must take it upon ourselves, each of us must take it upon himself (*auf sich nehmen* as Heidegger says concerning death, our death, concerning what is always 'my death,' and which no one can take on in place of me)" (p. 57). The wholly other is also manifested, without manifesting itself, in the total inaccessibility of the secrets in the hearts of other people.

> *Every other [one] is every [bit] other [tout autre est tout autre]*, "says Derrida," every one else is completely or wholly other. The simple concepts of alterity and of singularity constitute the concept of duty as much as that of responsibility. As a result, the concepts of responsibility, of decision, or of duty, are condemned a prioi to paradox, scandal, and aporia. . . . As soon as I enter into a relation with the other, with the gaze, look, request, love, command, or call of the other, I know that I can respond only by sacrificing ethics, that is, by sacrificing whatever obliges me to also respond, in the same way, in the same instant, to all the others. I offer a gift of death, I betray, I don't need to raise my knife over my son on Mount Moriah for that. Day and night, at every instant, on all the Mount Moriahs of this world, I am doing that, raising my knife over what I love ands must love, over those to whom I owe absolute fidelity, incommensurably (p. 68).

Included, finally, in this concept of the wholly other is literature. Literature too hides impenetrable secrets. A work of literature too is a response to a wholly other, which strongly recalls the relation of literature to death in Blanchot's thinking. This is made explicit in Derrida's reading of *Bartleby the Scrivener*, but also in the second, untranslated part of *Donner la mort*, entitled "*Ls literature au secret: Une filiation impossible.*" In this section, by way of further discussion of Abraham and Isaac, of Kierkegaard, and of Kafka, Derrida reaches the surprising conclusion not only that literature hides secrets that cannot be revealed. Literature is both irresponsible and at the same time works by "*aggravant d'autant, jusquà l'infini sa responsibilité pour l'événement singulier que constitue chaque oeuvre (respnsibilité nulle et infinie, comme celle de Abraham)* [by aggravating, moreover, even to infinity its responsibility for the singular event that constitutes each work (responsibility null and infinite, like Abraham's)]" (Derrida, 1999, p. 206, my trans.). Literature so defined is the unfaithful inheritor of a theological legacy without which it could not exist:

> *La literature hérite, certes, d'une histoire sainte dont le moment abrahamique reste le secret essentiel (et qui niera que la literature reste une reste de religion, un lien et un relais de sacro-sainteté dans une société sans Dieu?), mais elle renie aussi cette histoire, cette appartenance, cet heritage. Elle renie cette filiation. Elle la trahit au double sens du mot: Elle lui est infidèle, elle rompt avec elle au moment même d'en manifester la "vérité" et d'en dévoiler le secret. À savoir sa proper filiation: Possible impossible.*

> (Literature inherits, certainly, a sacred history of which the Abrahamic moment remains the essential secret (and who will deny that literature remains a remainder of religion, a connection and a relay of sacrosanctity in a society without God?), but it also denies that history, that belonging, that heritage. It denies that filiation. It betrays it in the double sense of the word: It is unfaithful to it, it breaks with it in the moment of manifesting its "truth" and of unveiling its secret. That is to say its own filiation: Possible impossible.)
> (P. 208, my trans.)

It is only necessary to add to what Derrida says here that literary study, as institutionalized in the university, is especially the place where the responsibility/irresponsibility of literature, its unconditionality, is received by professors and passed on to students, for example, the dissident notions of state sovereignty in Forster's *Howards End*.

I have now linked, across the gulf separating sovereignty and unconditionality, all six of the motifs in my title: Sovereignty Death Literature Unconditionality Democracy University. I have done this, however, apparently at the cost of blurring the difference between theologically based state sovereignty and the unconditional freedom of the university and of literary study there. Both, in the end, seem to be theological or quasi-theological concepts. What's the difference? That difference is easy to see, but perhaps not all that easy to accept. The distinction is "improbable" and "not provable," though it is essential to Derrida's thinking. For Derrida, and for me too, all claims by earthly sovereigns, such as those made implicitly by George W. Bush to wield power by mandate from God, are phantasms. They claim to see and to respond to something that is not there. A work of literature, on the other hand, and therefore the teaching of that work in a "university without condition," if there ever were to be such a thing, is a response to a call or command from the wholly other that is both impossible and yet may perhaps arrive. Each work is entirely singular, "counter, original, spare, strange" as Gerard Manley Hopkins puts it ("Pied beauty," l.7, Hopkins, 1948, p. 74). Each work is as different from every other work as each person differs from all others, or as each leaf differs from all other leaves. When I as reader or teacher respond to the wholly other as embodied in a literary work and try to mediate it to my students or to readers of what I write, I am, perhaps, just "perhaps," fulfilling my professional duty to put everything in question, and to help make or keep my university "without condition."

References

Austin, J. L. (1980). *How to Do Things with Words*, 2nd ed. Edited by J. O. Urmson and Marina Sbisà (Oxford: Oxford University Press).

Blanchot, M. (1981). "Literature and the right to death," in Lydia Davis (trans.), *The Gaze of Orpheus* (Barrytown, New York: Station Hill Press).

Derrida, J. (1992). *Acts of Literature*. Edited by Derek Attridge (New York: Routledge).

Derrida, J. (1995). *The Gift of Death*. Translated by David Wills (Chicago: The University of Chicago Press).

Derrida, J. (1999). *Donner la mort* (Paris: Galilée).

Derrida, J. (2001a). *Inconditionality ou souveraineté: L'Université aux frontières de l'Europe*. Bilingual edition in French and Greek; allocutions by Dimitris Dimiroulis and Georges Veltsos; annotations by Vanghelis Bitsoris (Athens: Éditions Patakis).

Derrida, J. (2001b). *L'Université sans condition* (Paris: Galilée).

Forster, E. M. (1989). *Howards End* (New York: Vintage International).

Hopkins, G. M. (1948). *Poems*, 3rd ed. Edited by W. H. Gardner (New York: Oxford University Press).

CHAPTER THREE

Right to Humanities: Of Faith and Responsibility

DENISE EGÉA-KUEHNE

In the current context of globalization[1] and sociopolitical conflicts, and of an increasingly bureaucratic approach to education through a business or industrial model, rights to Humanities education and the teaching of the Humanities take a new dimension and urgency, and present new challenges. Grounding this reflection in a reading of Derrida, I propose to explore the notion of heritage of a cultural memory before arguing the necessity of a right to the Humanities, and then I address the concurrent call for responsibility. The last section looks toward the concept of Humanities-to-come, and what Derrida calls "a profession of faith."

Of Cultural Legacy and the Humanities

A reading of Valéry's *La Liberté de l'esprit* and of Derrida's discussion of this text is helpful in understanding what lies behind the concept of cultural heritage. Valéry used a metaphor of economy to analyze the becoming of culture as a capital in a pre-war Europe undergoing major upheaval. He wrote, "Culture, civilization . . . are a kind of capital that grows and can be used and accumulated, can increase and diminish like all the imaginable kinds of capital."[2] This capital includes "material objects—books, artworks, instruments, etc.," but, Valéry stressed, these artifacts are not sufficient to constitute a cultural legacy. They also require individuals *"who need them* and *who know how to use them* [original

emphasis]."[3] On the eve of World War II, Valéry saw this capital threatened
and in a state of "crisis." He sent out a warning, "I say that our cultural
capital is in peril."[4] He perceived the danger as coming from the absence
of this essential human factor, of humanity. He highlighted the need for
knowledge and a yearning "for the power of inner transformation, for
the creations of . . . sensibility."[5] He insisted that a heritage is carried by
individuals, and that, in order to keep it alive, they need to be educated
about it; they need to know how "to acquire and exercise the habits, the
intellectual discipline, the conventions and methods" indispensable to
make use of the accumulated capital.[6] According to Valéry the disappearance
of those individuals who could keep the memory of a heritage, those
who knew "how to read . . . how to hear, and even how to listen . . . how
to see . . . to read, hear or see again"[7] is what constitutes the ultimate
threat to a cultural heritage and to the Humanities.

Commenting on Valéry's text in *The Other Heading*, a text exploring
the identity of the (new) "new Europe," Derrida discussed the question
of cultural legacy at length. He wondered whether there is "a completely
new 'today' of Europe beyond all the exhausted programs of *Eurocentrism*
and *anti-Eurocentrism*, these exhausting yet unforgettable programs."[8] Not
only did he stress repeatedly that we are unable to forget, but also that we
should not forget. However just any kind of memory will not do, and
Derrida argued the necessity of a "responsible memory," of both "repetition and memory," of individuals who are capable of assuming the
responsibility of this heritage, and, echoing Valéry's words, individuals
who are "prepared to respond, to respond *before*, to be responsible *for* and
to respond *to* what they had heard, seen, read, and known for the first
time [original emphasis]."[9] Valéry affirmed that it is this repetition and
this responsibility toward a cultural capital that guarantee the growth of
a "universal capital": "whatever they wished to read, hear, or see again
was, by recapitulation, turned into a *solid value*. And the world's wealth
was thus increased [original emphasis]."[10] The universal capital grew.

For Derrida the acknowledgment of our heritage is anything but passive,
and it entails a willingness to assume this legacy. It is not "received pas-
sively, but as a heritage one calls upon to form new questions and new
propositions," Derrida declared in an interview on French television in
May 2002.[11] According to him this recognition carries the necessity of a
response to two imperatives, to what he calls "a double injunction." First
we must learn what came "before us," then we must reaffirm it: "We must
know, and we must know how to *reaffirm* [original emphasis]."[12] Since
our heritage comes before us, Derrida says, it comes *to* us; it is received
by us without our having a chance to choose it. We are born to it, like we

are born to our language, which is part of it. What is left to us is the power to reaffirm it, to accept it, and to confirm it. The contradiction Derrida perceives is between "the passivity of the reception, and the decision to say 'yes,' "[13] yet not without a critical step.

For with this decision to accept our heritage comes the necessity to make choices, the necessity to "select, filter, interpret, and therefore transform, to not leave intact, unscathed."[14] While one reaffirms one's heritage, in order to do so, at the same time, one must question it, one must "reinterpret, critique, displace" this legacy.[15] With a constant reflection one must put this heritage into question, rethink and reevaluate its so-called or assumed certainties. Derrida understands the deconstruction, the unpacking of the sedimentations of this legacy, layer by layer, the uncovering of its composition, presumptions, and assumptions as "a tension between memory, fidelity, the preservation of something which has been given to us, and at the same time heterogeneity, something absolutely new."[16] The choice, if there is a choice, is then given and received through the experience of this reaffirmation and double injunction, experienced anew in each different context, through new steps of identification, selection, filtering, and interpretation. In "The deconstruction of actuality," Derrida explains:

> Whoever inherits chooses one spirit rather than another. One makes selections, one filters, one sifts through the ghosts or through the injunctions of each spirit. There is legacy only where assignations are multiple and contradictory, secret enough to defy interpretation, to carry the unlimited risk of active interpretation.[17]

To engage oneself Derrida believes that one must take "the unlimited risk of active interpretation," one must resist conditioning, escape enlisting, and challenge conformity. In his 2002 television interview, he declared: One "must do otherwise than merely follow up [*faire du suivisme*] and obey given watchwords or instructions. One must disengage oneself [*se désengager*]."[18] The paradox and the danger, the dangerous paradox is that one must negotiate a balance between engagement and disengagement. Derrida cautions that one "can engage politically . . . only in so far as one maintains as much freedom as possible with regard to all that is imposed . . . as hegemonic discourse, well-received axioms, etc."[19] He perceives his own engagement as concomitant with a necessary autonomy; for him it means, "being engaged without alienating [one's] freedom, [one's] right to disengage."[20] This notion is closely linked to his description of the aporia inherent in any responsible decision, to be addressed in the third section of this essay. However much Derrida can, and is willing to, account for the heterogeneity and complexity of a situation, "when it is necessary," he recognizes that there are times "when an urgent and binary choice" is called for in a specific instance; he believes that it is then his "duty to respond in a simple [i.e., straightforward] fashion," when it is necessary to take a definite stand, as "in the case of the Apartheid in South Africa, or for Mumia, or on the death penalty."[21]

Of Rights and the Humanities

Earlier we mentioned that Valéry stressed how in order for a cultural legacy not only to be sustained but to grow, it is essential for individuals to gain knowledge of their heritage as they learn "how to read . . . how to hear, and even how to listen . . . how to see . . . to read, hear or see again."[22] In order for the teaching of the Humanities to flourish and grow, one must cultivate the knowledge of one's heritage. One must "continue to develop, one must continue to read, the relation to tradition must be as cultivated as possible."[23] But at the same time, while being true to the memory of a culture, to what one receives from the past, while continuing to faithfully preserve and pass along a legacy, and the discipline and rigor of the profession, one must also break from the tradition, and strive to inaugurate something new. The pedagogy involved in the teaching of the Humanities cannot be one of mere reproduction, which would soon lead to a closing upon itself and asphyxiation. It must include putting into question past certitudes and assumptions.

Consequently and paradoxically one can be faithful to one's heritage only in as much as one accepts to be unfaithful to it, analyze, critique, and interpret it, relentlessly. Derrida goes one step further, declaring that it is precisely within this heritage that one can find the "conceptual tools," which will enable one to challenge the very limits of this heritage as traditionally defined and imposed. Derrida cites the example of human rights, which are, in essence, always in the making, "unfinished," perfectible beyond their own limits, limits which can be and should be, constantly pushed. Women's rights, children's rights, the right to work, to education, to culture, to Humanities education and to the teaching of the Humanities, and so on must be "torn" from the limits of human rights; but Derrida cautions, "this movement must be done in the name of an idea/ideal of right already present in the project of the Universal Declaration of Human Rights, which was itself founded on the 1789 declaration."[24] Hence the right to Humanities education and to the teaching of the

Humanities carries a right to questioning the Humanities itself. Derrida has widely addressed the mission of the university, and in his May 2002 interview he recalled what the concept of the university is: "A place of absolute independence in the questioning and in the quest for truth, in the face of any power, political, economic, religious, etc. That is the concept of the university, the principle of the unconditional freedom of the university," and within the university, of the Humanities.

In the same interview in May 2002, Derrida recalled that the founding principle of the university had a history, a heritage of several centuries, and that if it is to be faithful to its principle, it must not only allow questioning, even questioning itself, but it must in fact encourage it and nurture it: "It must not interdict any question, any putting to question, any discourse" within its own borders. The most challenging questions should not be excluded from inside the university, especially not according to "criteria external to the university," whether these criteria be issued from governmental, techno-scientific, ideological, religious, or economic concerns. Furthermore, within its borders, "the university can discuss, fight against, object, contest," these same questions and discourses.[25] The Humanities must question the question itself, its principle as well as its content. In fact in his various texts and lectures on the university without condition, Derrida insists repeatedly and under different forms that even questioning should not be beyond question, especially within the Humanities. He claims the university as the "ultimate place of critical resistance—and more than critical [i.e., deconstructive]—to all the powers of dogmatic and unjust appropriation."[26]

This is where the question of the unconditional university comes in (university as distinct from other research institutions serving "sponsored by," commercials and economic interests), the university without condition, where the new Humanities should be capable of taking on the task of deconstruction, as a right,

> as an unconditional right to ask critical questions . . . about the history even of the notion of critique, about the form and the authority of the question, about the interrogative form of thought. For this implies the right to do it affirmatively and performatively [original emphasis].[27]

Not only does the university have a "principial right to say everything," to question everything, but, at the same time, it should also, again especially through the new Humanities, "reflect, invent and pose," profess, and teach the "principle of unconditional resistance" as a fundamental right, questioning even the question.[28]

Of Responsibility and the Humanities

Never a given, the essence and purpose of the Humanities must ever be questioned, reinvented, and re-elaborated. The Humanities have a duty that entails the risk of asking questions, which are "unsettling" (*dérangeantes*), and which challenge established traditions, beliefs, and certitudes. "There is danger in thinking," declared Derrida in his May 2002 interview, and "it is first the danger to which I expose myself." He explained that the goal is not to frighten, but rather "to have it out with what in the thinkable remains unthinkable, or in any case threatening, unsettling; and there [for him] is the criterion of the experience of thinking." Assuming this risk is the responsibility of the Humanities, a responsibility anyone claiming a right to the Humanities and to the teaching of the Humanities must assume, a responsibility that is the essence of the Humanities and of the teaching of the Humanities.

In a 1999 conference Derrida discussed "the task of the philosopher, such as [he saw] it assigned and implied by the new 'world contract.' "[29] He was speaking before the UNESCO,[30] which hosted a conference on the general theme of The New World Contract being drawn up by Federico Mayor, the then director general of the institution. Derrida described the philosopher's task as also being "that of whoever tends to assume political and legal responsibilities in this matter"[31] in particular since "all the decisions . . . so-called ethical, theo-ethical, which must be taken today, questions of sovereignty, questions of international law, have been the objects of philosophical research for a very long time, and in a renewed fashion now."[32] To illustrate his point he offered four of the tightly linked themes around which have revolved his lectures, seminars, conferences, publications, and interviews in recent years (including several interventions before the UNESCO): Work, forgiveness, peace, and the death penalty. More recently, in his 2002 interview with France 3, Derrida insisted that philosophy and the Humanities are more necessary than ever to respond to the most urgent questions raised by today's sociopolitical context, questions of politics, ethics, and especially rights and law. These issues concern international institutions, including "the UN, the Security Council, the role of certain sovereign states in their relation of respect or non-respect toward these international institutions" (e.g., Apartheid, crimes against humanity, the death penalty, children's exploitation, etc.) all having to do with international law.[33] Derrida stressed that if international law is to be modified, "it can be done only on the grounds of a philosophical reflection."[34] Other burning issues concern cloning, genetic research, organ transplant, animals, and so on; they also require a questioning and a reflection guided by the philosophical and the Humanities models. In this reflection the Humanities heritage is indispensable to inform a responsible response. This entails an education to culture and to the Humanities, which is of paramount importance for an understanding of what is at stake.

Derrida discussed another responsibility of today's Humanities in the context of globalization and cosmopolitanism; it is the necessity to move beyond the opposition Eurocentrism versus anti-Eurocentrism. While upholding the memory of a heritage essentially Euro-Christian (Greek, Roman, Jewish, Christian, and Islamic, or Mediterranean/Central European, or Greco-Roman-Arab/Germanic), it is necessary to both recognize its origins, and go beyond its limits. It is also essential to be aware that the Humanities have been and are being transformed and appropriated by non-European languages and cultures. According to Derrida this is what a close, "long and slow" study of the historical roots and development of philosophy and the Humanities should reveal. He believes that

[w]hat is happening today, and has been for some time . . . are philosophical formations that will not let themselves be contained in this dialectic, which is basically cultural, colonial and neo-colonial, of appropriation and alienation. There are other ways [voies] of philosophy. . . . [Moreover, n]ot only are there other ways of philosophy, but philosophy, if there is such a thing, is the other way [l'autre voie].[35]

Derrida also believes that letting the Humanities, even under the label of cosmopolitanism, be determined by the opposition Eurocentrism versus. non-Eurocentrism would be limiting the right to the Humanities and to the teaching of the Humanities.

In an interview first published in Le Monde de l'Éducation, Derrida addressed pedagogical responsibilities. He indicated that for him "the task is infinite," with a necessity "to refine ever more scrupulously"[36] his thought, to do his utmost to address the heterogeneity or the complexity of a given situation. To this necessity, which he understands as a responsibility, he opposes that of the need sometimes to simplify in order to be able to transmit knowledge, the need for immediate or instant decision and communication, "not waiting, and at a precise moment, here, now, to take the risk (weighing it as best as possible) to speak, to teach, to publish."[37] To the traditional model of the intellectual, Derrida associates a specific responsibility, as he sees there not only "a guardian held responsible for the memory and culture," but also "a citizen entrusted with a sort of spiritual mission."[38] No doubt, with its memory, we are also given the responsibility of this legacy, a responsibility—Derrida pointed out again—that we did not choose, but which we must question and reaffirm.

Derrida described this responsibility toward a legacy as dual—as a duty to both keep and renew. Yet this is not without risk. Discussing European culture, Derrida stressed that an important characteristic of culture is that its history indicates a direction, "no doubt presupposes an identifiable heading, a *telos* toward which the movement, the memory, the promise, and the identity, even if it be as difference to itself, dreams of gathering itself."[39] For Derrida it is necessary to lay a path, "to anticipate and to keep the heading [*garder le cap*]," to maintain the direction, the goals, lest we repeat what has occurred before; for what is forgotten may surge again as the new threat. Under the guise of "the absolutely new, we can fear seeing return the phantom of the worst [evils], the one we have already identified" as such.[40] Examples abound, especially in education, of the "new," which is nothing but a repetition of the old rhetoric.[41] On the other hand history presupposes that we have no knowledge of the future, no way to anticipate or identify before the fact. Derrida stressed that "the unicity of the other *today* should be awaited *as such* . . . it should be anticipated *as* the unforeseeable, the *unanticipatable*, the non-masterable, non-identifiable, in short, as that of which one does not yet have a memory [original emphasis]."[42] Many a time, and more recently in his texts on the university without condition, Derrida explained how this unpredictability, this experience with the incalculable is precisely what constitutes the event, which must remain unpredictable, incalculable, in order to qualify as an event, to be "an event worthy of the name."[43] One must grasp "the incalculable *and* the calculable [original emphasis]" both and at the same time as well as "the transaction between the two."[44]

Consequently our responsibility entails being wary of "*both* repetitive memory *and* the completely other, the absolutely new [original emphasis]."[45] Derrida prompts us to be vigilant about "*both* anamnestic capitalization *and* the amnesic exposure to what would no longer be identifiable at all [original emphasis]."[46] The difficulty is in assuming a responsibility that is double and contradictory, for while we must preserve and guard an ideal of culture, an ideal of Humanities, we must also remain aware that a culture, a heritage of Humanities (be it of Europe or any other culture) cannot enclose itself within the borders of the university, and within the university, in the Humanities. For the cultural legacy, the heritage of the Humanities "consists precisely in not closing itself off in its own identity and in advancing itself in an exemplary way toward what it is not . . . indeed . . . perhaps something else altogether."[47] This touches upon the concepts of "to come," "promise," and "faith," which will be discussed in the next section.

Double injunctions, contradictions, aporias are, for Derrida, the essence of responsibility. He has described and discussed extensively in most of his texts how these dilemmas are inherent in the concept of responsibility, are in fact *the very condition* of its possibility. For "at a certain point promise and decision, which is to say responsibility, owe their possibility to the ordeal of undecidability which will always remain their condition."[48] Derrida further defined "the condition of possibility of this thing called responsibility" as "a certain *experience and experiment of the possibility of the impossible: The testing of the aporia* from which one may invent the only *possible invention, the impossible invention* [original emphasis]."[49] He stressed repeatedly, and again in his more recent texts on the unconditional university, that if there is an easy decision to make, and only a set of rules to follow, or a program to implement, there is, in fact, no decision to be made and therefore no responsibility to be taken.

Of Faith and the New Humanities

Derrida links this concept—this condition of possibility as being dependent on the simultaneous necessity of a condition of impossibility—to the experience of the university and, within the university, of the Humanities *à venir*, to come, to the promise, to a notion of messianism, to faith.

Talking about the Humanities, especially what he calls the *new* Humanities, Derrida returns to his concept of to come, developed in particular when discussing democracy, and complexified more recently with the notions of "as if" and "perhaps," analyzed at length in his various versions on the theme of the unconditional university.[50] These new Humanities, which would be characteristic of the unconditional, unconditionally free, autonomous university, are an idea, an ideal toward which we must strive. Derrida recognized that the concept of the university without condition, of the unconditional university, has been repeatedly betrayed throughout the years. A university as defined earlier by Derrida as a place of absolute independence in its questioning, its research, its quest for, and commitment to, truth as regards any political, economic, ideological, or religious power has never existed as such. This is repeatedly stated in the texts on the university without condition, for example,

"This university without conditions does not, *in fact*, exist, as we know only too well," and further, "One must insist on this again: If this uncon-ditionality, in principle and *de jure*, constitutes the invincible force of the university, it has never been in effect."[51]

However when talking about the Humanities to come, Derrida's reference is not to Humanities as we know them, as determined by their history in Western universities. He makes it clear that the social, political, philosophical, and economic dimensions of our world have changed, are still changing, and that intellectuals the world over have to rethink, reevaluate, reconceptualize the meaning of "old" paradigms and develop new ones. This does not mean some new brand of Humanities, which will realize itself only in a future time, nor "a regulating idea, in the Kantian sense, or . . . a utopia."[52] What it offers is some openness to the future and to the other, to the new, to renewal, which Derrida sees as an enlarged and re-elaborated concept including, but broader than, the traditional conservative and humanist project.

> This deconstructive task of the Humanities to come will not let itself be contained within the traditional limits of the departments that today belong, by their very status, to the Humanities. These Humanities to come will cross disciplinary borders without, all the same, dissolving the specificity of each discipline into what is called, often in a very confused way, interdisciplinarity, or into what is lumped with another good-for-everything concept, "cultural studies."[53]

Furthermore,

> They should include law, "legal studies," as well as . . ."theory" (an original articulation of literary theory, philosophy, linguistics, psychoanalysis, and so forth), but also, of course, in all these places, deconstructive practices.[54]

By Humanities to come Derrida refers to the very concept of Humanities "as the concept of a promise." For Derrida the future of the Humanities, of the university, and of the profession holds a promise; at the core of the idea of Humanities, he sees a promise, that of the ideal of Humanities. He described at length the "deconstructive task of the Humanities to come,"[55] which can manifest themselves only where there is disruption, where there exists a gap between the present state of the Humanities and the idea, the ideal of Humanities. In fact it is in this very gap that the new Humanities can be shaped,

> between an infinite promise (always untenable at least for the reason
> that it calls for the infinite respect of singularity *and* infinite alterity
> of the other as much as for the respect of the countable, calculable,
> subjectal equality between anonymous singularities) and the deter-
> mined, necessary, but also necessarily inadequate forms of what has
> to be measured against this promise.[56]

In this gap must be preserved heterogeneity, "as the only chance of an
affirmed or rather reaffirmed future."[57] Without this gap, without this
disjunction, the Humanities may simply believe, in all good conscience,
that they have succeeded, that their duty is accomplished, and therefore
they may miss their "chance of the future, of the promise or the appeal,
or the desire also (that is [their] 'own' possibility)."[58] It is by opening a
space for the affirmation of this promise, of the impossible event as a
promise, of the "messianic and emancipatory promise as promise,"[59] that
the Humanities will preserve their capital of possibilities, of dynamic
ideal in-the-making, to come.

The possibility, the eventuality of this promise of the Humanities to
come is absolutely dependent on its preserving within itself a hope, but a
hope that can never be expected, anticipated, or identified as such. For the
moment it is, it loses its very possibility of being a promise. Derrida writes:
"If one could *count* on what is coming, hope would be but the calculation
of a program."[60] His words about democracy to come can aptly be applied
to the promise of the Humanities, which cannot be a promise unless it
"always keeps within . . . this absolutely undetermined messianic hope at
its heart, this eschatological relation to the to-come of an event *and* of a
singularity, of an alterity that cannot be anticipated [original emphasis],"[61]
which must not be anticipated lest it would simply not be. For Derrida the
messianic and the promise are "inseparable." But unlike Benjamin for
whom messianism still carries traces of Jewish or Marxist messianism,
Derrida considers messianicity "as a universal structure of experience."[62]
For him messianicity is messianism without religion, without a messiah. In
the sense that it is not utopian and that it has to do with "the coming of an
eminently real, concrete event,"[63] it is tightly linked to the promise and to
the concept of to come. Caputo underscored this link when he declared
that "the Messiah is a very special promise." Like the promise whose very
existence depends on its not being kept, which, the moment it is kept is no
longer a promise, the possibility of its coming is what makes a messiah
a possibility, which can only be sustained by its being forever deferred.

Derrida described the messianic as belonging to "a universal structure, to that irreducible movement of the historical opening to the future, therefore to experience itself and to its language (expectation, promise, commitment . . .)."[64] He sees the "messianic structure," what he calls messianicity, as having everything to do with faith. For him the concepts of to come and the promise are closely tied to the pledge, to commitment, and his texts on the university without condition repeatedly utilize these terms along with engagement, responsibility, profession, profession of faith, act of faith, declaration of faith, and act of sworn faith. He declared: "I would like to connect this problematic of the university without condition to a pledge, a commitment, a promise, an act of faith, a declaration of faith, a profession of faith."[65]

Derrida opened each one of the three texts on the unconditional university with the same words, "This will no doubt be like a profession of faith," words he repeated a second time in that first line. In these texts the words "profession of faith" are mentioned no less than nearly thirty times, the word faith alone almost fifty times, and they all conclude with the statement of "seven professions of faith." Six are a recapitulation, while the seventh "attempt[s] a step beyond the others." Between these six theses, which he called professions of faith, and the seventh, one can see a leap of faith into the promised event (the Humanities to come) brought on by the as if and the perhaps, beyond the distinction he discussed at length between the constative and performative acts.

These new Humanities would treat . . . in the same style . . .

1. the history of man, the idea, the figure, and the notion of "what is proper to man" [in particular the "Declarations[66] of the Rights of Man" and the concept of "crime against humanity"] . . .
2. the history of democracy and the idea of sovereignty . . .
3. the history of "professing," of the "profession," and of the professoriat— a history articulated with that of the premises or presuppositions . . . of work and of the worldwide-ized confession . . .
4. the history of literature . . .
5. the history of profession, the profession of faith, professionalization, and the professoriat . . . [in terms of the profession of faith of the professor] . . .
6. finally . . . the history of the as if and especially the history of this precious distinction between performative acts and constative acts . . .[67]

The event of the seventh point (the seventh profession of faith)

7. by taking place or having place, revolutionizes, overturns, and puts
    to rout the very authority that is attached in the university, in the
    Humanities,

    (i)   to knowledge (or at least to its model of constative language),
    (ii) to the profession or to the profession of faith (or at least to its
          model of performative language),
    (iii) to the *mise en oeuvre*, the putting to work, at least of the per-
          formative putting to work of the as if.[68]

Going back to the etymology of "profess" and its Latin roots, Derrida
explains how he understands the profession of professor as a profession of
faith, and how he "would like to connect this problematic of the university without condition to a pledge, a commitment, a promise, an act of
faith, a declaration of faith."[69] Linking faith to knowledge Derrida
prompts us to reaffirm our faith in knowledge, in the Humanities, in a
university, which would be unconditional:

> I am thus referring to a university that would be what it should have
> been or always should have represented, that is, from its inception and
> in principle: Autonomous, unconditionally free in its institution, in its
> speech, in its writing, in its thinking. In a thinking, a writing, a speech
> that would not be only the archives or the product of *knowledge* but
> also performative works, which are far from being neutral utopias.[70]

In *Marx & Sons* Derrida explains how by faith, he means "thinking," as in
Heidegger's *denken*.This thinking is not limited to theoretical thinking or
to knowledge in its general sense. In fact it could not be further from
utopia and utopic thinking. On the contrary, if met with responsibility, it
is a thinking, a faith, which calls for action, that strives toward a possible
future which, because it is always in the making, *à venir*, remains a
dynamic hope and promise of something to come.This tension between
the state of the Humanities today and the hope for the faith in the
Humanities to come is the force behind a thinking that "calls for the
coming of an event, i.e., calls precisely for that which 'changes,' "[71] that
which helps shape the new Humanities.

Conclusion

Reading Derrida helps understand how important and necessary our
cultural and Humanities heritage is for us to be aware of, and respond to,

the most urgent questions and dilemmas posed by the current socio-political context. At a time when education faces the pressures of "accountability," of test-driven educational objectives, and of an increasingly bureaucratic approach to education through the business or industrial model, rights to the Humanities and Humanities education take a new dimension and urgency, and present new challenges. The necessity of a right to the Humanities must be upheld, as well as the responsibility it entails. The link Derrida establishes between faith and knowledge in the university and, within the university, the Humanities, reminds us all of what professing, the profession of professor, is about, and calls us into action to help shape the possibility of the new Humanities.

Notes

1. To the term "globalization," Derrida prefers the French word *mondialisation*, i.e., "worldwide-ization" to retain the reference to the world, which he points out is "neither the globe nor the cosmos."
2. Paul Valéry (1960). "Notes sur la grandeur et la décadence de l'Europe," in *Oeuvres Complètes*, vol. 2 (Paris: Pléiade), p. 1089. Denise Folliot and Jackson Matthews (trans.) (1962). "Notes on the greatness and decline of Europe," in *History and Politics* (New York: Bollingen), p. 200.
3. Ibid., p. 1089/200.
4. Ibid., p. 1090/201.
5. Ibid., p. 1090/201.
6. Ibid., p. 1090/201.
7. Ibid., p. 1091/202.
8. Jacques Derrida (1992). *The Other Heading: Reflections on Today's Europe*. Translated by Pascale-Anne Brault and Michael B. Naas (Indianapolis: Indiana University Press), pp. 12–13.
9. Ibid., p. 70.
10. Valéry, "Notes," p. 1091/202.
11. Jacques Derrida, "Cultures et dépendances—Spécial Jacques Derrida." Presented by Franz-Olivier Giesbert, with the participation of Elizabeth Levy, Charles Pépin, Daniel Schick, and Séverine Werba (France 3 Television, May 2002). Translated by Denise Egéa-Kuehne; not available in print.
12. Jacques Derrida and Elizabeth Roudinesco (2001). *De quoi demain . . . Dialogue* (Paris: Fayard/Galilée), p. 15.
13. Ibid., p. 16.
14. Ibid., p. 16.
15. Ibid., p. 16.
16. Roundtable discussion with Jacques Derrida (Villanova University, October 3, 1994), http://www.hydra.umn.edu/derrida/vill.html.
17. Jacques Derrida (2002). *Negotiations: Interventions and Interviews, 1971–2001*. Translated by Elizabeth Rottenberg (Stanford: Stanford University Press), p. 111.
18. Derrida, "Cultures et dépendances."
19. Ibid.
20. Ibid.
21. Ibid. Examples of Derrida's political engagement are numerous throughout the years, be it Apartheid in South Africa, Mumia Abu-Jamal, the death penalty, or as recalled by Giesbert in this interview, his imprisonment in Prague.

22. Valéry, "Notes," p. 1091/202.
23. Derrida, *Negotiations*, p. 15.
24. Derrida and Roudinesco, *De quoi demain*, pp. 39–40.
25. The preceding quotes are from Derrida's 2002 interview with France 3. However he has spoken and published numerous times about "the university without condition." See, e.g., the Stanford lecture written in response to an invitation for the Presidential Lecture Series in the Humanities and Arts hosted by President Gerhard Casper of Stanford University and organized by Hans Ulrich Gumbrecht in 1999. Originally titled "The Future of the Profession or The University Without Condition" (Thanks to the "Humanities," What *Could Take Place* Tomorrow), it was published under the shorter title "The University Without Condition," in *Without Alibi*, ed. Peggy Kamuf (Stanford: Stanford University Press, 2002), pp. 202–237. With minor variations, the same lecture was delivered at the University of SUNY Albany on October 11, 1999, under the title "The Future of the Profession or the Unconditional University." It was hosted by Tom Cohen, chair of the English Department, and David Wills, chair of Languages, Literatures, and Cultures. Derrida can be heard delivering this lecture at http://www.albany.edu/history/derrida.html. Under its longer title Tom Cohen included this text in the collection he edited titled *Jacques Derrida and the Humanities: A Critical Reader* (Cambridge: Cambridge University Press, 2001), pp. 24–57.
26. Ibid., p. 204.
27. Ibid., p. 204. On the next page (p. 205) Derrida writes: "The university should thus also be the place in which nothing is beyond question . . . not even the traditional idea of critique, meaning theoretical critique, and not even the authority of the 'question' form, of thinking as 'questioning.' This is why I spoke without delay and without disguise of deconstruction."
28. Ibid., pp. 204–205.
29. Derrida, "Globalization, Peace, and Cosmopolitanism," *Negotiations*, p. 376.
30. The United Nations Educational, Scientific, and Cultural Organization, an independent organization related to, and recognized by, the United Nations as one of its specialized agencies. "La mondialisation et la paix cosmopolitique" was first delivered at the UNESCO's headquarters in Paris on November 6, 1999, as part of the "Discussions of the twenty-first century." Transcribed and published in *Regards* 54 (February 2000, 16–19). Translated by Elizabeth Rottenberg, in *Negotiations*, pp. 371–386.
31. Derrida, "Globalization, peace, and cosmopolitanism," *Negotiations*, p. 376.
32. Derrida, "Cultures et dépendences."
33. See also Jacques Derrida (2001). *On Cosmopolitanism and Forgiveness* (London & New York: Routledge).
34. Derrida, "Cultures et dépendences."
35. Derrida, "The right to philosophy," *Negotiations*, p. 337.
36. Jacques Derrida (2000). "Autrui est secret parce qu'il est autre," *Le Monde de l'Éducation*, no. 284, 14–21. Reprinted in "21 penseurs pour comprendre le XXIe siècle . . . et 21 regards critiques," Numéro Spécial, *Le Monde de l'Éducation*, no. 194 (2001), 104–112. Translated by Denise Egéa-Kuehne.
37. Derrida, "Autrui est secret," 18.
38. Derrida, *The Other Heading*, p. 23.
39. Ibid., pp. 17–18.
40. Ibid., p. 18.
41. Examples abound also in politics, to mention only recent elections (e.g., David Duke in Louisiana gubernatorial elections, Le Pen in France's last presidential elections) and international conflicts (e.g., Bosnia, Afghanistan, Iraq, Africa).
42. Derrida, *The Other Heading*, p. 18.
43. Derrida, "The University Without Condition," p. 234.
44. Derrida, "Culture et dépendences."
45. Derrida, *The Other Heading*, p. 19.
46. Ibid., p. 19.

47. Derrida, *The Other Heading*, p. 29.

48. Jacques Derrida (1994). *Specters of Marx*. Translated by Peggy Kamuf (New York & London: Routledge), p. 75.

49. Derrida, *The Other Heading*, p. 41.

50. "What I would like to attempt with you is this apparently impossible thing: to link this 'as if' to the thinking of an event, that is, to the thinking of this thing that *perhaps* happens, that is supposed to *take place* . . . . I will speak of an event that, without necessarily coming about tomorrow, would remain perhaps—and I underscore *perhaps*—to come." (Derrida, "The University Without Condition," p. 213).

51. Derrida, "The University Without Condition," pp. 204 and 206.

52. Derrida, *Specters of Marx*, p. 65.

53. Derrida, "The University Without Condition," p. 230.

54. Ibid., p. 208.

55. Ibid., p. 230.

56. Derrida, *Specters of Marx*, p. 65.

57. Ibid., p. 37.

58. Ibid., p. 28.

59. Ibid., p. 75.

60. Ibid., p. 169.

61. Ibid., p. 65.

62. Jacques Derrida (1999). "Marx & Sons," in Michael Sprinker (ed.), *Ghastly Demarcations: A Symposium on Jacques Derrida's* Specters of Marx (New York: Verso), p. 248.

63. Ibid., p. 248.

64. Derrida, *Specters of Marx*, p. 167.

65. Derrida, "The University Without Condition," p. 208.

66. Plural in Derrida's text, referring to the several versions of the Declaration of the Rights of Man throughout its history.

67. Derrida, "The University Without Condition," pp. 231–233.

68. Ibid., p. 233.

69. Ibid., p. 208.

70. Ibid., pp. 213–214.

71. Derrida, "Marx & Sons," p. 257.

CHAPTER FOUR

Higher Education and Democracy's Promise: Jacques Derrida's Pedagogy of Uncertainty

HENRY A. GIROUX

Introduction

During the last two decades Jacques Derrida has made a number of important and crucial interventions regarding the relationship between democracy and the purpose and meaning of higher education. Democracy, for Derrida, is not merely a social–historical creation, but also contains a promise of what is to come. And it is precisely in the tension between the dream and the reality of democracy that a space of agency, critique, and education opens up, which signals both the normative and political character of democracy. But, as Derrida is well aware, democracy also demands a pedagogical intervention organized around the need to create the conditions for educating citizens who have the knowledge and skills to participate in public life, question institutional authority, and engage the contradiction between the reality and promise of democracy. Pedagogy, in this sense, is central to democracy because it represents an essential dimension of justice, offering the conditions necessary for individuals to become autonomous in order to make choices, participate in and shape public life, and develop a socially committed notion of justice. If politics represents an intervention into the social, education provides the resources to translate "individual problems into public issues and common interests into individual rights and duties,"[1] and opens up strategic space for rupturing those modes of authority that freeze society by claiming it has become just enough, no longer sanctioning those pedagogical practices dedicated to the perception that society can never attain a definitive level of justice. For Derrida democracy must not only contain the structure of a promise, it must also be nurtured in those public spaces in which "the unconditional freedom to question"[2] becomes central to any viable definition of individual and social agency. At stake here is the recognition that if democracy is to become vital, it needs to create citizens who are critical, interrogate authority, hold existing institutions accountable for their actions, and be able to assume public responsibility through the very process of governing.[3] Hence, for Derrida, higher education is one of the few public spaces left where unconditional resistance can be both produced and subject to critical analysis. In Derrida's perspective the university "should thus be a place in which nothing is beyond question, not even the current and determined figure of democracy, and not even the traditional idea of critique."[4] The role of the university in this instance, and particularly the Humanities, should be to create a culture of questioning and resistance aimed at those ideologies, institutions, social practices, and "powers that limit democracy to come."[5] Derrida's views on higher education, democracy, and the role of intellectuals raise important questions about the state of democracy in the United States today, and how the latter is shaping the purpose of higher education and the social contract between society and young people, which has always been at the heart of how higher education defined its future and legitimated a particular view of democracy itself. In what follows I want to briefly say something about the state of democracy under the presidency of George Bush with particular reference to youth and the crisis of the future. I will conclude by talking about the changing nature of higher education and the implications this raises for both democracy to come and for the role of academics as engaged intellectuals.

The Crisis of Democracy and the Crisis of Youth

As the state is restructured due to right wing assaults by the Bush administration, it has dramatically shifted its allegiance away from providing for people's welfare, protecting the environment, and expanding the realm of public good. As a result of such a shift, the state has nullified the social contract that lies at the heart of a substantive democracy, a contract that provides for social provisions against life's hazards, that ensures a decent education, health care, food, and housing for all, but especially for those who are marginalized by virtue of sickness, age, race, gender, and youth. As the social contract is torn up by Bush's army of neoliberal evangelicals, neoconservative hard-liners, and religious fundamentalists, government relies more heavily on its militarizing functions giving free reign to security at the expense of public service and endorsing property rights over human rights. Under such circumstances we are witnessing a society organized increasingly around a culture of fear, cynicism, and unbridled self interest—a society where the government promotes legislation urging neighbors to spy on each other and the president of the United States endorses a notion of patriotism based on moral absolutes and an alleged mandate to govern, which, if John Ashcroft is to be believed, comes directly from God. Increasingly we are told by Bush, Rumsfeld, and Ashcroft that patriotism is now defined through the simple decision of either being with the government or being against it. Such absolutes, of course, have little respect for difference, dissent, or for that matter democracy itself. Politics in this instance has much less in common with public engagement, dialogue, and democratic governance than with a heavy reliance on institutions that rule through an appeal to fear and, if necessary, brute force. With such a set of circumstance the criminal justice system rather than public and higher education increasingly serves as one of the primary models for managing and containing populations within a wide range of public spheres, especially poor people of color. Not only do many states spend more money for building and maintaining prisons than on higher education, but in a state like New York "more Blacks entered prison just for drug offenses than graduated from the state's massive university system with undergraduate, masters, and doctoral degrees combined in the 1990s." In this context the prison–industrial complex can best be understood as a model for enforcing the criminalization of social problems, policing communities, suppressing dissent, punishing and containing students of color, and reconstructing the state as a force for domestic militarization. The importance of the prison–industrial complex can be seen in the fact that the United States imprisons more people than any other country in the world–more than 2 million—and though it comprises only 5 percent of the world's population it houses more than 25 percent of the world's prisoners.

Democracy has never appeared more fragile and endangered in the United States than in this time of civic and political crisis. This is especially true for young people. While a great deal has been written about war and the occupation of Iraq and the passing of new antiterrorist laws, which make it easier to undermine basic civil liberties, there is a thunderous silence on the part of many critics and academics regarding the ongoing "war" waged against the young people in this country, which is now being intensified as a result of the state's increasing resort to repression and punitive social policies. Any discourse about the future has to begin with the issue of youth because more than any other group youth embody the projected dreams, desires, and commitment of a society's obligations to the future. This echoes a classical principle of modernity in which youth both symbolize society's responsibility to the future and offer a measure of its progress. For most of this century Americans have embraced as a defining feature of politics that all levels of government would assume a large measure of responsibility for providing the resources, social provisions, security, and modes of education that simultaneously offers young people a future as it expands the meaning and depth of a substantive democracy. In many respects youth not only registered symbolically the importance of modernity's claim to progress, they also affirmed the importance of the liberal, democratic tradition of the social contract in which adult responsibility was mediated through a willingness to fight for the rights of children, enact reforms that invested in their future, and provide the educational conditions necessary for them to make use of the freedoms they have while learning how to be critical citizens. Within such a modernist project democracy was linked to the well-being of youth, while the status of how a society imagined democracy and its future was contingent on how it viewed its responsibility toward future generations.

But the category of youth did more than affirm modernity's social contract rooted in a conception of the future in which adult commitment and intergenerational solidarity were articulated as a vital public service, it also affirmed those vocabularies, values, and social relations central to a politics capable of both defending vital institutions as a public good, and contributing to the quality of public life. Such a vocabulary was particularly important for higher education, which often defined and addressed its highest ideals through the recognition that how it educated youth was connected to both the democratic future it hoped for and its claim as an important public sphere.

Yet at the dawn of the new millennium it is not at all clear that we believe any longer in youth, the future, or the social contract, even in its minimalist version. Since the Reagan/Thatcher revolution of the 1980s, we have been told that there is no such thing as society and, indeed, following that nefarious pronouncement, institutions committed to public welfare have been disappearing. Those of us who, against prevailing common sense, insist on the relationship between higher education and the future of democracy have to face a disturbing reversal in priorities with regard to youth and education, which now defines the United States and other regions under the reign of neoliberalism.[6] Rather than being cherished as a symbol of the future, youth are now seen as a threat to be feared and a problem to be contained. A seismic change in which youth are being framed as both a generation of suspects and a threat to public life has now taken place. If youth once symbolized the moral necessity to address a range of social and economic ills, they are now largely portrayed as the source of most of society's problems. Hence youth now constitute a crisis that has less to do with improving the future than with denying it. A concern for children is the defining absence in almost any discourse about the future and the obligations this implies for adult society. To witness the abdication of adult responsibility toward children we need look no further than the current state of children in America who once served as a "kind of symbolic guarantee that America still had a future, which it still believed in a future, and that it was crucial to America to invest in that future."[7]

No longer "viewed as a privileged sign and embodiment of the future,"[8] youth are now demonized by the popular media and derided by politicians looking for quick-fix solutions to crime, joblessness, and poverty. In a society deeply troubled by their presence, youth prompt a public rhetoric of fear, control, and surveillance, which translates into social policies that signal the shrinking of democratic public spheres, the highjacking of civic culture, and the increasing militarization of public space. Equipped with police and drug-sniffing dogs, though not necessarily teachers or textbooks, public schools increasingly resemble prisons. Students begin to look more like criminal suspects who need to be searched, tested, and observed under the watchful eye of administrators who appear to be less concerned with educating them than with containing their every move. Nurturance, trust, and respect now give way to fear, disdain, and suspicion. In many suburban malls young people, especially urban youth of color, cannot shop or walk around without having appropriate identification cards or being in the company of a parent. Children have fewer rights than almost any other group and fewer institutions protecting these rights. Consequently their voices and needs are almost completely absent from the debates, policies, and legislative practices that are constructed in terms of their needs.

While the United States ranks first in military technology, military exports, defense expenditures, and the number of millionaires and billionaires, it is ranked eighteenth among the advanced industrial nations in the gap between rich and poor children, twelfth in the percentage of children in poverty, seventeenth in the efforts to lift children out of poverty, and twenty-third in infant mortality.[9] The U.S. Government plans to spend up to $400 billion to finance the Iraq War and the ongoing occupation, while it allocates only $16 billion to welfare programs that cannot possibly address the needs of over 33 million people who live below the poverty line, many of them children, or the 75 million without health insurance, or the millions now unemployed because of the gutting of public services and state resources. While $350 billion dollars (the amount goes up to $1 trillion over a 10-year period) are allocated for tax cuts for the rich, state governments are cutting a total of $75 billion in public services, health, welfare benefits, and education. The sheer inhumanity this government displays toward the working poor and children living below and slightly above poverty level can be seen in the decision by Republicans in Congress to eliminate from the recent tax bill the $400 child credit for families with incomes between $10,000 and $26,000. The money saved by this cut will be used to pay for the cut on dividend taxes. As a result, as Bill Moyers observes, "Eleven million children punished for being poor, even as the rich are rewarded for being rich."[10] But Bush's insensitivity to American children represents more than a paean to the rich, it also represents an attempt to shrink the government, dismantle public services, and usurp the most fundamental dimensions of the social contract.

Youth have become the central site onto which class and racial anxieties are projected. Their very presence in an age where there is no such thing as society represents *both* the broken promises of democracy. Corporate deregulation and downsizing and a collective fear of the consequences wrought by systemic class inequalities, racism, and a culture of "infectious greed" has created a generation of displaced and unskilled youth who have been expelled from the "universe of moral obligations."[11] Youth within the economic, political, and cultural geography of neoliberal capitalism occupy a degraded borderland in which the spectacle of commodification exists side by side with the imposing threat of the prison–industrial complex and the elimination of basic civil liberties. As neoliberalism disassociates economics from its social costs, "the political state has become the corporate state."[12] Under such circumstances the state does not disappear, but, as Pierre Bourdieu has brilliantly reminded us,[13] is refigured as its role in providing social provisions, intervening on behalf of public welfare, and regulating corporate plunder is weakened. The neoliberal state no longer invests in solving social problems; it now punishes those who are caught in the downward spiral of its economic policies. Punishment, incarceration, and surveillance represent the face of the new state. One consequence is that the implied contract between the state and the citizens is broken and social guarantees for youth as well as civic obligations to the future vanish from the agenda of public concern. Similarly, as market values supplant civic values, it becomes increasingly difficult "to translate private worries into public issues and, conversely, to discern public issues in private troubles."[14] Alcoholism, homelessness, poverty, and illiteracy, among other issues, are not seen as social but as individual problems—matters of character, individual fortitude, and personal responsibility. In the light of increased antiterrorism campaigns waged by the Bush administration, it becomes easier to militarize domestic space, criminalize social problems, and escape from the responsibilities of the present while destroying all possibilities of a truly democratic future. Moreover the social costs of the complex cultural and economic operations of this assault can no longer be ignored by educators, parents, and other concerned citizens.

The war against youth, in part, can be understood within those fundamental values and practices that characterize a rapacious, neoliberal capitalism. For many young people and adults today, the private sphere has become the only space in which to imagine any sense of hope, pleasure, or possibility. Culture as an activity in which people actually produce the conditions of their own agency through dialogue, community participation, resistance, and political struggle is being replaced by a "climate of cultural and linguistic privatization"[15] in which culture becomes something you consume, and the only kind of speech that is acceptable is that of the savvy shopper. Neoliberalism, with its emphasis on market forces and profit margins, narrows the legitimacy of the public sphere by redefining it around the related issues of privatization, deregulation, consumption, and safety. Big government, recalled from exile after 9/11, is now popularly presented as a guardian of security—security not in terms of providing adequate social provisions or a social safety net, but in terms of increasing the state's role as a policing force. The new emphasis on national security has resulted in the ongoing abridgement of basic freedoms and dissent, the criminalization of social problems, and the prioritizing of penal methods over social investments. Ardent consumers and disengaged citizens provide fodder for a growing cynicism and depoliticization of public life at a time when there is an increasing awareness not just of corporate corruption, financial mismanagement, and systemic greed, but also of the recognition that a democracy of critical citizens is being replaced quickly by an eratz democracy of consumers. Ironically the desire to protect market freedoms and wage a war against terrorism has not only ushered in a culture of fear but has also dealt a lethal blow to civil freedoms. Resting in the balance of this contradiction is both the fate of democracy and the civic health and future of a generation of children and young people.

Under this insufferable climate of increased repression and unabated exploitation, young people become the new casualties in an ongoing war against justice, freedom, citizenship, and democracy. What is happening to children in America and what are its implications for addressing the future of higher education? Lawrence Grossberg argues that "the current rejection of childhood as the core of our social identity, is at the same time, a rejection of the future as an affective investment."[16] But the crisis of youth not only signals a dangerous state of affairs for the future, it also portends a crisis in the very idea of the political and ethical constitution of the social and the possibility of articulating the relevance of democracy itself; it is in reference to the crisis of youth, the social, and democracy that I want to address the relationship between higher education and the future.

Higher Education and the Crisis of the Social

Within the last two decades a widespread pessimism about public life and politics has developed in the United States. Individual interests now outweigh collective concerns as market ideals have taken precedence over democratic values. Moreover the ethos of citizenship has been stripped of its political dimensions and is now reduced to the obligations of consumerism. In the vocabulary of neoliberalism the public collapses into the personal, and the personal becomes "the only politics there is, the only politics with a tangible referent or emotional valence,"[17] and it is within such an utterly personal discourse that human actions are shaped and agency is privatized. Under neoliberalism hope becomes dystopian as the public sphere disappears and, as Peter Beilharz argues, "politics becomes banal, for there is not only an absence of citizenship but a striking absence of agency."[18] As power is increasingly separated from the specificity of traditional politics and public obligations, corporations are less subject to the control of the state and "there is a strong impulse to displace political sovereignty with the sovereignty of the market, as if the latter has a mind and morality of its own."[19] Under the auspices of neoliberalism the language of the social is either devalued or ignored altogether as the idea of the public sphere is equated with a predatory space, rife with danger and disease—as in reference to public restrooms, public transportation, and urban public schools. Dreams of the future are now modeled on the narcissistic, privatized, and self-indulgent needs of consumer culture and the dictates of the alleged free market. Mark Taylor, a social critic turned apologist for the alleged free market, both embodies and captures the sentiment well with his comment: "Insofar as you want to engage in practice responsibly, you have to play with the hand you're dealt. And the hand we're dealt seems to me to be one in which the market has certainly won out over other kinds of systems."[20] There is more at stake here than another dominant media story about a left academic who finally sees the entrepreneurial halo. The narrative points to something much larger. Samuel Weber has suggested that what seems to be involved in this transformation is "a fundamental and political redefinition of the social value of public services in general, and of universities and education in particular."[21]

Within this impoverished sense of politics and public life the university is gradually being transformed into a training ground for the corporate workforce, rendering obsolete any notion of higher education as a crucial public sphere in which critical citizens and democratic agents are formed. As universities become increasingly strapped for money, corporations provide the needed resources for research and funds for endowed chairs, exerting a powerful influence on both the hiring of faculty, and how research is conducted and for what purposes. In addition universities now offer up buildings and stadiums as billboards for brand name corporations in order to procure additional sources of revenue while also adopting the values, management styles, cost-cutting procedures, and the language of excellence that has been the hallmark of corporate culture. Under the reign of neoliberalism and corporate culture, the boundaries between commercial culture and public culture become blurred as universities rush to embrace the logic of industrial management while simultaneously forfeiting those broader values both central to a democracy and capable of limiting the excesses of corporate power. Although the university has always had ties with the industry, there is a new intimacy between higher education and corporate culture, characterized by what Larry Hanley calls a "new, quickened symbiosis."[22] As Masao Miyoshi points out the result is "not a fundamental or abrupt change perhaps, but still an unmistakable radical reduction of its public and critical role."[23] What was once the hidden curriculum of many universities—the subordination of higher education to capital—has now become an open and much celebrated policy of both public and private higher education.[24] How do we understand the university in light of both the crisis of youth and the related crisis of the social, which have emerged under the controlling hand of neoliberalism? How can the future be grasped given the erosion of the social and public life over the last 20 years? What are the implications for the simultaneous corporatization of higher education in light of these dramatic changes? Any concern about the future of the university has to both engage and challenge this transformation while reclaiming the role of the university as a democratic public sphere. In what follows I want to analyze the university as a corporate entity within the context of a crisis of the social. In particular I will focus on how this crisis is played out not only through the erosion of public space, but also through the less explained issues of public versus corporate time, on the one hand, and the related issues of agency, pedagogy, and public mission on the other.

Public Time versus Corporate Time

Questions of time are crucial to how a university structures its public mission, the role of faculty, the use of space, student access, and the legitimation of particular forms of knowledge, research, and pedagogy. Time is not simply a question of how to invoke the future, but is also used to legitimate particular social relations and make claims on human behavior, representing one of the most important battlefields for determining how the future of higher education is played out in political and ethical terms. Time refers not only to the way in which it is mediated differently by institutions, administrators, faculty, and students but also how it shapes and allocates power, identities, and space through a particular set of codes and interests. But more importantly time is a central feature of politics and orders not merely the pace of the economic, but the time available for consideration, contemplation, and critical thinking. When reduced to a commodity time often becomes the enemy of deliberation and thoughtfulness and undermines the ability of political culture to function critically.

For the past 20 years, time as a value and the value of time have been redefined through the dictates of neoliberal economics, which has largely undermined any notion of public time guided by non-commodified values central to a political and social democracy. As Peter Beilharz observes,

> time has become our enemy. The active society demands of us that we keep moving, keep consuming, experience everything, travel, work as good tourists more than act as good citizens, work, shop and die. To keep moving is the only way left in our cultural repertoire to push away . . . meaning . . . [and consequently] the prospects, and forms of social solidarity available to us shrink before our eyes.[25]

Without question the future of the university will largely rest on the outcome of the current struggle between the university as a public space with the capacity to slow time down in order to question, once again, what Jacques Derrida calls the powers that limit "a democracy to come"[26] and a corporate university culture wedded to a notion of accelerated time in which the principle of self-interest replaces politics and consumerism replaces a broader notion of social agency. A meaningful and inclusive democracy is indebted to a notion of public time, while neoliberalism celebrates what I call corporate time. In what follows I want to briefly comment on some of the theoretical and political work performed by each of these notions of time and the implications they have for addressing the future of higher education. Public time as a condition and critical referent makes visible how politics is played out through the unequal access different groups have to "institutions, goods, services, resources, and power and knowledge."[27] That is, it offers a critical category for understanding how the ideological and institutional mechanisms of higher education work to grant time to some faculty and students and to withhold it from others, how time is mediated differently within different disciplines and among diverse faculty and students, how time can work across the canvas of power and space to create new identities and social formations capable of "intervening in public debate for the purpose of affecting positive change in the overall position and location in society."[28] When linked to issues of power, identity, ideology, and politics, public time can be an important social construct for orientating the university toward a vision of the future in which critical learning becomes central to increasing the scope of human rights, individual freedom, and the operations of a substantive democracy. In this instance public time resonates with a project of leadership, teaching, and learning in which higher education seems an important site for investing democratic public life with substance and vibrancy.

Public time rejects the fever-pitch appeals of "just in time" or "speed time," demands often made within the context of "ever faster technological transformation and exchange,"[29] and buttressed by corporate capital's golden rule: "time is money." Public time slows time down not as a simple refusal of technological change or a rejection of all calls for efficiency but as an attempt to create the institutional and ideological conditions that promote long term analyses, historical reflection, and deliberations over what our collective actions might mean for shaping the future. Rejecting an instrumentality that evacuates questions of history, ethics, and justice, public time fosters dialogue, thoughtfulness, and critical exchange. It offers room for knowledge that contributes to society's self-understanding, enables it to question itself, and seeks to legitimate intellectual practices, which are not only collective and noninstrumental but deepen democratic values while encouraging pedagogical relations that question the future in political, ethical, and social terms. As Cornelius Castoriadis observes public time puts into question established institutions and dominant authority, rejecting any notion of the social that either eliminates the question of judgment or "conceals . . . the question of responsibility." Rather than maintaining a passive attitude toward power, public time demands and encourages forms of political agency based on a passion for self-governing, actions informed by critical judgment, and a commitment to linking social responsibility and transformation. Public time legitimates those pedagogical practices that provide the basis for a culture of questioning, one that enables the knowledge, skills, and social practices necessary for resistance, a space of translation, and a proliferation of discourses. Public time unsettles common sense and disturbs authority while encouraging critical and responsible leadership. As Roger Simon observes public time "presents the question of the social—not as a space for the articulation of pre-formed visions through which to mobilize action, but as the movement in which the very question of the possibility of democracy becomes the frame within which a necessary radical learning (and questioning) is enabled."[30] Put differently public time affirms a politics without guarantees and a notion of the social that is open and contingent. It also provides a conception of democracy that is never complete and determinate but constantly open to different understandings of the contingency of its decisions, mechanisms of exclusions, and operations of power.[31] Public time challenges neoliberalism's willingness to separate the economic from the social as well as its failure to address of human needs and social costs.

At its best public time renders governmental power explicit, and in doing so it rejects the language of religious rituals and the abrogation of the conditions necessary for the assumption of basic freedoms and rights. Moreover public time considers civic education the basis, if not essential dimension, of justice because it provides individuals with the skills, knowledge, and passions to talk back to power while simultaneously emphasizing both the necessity to question, which accompanies viable forms of political agency, and the assumption of public responsibility through active participation in the very process of governing. Expressions of public time in higher education can be found in shared notions of governance between faculty and administration, in modes of academic labor that encourage forms of collegiality tied to vibrant communities of exchange and democratic values, and in pedagogical relations in which students do not just learn about democracy but experience it through a sense of active participation, critical engagement, and social responsibility. The notion of public time has a long history in higher education and has played a formative role in shaping some of the most important principles of academic life. Public time, in this instance, registers the importance of pedagogical practices, which provide the conditions for a culture of questioning where teachers and students engage in critical dialogue and unrestricted discussion in order to affirm their role as social agents, inspect their own past, and engage the consequences of *their own actions in shaping the future*.

As higher education becomes increasingly corporatized, public time is replaced by corporate time. In corporate time the "market is viewed as a master design for all affairs,"[32] profit-making becomes the defining measure of responsibility, and consumption is the privileged site for determining value between the self and the larger social order. Corporate time fosters a narrow sense of leadership, agency, and public values and is largely indifferent to those concerns that are critical to a just society, but are not commercial in nature. The values of hierarchy, materialism, competition, and excessive individualism are enshrined under corporate time and play a defining role in how it allocates space, manages the production of particular forms of knowledge, and regulates pedagogical relations. Hence it is not surprising that corporate time accentuates privatized and competitive modes of intellectual activity, largely removed from public obligations and social responsibilities. Divested of any viable democratic notion of the social, corporate time measures relationships, productivity, space, and knowledge according to the dictates of cost efficiency, profit, and a market-based rationality. Time, within this framework, is accelerated rather than slowed down and reconfigures academic labor, increasingly through, though not limited to, new computer-generated technologies, which are making greater demands on faculty time, creating larger teaching loads, and producing bigger classes. Under corporate time speed controls and organizes place, space, and communication as a matter of quantifiable calculation. And as Peter Euben observes, under such circumstances a particular form of rationality emerges as common sense:

> When speed rules so does efficient communication. Calculation and logic are in, moral imagination and reasoned emotions are out. With speed at a premium, shorthand, quantification and measurements become dominant modes of thought. Soon we will talk in cliches and call it common sense and wisdom.[33]

Corporate time maps faculty relationships through self-promoting market agendas and narrow definitions of self-interest. Caught on the treadmill of getting more grants, teaching larger classes, and producing more revenue for the university, faculty become another casualty of a business ideology that attempts to "extract labor from campus workers at the lowest possible cost, one willing to sacrifice research independence and integrity for profit."[34] Under corporatization time is accelerated and fragmented. Overworked and largely isolated, faculty are now rewarded for intellectual activities privileged as entrepreneurial, "measured largely in the capacity to transact and consume."[35] Faculty are asked to spend more time in larger classrooms while they are simultaneously expected to learn and use new instructional technologies such as Power Point, the Web, and various multimedia pedagogical activities. Faculty now interact with students not only in their classes and offices, but also in chat rooms and through e-mail.

Grounded in the culture of competitiveness and self-interest, corporate time reworks faculty loyalties. Faculty interaction is structured less around collective solidarities built upon practices that offer a particular relationship to public life than through corporate-imposed rituals of competition and production, which conform to the "narrowly focused ideas of the university as a support to the economy."[36] For instance many universities are now instituting post-tenure review as an alleged measure of faculty accountability and an efficient way to eliminate "deadwood" professors. As Ben Agger points out, what is "Especially pernicious is the fact that faculty are supposed to axe their own colleagues, thus pitting them against each other and destroying whatever remains of the fabric of academic community and mutuality."[37]

Corporate time also fragments time by redefining academic labor "as part-time labor versus academic work as full-time commitment and career."[38] Under such conditions faculty solidarities are weakened ever more as corporate time evokes cost-efficient measures by outsourcing instruction to part-time faculty who are underpaid, overworked, who lack health benefits, and are deprived of any power to shape the conditions under which they work. Powerlessness breeds resentment and anger among part-time faculty, and fear and insecurity among full-time faculty, who no longer believe that their tenure is secure. Hence the divide between part- and full-time faculty is reproduced by the heavy hand of universities as they downsize and outsource under the rubric of fiscal responsibility and accountability, especially in a post–9/11 era. But more is reproduced than structural dislocations among faculty; there is also a large pool of crippling fear, insecurity, and resentment, which makes it difficult for them to take risks, forge bonds of solidarity, engage in social criticism, and perform as public intellectuals rather than as technicians in the service of corporate largesse.

Leadership under the reign of corporate culture and corporate time has been rewritten as a form of homage to business models of governance. As Stanley Aronowitz points out, "Today . . . leaders of higher education wear the badge of corporate servants proudly."[39] Gone are the days when university presidents were hired for intellectual status and public roles. College presidents are now labeled as chief executive officers, and are employed primarily because of their fund raising abilities. Deans of various colleges are often pulled from the ranks of the business world and pride themselves on the managerial logic and cost-cutting plans they adopt from the corporate culture of Microsoft, Disney, and IBM. Bill Gates and Michael Eisner replace John Dewey and Robert Hutchins as models of educational leadership. Rather than defend the public role of the university, academic freedom, and worthy social causes, the new corporate heroes of higher education now focus their time selling off university services to private contractors, forming partnerships with local corporations, searching for new patent and licensing agreements, and urging faculty to engage in research and grants, which generate external funds. Under this model of leadership the university is being transformed from a place to think to a place to imagine stock options and profit windfalls.

Corporate time provides a new framing mechanism for faculty relations and modes of production and suggests a basic shift in the role of the intellectual. Academics now become less important as a resource to provide students with the knowledge and skills they need to engage the future as a condition of democratic possibilities. In the "new economy," they are entrepreneurs who view the future as an investment opportunity and research as a private career opportunity rather than as a civic and collective effort to improve the public good. Increasingly academics find themselves being deskilled as they are pressured to teach more service-oriented and market-based courses and devote less time to their roles either as well-informed public intellectuals or as "cosmopolitan intellectuals situated in the public sphere."[40]

Corporate time not only transforms the university as a democratic public sphere into a space for training while defining faculty as market-oriented producers, it also views students as both customers, potential workers, and as a source of revenue. As customers students "are conceptualized in terms of their ability to pay. . . . and the more valued customers are those who can afford to pay more."[41] One consequence, as Gary Rhoades points out, is that student access to higher education is "now shaped less by considerations of social justice than of revenue potential."[42] Consequently those students who are poor and under-serviced are increasingly denied access to the benefits of higher education. Of course the real problem, as Cary Nelson observes, is not merely one of potential decline, but "long term and continuing failure to offer all citizens, especially minorities of class and color, equal educational opportunities,"[43] a failure that has been intensified under the authority of the corporate university. As a source of revenue students are now subjected to higher fees, tuition costs, and are bombarded by brand name corporations who either lease space on the university commons to advertise their goods or run any one of a number of students services from the dining halls to the university bookstore. Almost every aspect of public space in higher education is now designed to attract students as consumers and shoppers, constantly subjecting them to forms of advertisements mediated by the rhythms of corporate time, which keeps students moving through a marketplace of brand name products rather than ideas. Such hyper-commercialized spaces increasingly resemble malls, transforming all available university space into advertising billboards, and bringing home the message that the most important identity available to students is that of a consuming subject. As the line between public and commercial space disappears, the gravitational pull of Taco Bell, McDonald's, Starbucks, Barnes and Noble, American Express, and Nike, among others, creates a "geography of nowhere,"[44] a consumer placelessness in which all barriers between a culture of critical ideas and branded products simply disappear.[45] Education is no longer merely a monetary exchange in which students buy an upscale, lucrative career, it is also an experience designed to evacuate any broader, more democratic notion of citizenship, the social, and the future that students may wish to imagine, struggle over, and enter. In corporate time students are disenfranchised "as future citizens and reconstitute[d] . . . as no more than consumers and potential workers."[46]

Corporate time not only translates faculty as multinational operatives and students as sources of revenue and captive consumers, it also makes a claim on how knowledge is valued, how the classroom is to be organized, and how pedagogy is defined. Knowledge under corporate time is valued as a form of capital. As Michael A. Peters observes entire disciplines and bodies of knowledge are now either valued or devalued on the basis of their "ability to attract global capital and . . . potential for serving transnational corporations. Knowledge is valued for its strict utility rather than as an end in itself or for its emancipatory effects."[47] Good value for students means taking courses labeled as "relevant" in market terms, which are often counterposed to courses in the social sciences, humanities, and the fine arts that are concerned with forms of learning that do not readily translate into either private gain or commercial value. Under the rule of corporate time the classroom is no longer a public sphere concerned with issues of justice, critical learning, or the knowledge and skills necessary for civic engagement. As training replaces education, the classroom, along with pedagogy itself, is transformed as a result of the corporate restructuring of the university.

As the structure and content of education change, intellectual and pedagogical practices are less identified with providing the conditions for students to learn how to think critically, hold institutional authority accountable for its actions, and act in ways that further democratic ideals. Rather than providing the knowledge and skills for asserting the primacy of the political, social responsibility, and the ethical as central to preparing students for the demands of an inclusive democracy, intellectual practice is subordinated to managerial, technological, and commercial considerations. Not only is classroom knowledge and intellectual practice bought and traded as a marketable commodity, but they are also defined largely within what Zygmunt Bauman calls "the culture of consumer society, which is more about forgetting, [than] learning"[48]—that is, forgetting that knowledge can be emancipatory, that citizenship is not merely about being a consumer, and that the future cannot be sacrificed to ephemeral pleasures and values of the market. When education is reduced to training the meaning of self-government is devalued and democracy is rendered meaningless.

What is crucial to recognize in the rise of corporate time is that while it acknowledges that higher education should play a crucial role in offering the narratives that frame society, it presupposes that faculty, in particular, will play a different role and assume a "different relation to the framing of cultural reality."[49] Many critics have pointed to the changing nature of governance and management structures in the university as a central force in redefining the relationship of the university to the larger society, but little has been said about how the changing direction of the university impacts on the nature of academic activity and intellectual relations.[50] While at one level the changing nature of the institution suggests greater control of academic life by administrators and an emerging class of managerial professionals, it also points to the privileging of those intellectuals in the techno-sciences whose services are indispensable to corporate power, while recognizing information as the reigning commodity of the new economy. Academic labor is now prized for how it fuses with capital, rather than how it contributes to what Geoff Sharp calls "society's self-understanding."[51] The changing institutional and social forms of the university reject the elitist and reclusive models of intellectual practice, which traditionally have refused to bridge the gap between higher education and the larger social order, theory and practice, the academic and the public. Within the corporate university transformation rather than contemplation is now a fundamental principle for judging and rewarding intellectual practice. Removed from matters of either social justice or democratic possibilities, transformation is defined through a notion of the social that is entirely rooted in privileging the material interests of the market. Higher education's need for new sources of funding neatly dovetails with the inexhaustible need on the part of corporations for new products. Within this symbiotic relationship knowledge is directly linked to its application in the market, mediated by a collapse of the distinction between knowledge and the commodity. Knowledge has become capital to invest in the market but has little to do with the power of self-definition, civic commitments, or ethical responsibilities, which "require an engagement with the claims of others"[52] and with questions of justice. At the same time the conditions for scholarly work are being transformed through technologies that eliminate face-to-face contact, speed up the labor process, and define social exchange in terms that are more competitive, instrumental, and removed from face-to-face contact.

Electronic, digital, and image-based technologies shape notions of the social in ways that were unimaginable a decade ago. Social exchanges can now proceed without the presence of "real" bodies. Contacts among faculty and between teachers and students are increasingly virtual, yet these practices profoundly delineate the nature of the social in instrumental, abstract, and commodified terms. As John Hinkson and Geoff Sharp have pointed out, these new intellectual practices and technological forms are redefining the nature of the social in higher education in ways in which the free sharing of ideas and cooperativeness as democratic and supportive forms of collegiality seem to be disappearing among faculty.[53] This is not just an issue that can be taken up strictly as an assault on academic labor, it also raises fundamental questions about where those values that support democratic forms of solidarity, sharing, dialogue, and mutual understanding are to be found in university life. This is an especially important issue since such values serve as a "condition for the development of intellectual practices devoted to public service."[54] Within these new forms of instrumental framing and intellectual practice, the ethic of public service, which once received some support in higher education, is being eliminated and with it those intellectual relations, scholarly practices, and forms of collegiality that leave some room for addressing a less commodified and democratic notion of the social.

In opposition to this notion of corporate time, instrumentalized intellectual practices, and a deracinated view of the social, I want to reassert the importance of academic social formations that view the university as a site of struggle and resistance. Central to such a challenge is the necessity to define intellectual practice "as part of an intricate web of morality, rigor and responsibility"[55] that enables academics to speak with conviction, enter the public sphere in order to address important social problems, and demonstrate alternative models for what it means to bridge the gap between higher education and the broader society. This is a notion of intellectual practice that refuses both the instrumentality and privileged isolation of the academy, while affirming a broader vision of learning, which links knowledge to the power of self-definition and the capacities of administrators, academics, and students to expand the scope of democratic freedoms, particularly as they address the crisis of the social as part and parcel of the crisis of both youth and democracy itself. Implicit in this notion of social and intellectual practice is a view of academics as public intellectuals. Following Edward Said I am referring to those academics engaged in intellectual practices who interpret and question power rather than merely consolidate it, enter into the public sphere in order to alleviate human suffering, make the connections of power visible, and work individually and collectively to create the pedagogical and social conditions necessary for what the late Pierre Bourdieu has called "realist utopias."[56] I want to conclude this essay by taking up how the role of both the university as a democratic public sphere and the function of academics as public intellectuals can be further enabled through the pedagogical possibilities of what Derrida calls democracy's promise.

Democracy as a Promise or Reclaiming the University as a Democratic Public Sphere

If the rise of the corporate university is to be challenged, educators and others need to reclaim the meaning and purpose of higher education as an ethical and political response to the demise of democratic public life. At stake here is the need to insist, as Derrida does, on the role of the university as a public sphere committed to deepening and expanding the possibilities of democratic identities, values, and relations. This approach suggests new models of leadership based on the understanding that the real purpose of higher education means encouraging people to think beyond the task of simply getting a lucrative job. Beyond this ever narrowing instrumental justification there is the more relevant goal of opening higher education up to all groups, creating a critical citizenry, providing specialized work skills for jobs that really require them, democratizing relations of governance among administrators, faculty, and students, and taking seriously the imperative to disseminate an intellectual and artistic culture. Higher education may be one of the few sites left in which students learn how to mediate critically between democratic values and the demands of corporate power, between identities founded on democratic principles and identities steeped in forms of competitive, atomistic individualism that celebrate self-interest, profit making, and greed. This view suggests that higher education be defended through intellectual work that self-consciously recalls the tension between the democratic imperatives and possibilities of public institutions and their everyday realization within a society dominated by market principles. Only if this struggle is taken seriously by educators and others can the university be reclaimed as a space of debate, discussion, and at times dissidence. Within such a pedagogical space, time can be unconditionally apportioned to what Cornelius Castoriadis calls "an unlimited interrogation in all domains"[57] of society, especially with regard to the operations of dominant authority and power and the important issues that shape public life, practices ultimately valued for their contribution to the unending process of democratization.

Higher education should be defended as a form of civic education where teachers and students have the chance to resist and rewrite those modes of pedagogy, time, and rationality that refuse to include questions of judgment and issues of responsibility. Understood as such higher education is viewed neither as a consumer-driven product nor as a form of training and career preparation but as a mode of critical education that renders all individuals fit "to participate in power . . . . to the greatest extent possible, to participate in a common government,"[58] to be capable as Aristotle reminds us of both governing and being governed. If higher education is to bring democratic public culture and critical pedagogy back to life, educators need to provide students with the knowledge and skills that enable them not only to judge and choose between different institutions but also to create those institutions they deem necessary for living lives of decency and dignity. In this instance education provides not only the tools for citizen participation in public life, but also for exercising leadership. As Castoriadis insists, "People should have not just the typical right to participate; they should also be educated in every aspect (of leadership and politics) in order to be able to participate"[59] in governing society.

Reclaiming higher education as a public sphere begins with the crucial project of challenging corporate ideology and its attending notions of time, which covers over the crisis of the social by dissociating all discussions about the goals of higher education from the realm of democracy. This project points to the important task of redefining higher education as a democratic public sphere not only to assert the importance of the social, but also to reconfigure it so that "economic interests cease to be the dominant factor in shaping attitudes"[60] about the social as a realm devoid of politics and democratic possibilities. Education is not only about issues of work and economics, but also about questions of justice, social freedom, and the capacity for democratic agency, action, and change as well as the related issues of power, exclusion, and citizenship. These are educational and political issues and should be addressed as part of a broader concern for renewing the struggle for social justice and democracy. Such a struggle demands, as the writer Arundhati Roy points out, that as intellectuals we ask ourselves some very "uncomfortable questions about our values and traditions, our vision for the future, our responsibilities as citizens, the legitimacy of our 'democratic institutions,' the role of the state, the police, the army, the judiciary, and the intellectual community."[61]

While it is crucial for educators and others to defend higher education as a public good, it is also important to recognize that the crisis of higher education cannot be understood outside of the overall restructuring of the social and civic life. The death of the social, the devaluing of political agency, the waning of noncommercial values, and the disappearance of noncommercialized public spaces have to be understood as part of a much broader attack on public entitlements such as healthcare, welfare, and social security, which are being turned over to market forces and privatized so that "economic transactions can subordinate and in many cases replace political democracy."[62]

Jacques Derrida has observed in another context that if higher education is going to have a future that makes a difference in promoting democracy, it is crucial for educators to take up the "necessity to rethink the concepts of the possible and the impossible."[63] What Derrida is suggesting is that democracy as a promise demands a new vocabulary for challenging the presupposition that there are no alternatives to the existing social order, while simultaneously stressing the dynamic, still unfinished elements of a democracy to be realized.[64] Derrida's promise of democracy or democracy "as if" accentuates the ways in which the political can become more pedagogical and the pedagogical more political. In the first instance pedagogy merges politics and ethics with revitalized forms of civic education, which provide the knowledge, skills, and experiences enabling individual freedom and social agency. Making the pedagogical more political demands that educators become more attentive to the ways in which institutional forces and cultural power are tangled up with everyday experience. It means understanding how higher education in the information age now interfaces with the larger culture, how it has become the most important site for framing public pedagogies and authorizing specific relations between the self, the other, and the larger society that often shut down democratic visions. Any viable politics based on a democracy to come must tap into individual experiences while at the same time linking individual responsibility with a progressive sense of social agency. Politics and pedagogy alike spring "from real situations and from what we can say and do in these situations."[65]

Emphasizing politics as a pedagogical practice and performative act, democracy as a promise accentuates the notion that politics is played out not only on the terrain of imagination and desire, but is also grounded in material relations of power and concrete social formations through which people live out their daily lives. Freedom and justice, in this instance, have to be mediated through the connection between civic education and political agency, which presupposes that the goal of critical education is not to liberate the individual from the social—a central tenet of neoliberalism—but to take seriously the notion that the individual can only be liberated through the social. If critical pedagogy is to be meaningful, it should provide a link, however transient, provisional, and contextual, between vision and critique, on the one hand, and engagement and transformation on the other. But for such a notion of pedagogy to be meaningful it has to be grounded in a vision that has some hold on the present.

The limits of politics as an intervention into the promise of democracy are related, in part, to the failure of academics and intellectuals in a variety of public spheres not only to conceive of life beyond profit margins, but also to imagine what pedagogical conditions might be necessary to bring into being forms of political agency that might expand the operations of individual rights, social provisions, and democratic freedoms. Against such failures and dystopian notions it is crucial for educators to address democracy's promise as anticipatory rather than messianic, as temporal rather than merely spatial, forward looking rather than backward. Democracy as a promise in this view is neither a blueprint for the future nor a form of social engineering, but a belief that different futures are possible. For Derrida this position rejects a politics of certainty and holds open matters of contingency, context, and indeterminancy as central to any notion of agency and the future. This suggests a view of democracy as a performative act that is based on the recognition that it is only through education that human beings can learn about the limits of the present and the conditions necessary for them to "combine a gritty sense of limits with a lofty vision of possibility."[66] Democracy as a promise poses the important challenge of how to reclaim social agency within a broader discourse of ethical advocacy while addressing those essential pedagogical and political elements necessary for envisioning alternatives to global neoliberalism and its attendant forms of corporate time and its attendant assault on public time and space.

Democracy as a promise takes as a political and ethical necessity the need to address those modes of education required for a democratic future and further requires that we ask such questions as: What pedagogical projects, resources, and practices can be put into place that would convey to students the vital importance of public time and its attendant culture of questioning as an essential step toward self-representation, agency, and a substantive democracy? How might public time with its imperative to "take more time," compel respect rather than reverence, critique rather than silence, while challenging the narrow and commercial nature of corporate time? What kinds of social relations necessarily provide students with time for deliberation as well as spaces of translation in which they can critically engage those forms of power and authority that speak directly to them both within and outside of the academy? How might public time, with its unsettling refusal to be fixed or to collapse in the face of corporate time, be used to create pedagogical conditions, which foster forms of self and social critique as part of a broader project of constructing alternative desires and critical modes of thinking, on the one hand, and democratic agents of change on the other? How to deal with these issues is a major question for intellectuals in the academy today and their importance resides not just in how they might provide teachers and students with the tools to fight corporatization in higher education, but also how they address the need for fundamental institutional change in the ongoing struggles for freedom and justice in a revitalized democracy.

There is a long-standing tradition among critical theorists that pedagogy as a moral and political practice plays a crucial role in constituting the social. Far from innocent, pedagogical practices operate within institutional contexts that carry great power in determining what knowledge is of most worth, what it means for students to know something, and how such knowledge relates to a particular understanding of the self and its relationship to both others and the future. Connecting teaching as knowledge production to teaching as a form of self-production, pedagogy presupposes not only a political and ethical project that offers up a variety of human capacities, it also propagates diverse meanings of the social. Moreover as an articulation of and intervention in the social, pedagogical practices always sanction particular versions of what knowledge is of most worth, what it means to know something, how to be attentive to the operations of power, and how we might construct representations of ourselves, others, and our physical environment. In the broadest sense pedagogy is a principal feature of politics because it provides the capacities, knowledge, skills, and social relations through which individuals recognize themselves as social and political agents. As Roger Simon points out, "talk about pedagogy is simultaneously talk about the details of what students and others might do together and the cultural politics such practices support."[67]

While many critical educators and social theorists recognize that education, in general, and pedagogy, more specifically, cannot be separated from the dual crisis of representation and political agency, the primary emphasis in many of these approaches to critical pedagogy suggests that its foremost responsibility is to provide a space where the complexity of knowledge, culture, values, and social issues can be explored by means of open and critical dialogue through a vibrant culture of questioning. This position is echoed by Judith Butler who argues "For me there is more hope in the world when we can question what is taken for granted, especially about what it is to be human."[68] Derrida goes further, arguing that the resurrection of any viable notion of political and social agency is dependent upon a culture of questioning, whose purpose is not simply the "unconditional right to ask questions . . . but the right to do it performatively."[69]

Central to any viable notion of critical pedagogy is its willingness to take seriously those academic projects, intellectual practices, and social relations in which students have the basic right to raise, if not define, questions, both within and outside of disciplinary boundaries. Such a pedagogy must also bear the responsibility of being self-conscious about those forces that sometimes prevent people from speaking openly and critically, whether they are part of a hidden curriculum of either racism, class oppression, or gender discrimination or part of those institutional and ideological mechanisms that silence students under the pretext of a claim to professionalism, objectivity, or unaccountable authority. Crucial here is the recognition that a pedagogical culture of questioning is not merely about the dynamics of communication but also about the effects of power and the mechanisms through which it either constrains, denies, or excludes particular forms of agency—preventing some individuals from speaking in specific ways, in particular spaces, under specific circumstances. Clearly such a pedagogy might include a questioning of the corporatization of the educational context itself, the role of foreign policy, the purpose and meaning of the burgeoning prison–industrial complex, and the declining nature of the welfare state. Pedagogy makes visible the operations of power and authority as part of its processes of disruption and unsettlement—an attempt, as Larry Grossberg points out, "to win an already positioned, already invested individual or group to a different set of places, a different organization of the space of possibilities."[70]

At its best such a pedagogy is self-reflective, and views its own practices and effects not as pregiven but as the outcome of previous struggles. Rather than defined as either a technique, method, or "as a kind of physics which leaves its own history behind and never looks back," critical pedagogy is grounded in a sense of history, politics, and ethics, which uses theory as a resource to respond to particular contexts, problems, and issues. I want to suggest that as educators we need to extend this approach to critical pedagogy beyond the project of simply providing students with the critical knowledge and analytic tools that enable them to use them in any way they wish. While this pedagogical approach rightly focuses on the primacy of dialogue, understanding, and critique, it does not adequately affirm the experience of the social and the obligations it evokes regarding questions of responsibility and social transformation. Such a pedagogy attempts to open up for students important questions about power, knowledge, and what it might mean for students to critically engage the conditions under which life is presented to them, but it does not directly address what it would mean for them to work to overcome those social relations of oppression that make living unbearable for those youths and adults who are poor, hungry, unemployed, refused adequate social services, and under the aegis of neoliberalism, viewed largely as disposable.

A pedagogy that simply promotes a culture of questioning says nothing about what kind of future is or should be implied by how and what educators teach; nor does it address the necessity of recognizing the value of a future in which matters of liberty, freedom, and justice play a constitutive role. While it is crucial for education to be attentive to those practices in which forms of social and political agency are denied, it is also imperative to create the conditions in which forms of agency are available for students to learn how to not only think critically but to act differently. People need to be educated for democracy not only by expanding their capacities to think critically, but also for assuming public responsibility through active participation in the very process of governing and engaging important social problems. This suggests connecting a pedagogy of understanding with pedagogical practices that are empowering and oppositional, practices that offer students the knowledge and skills needed to believe that a substantive democracy is not only possible but is worth both taking responsibility for and struggling over. Any notion of critical pedagogy has to foreground issues not only of understanding but also of social responsibility and address the implications the latter has for a democratic society.

Pedagogy plays a crucial role in nurturing this type of responsibility and suggests that students should learn about the relevance of translating critique and understanding to civic courage, of translating what they know as a matter of private privilege into a concern for public life. Responsibility breathes politics into educational practices and suggests both a different future and the possibility of politics itself. Responsibility makes politics and agency possible because it does not end with matters of understanding since it recognizes the importance of students becoming accountable for others through their ideas, language, and actions. Being aware of the conditions that cause human suffering and the deep inequalities that generate dreadfully undemocratic and unethical contradictions for many people is not the same as resolving them. If pedagogy is to be linked to critical citizenship and public life, it needs to provide the conditions for students to learn in diverse ways how to take responsibility for moving society in the direction of a more realizable democracy. In this case the burden of pedagogy is linked to the possibilities of understanding and acting, engaging knowledge and theory as a resource to enhance the capacity for civic action and democratic change.

Derrida has insisted rightly that democracy demands the most concrete urgency. Of course urgency is not only a response to the crisis of the present, increasingly shaped by the footprint of fascism wielded through the anonymous presence of neoliberal capitalism, but also connected to the future that we make available to the next generation of young people. How much longer can we allow the promise of democracy to be tainted by its reality? At stake are not only the fates of higher education and democracy, but also the very future educators provide for coming generations of young people. Democracy's promise demands more justice, more hospitality, more struggle, not less. Democracy is more than an event and a ritual; it is a site of struggle whose outcome is always uncertain but whose future should never remain in doubt.

Notes

1. Zygmunt Bauman (2002). *Society under Siege* (Malden, MA: Blackwell), p. 170.
2. Jacques Derrida (2001). "*The future of the profession or the unconditional university,*" in *Laurence Simmons and Heather Worth (eds) Derrida Downunder* (Auckland, New Zealand: Dunmore Press), p. 233.

3. Cornelius Castoriadis (1997). "Democracy as procedure and democracy as regime." *Constellations*, 4: 1, 10.

4. Derrida, "The future of the profession," p. 253.

5. Ibid., p. 253.

6. For some excellent critical commentaries on various aspects of neoliberalism and its consequences, see Noam Chomsky (1999). *Profit over People: Neoliberalism and the Global Order* (NewYork: Seven Stories Press); Pierre Bourdieu (1998). *Acts of Resistance; Against the Tyranny of the Market* (New York: The New Press); Pierre Bourdieu et al. (1999). *The Weight of the World: Social Suffering in Contemporary Society* (Stanford: Stanford University Press; Robert W. McChesney (1999). *Rich Media, Poor Democracy: Communication Politics in Dubious Times* (New York: The New Press); Zygmunt Bauman (1998). *Work, Consumerism, and the New Poor* (Philadelphia: Open University Press); *Society under Siege*.

7. Lawrence Grossberg (2001). "Why does neo-liberalism hate kids? The war on youth and the culture of politics." *The Review of Education / Pedagogy / Cultural Studies*, 23: 2, 133.

8. Ibid., 133.

9. These figures largely come from Children's Defense Fund, *The State of Children in America's Union: A 2002 Action Guide to Leave No Child Behind* (Washington, DC: Children's Defense Fund Publication, 2002), pp. iv–v, 13.

10. Bill Moyers (May 30, 2003). "Deep in a black hole of red ink," Common Dreams News Center. Available on line at www.commondreams.org/views03/0530-11.htm

11. Bauman. *Work, Consumerism*, p. 77.

12. Noreena Hertz (2001). *The Silent Takeover: Global Capitalism and the Death of Democracy* (NewYork: The Free Press), p. 11.

13. Bourdieu, *Acts of Resistance*; Bourdieu et al., *Weight of the World*.

14. Zygmunt Bauman (1999). *In Search of Politics* (Stanford, CA: Stanford University Press), p. 2.

15. Naomi Klein (1999). *No Logo* (NewYork: Picador), p. 177.

16. Grossberg "Why does neo-liberalism hate kids?," 133.

17. Jean Comaroff and John L. Comaroff (2000). "Millennial capitalism: First thoughts on a second coming." *Public Culture*, 12: 2 (North Carolina: Duke University Press), pp. 305–306.

18. Peter Beilharz (2000). *Zygmunt Bauman: Dialectic of Modernity* (London: Sage), p. 160.

19. Comaroff and Comaroff, "Millennial capitalism," p. 332.

20. James Traub (November 19, 2000). "This campus is being simulated." *The New York Times Magazine*, p. 93.

21. Cited in Roger Simon (2001). "The university: A place to think?," in Henry A. Giroux and Kostas Myrsiades (eds), *Beyond the Corporate University: Culture and Pedagogy in the New Millenium* (Lanham, MD: Rowman and Littlefield), pp. 47–48.

22. Larry Hanley, "Conference roundtable." *Found Object*, 10 (spring 2001), 103.

23. Masao Miyoshi (1998). " 'Globalization,' culture, and the university," in Fredric Jameson and Masao Miyoshi (eds), *The Cultures of Globalization* (Durham: Duke University Press), p. 263.

24. Stanley Aronowitz (March/April 1998) "The new corporate university." *Dollars and Sense*, p. 32.

25. Beilharz, *Dialectic of Modernity*, p. 161.

26. Jacques Derrida (2000). "Intellectual courage: An interview." *Culture Machine*, 2, 9.

27. Michael Hanchard (Winter 1999). "Afro-modernity: Temporality, politics, and the African diaspora." *Public Culture*, 11: 1, 253.

28. Ibid., 256.

29. Jerome Bind (2000). "Toward an ethic of the future." *Public Culture*, 12: 1, 52.

30. Roger I. Simon (April 1, 2002). "On public time," Ontario Institute for Studies in Education. Unpublished paper, p. 4.

31. Simon Critchley, "Ethics, politics, and radical democracy—The History of a Disagreement," *Culture Machine*, available at www.culturemachine.tees.ac.uk/frm_f1.htm

32. James Rule (Winter 1998). "Markets in their place." *Dissent*, 30.

33. Peter Euben (Summer–Fall, 2000). "Reforming the liberal arts." *The Civic Arts Review*, 2, 8.

34. Cary Nelson (July 2002). "Between anonymity and celebrity: The zero degrees of professional identity." *College English*, 64:6, 717.
35. Comaroff and Comaroff, "Millennial capitalism," p. 306.
36. Geoff Sharp (2002). "The idea of the intellectual and after," in Simon Cooper, John Hinkson, and Geoff Sharp (eds), *Scholars and Entrepreneurs* (Melbourne, Australia: Arena Publications), p. 280.
37. Ben Agger (November 4, 2002). "Sociological writing in the wake of postmodernism." *Cultural Studies/Cultural Methodologies*, 2:4, 444.
38. Gary Rhoades (Spring 2001). "Corporate, Techno Challenges, and Academic Space," *Found Object* 10, p. 143.
39. Aronowitz, "The new corporate university," 32.
40. Agger, "sociological writing," 444.
41. Rhoades, "Corporate, Techno Challenges," 122.
42. Rhoades, "Corporate, Techno Challenges," 122.
43. Nelson, "Anonymity and Celebrity," 713.
44. Taken from James Howard Kunstler (1993). *The Geography of Nowhere* (New York: Touchstone).
45. The most extensive analysis of the branding of culture by corporations can be found in Klein, *No Logo*.
46. Jeffrey L. Williams, "Franchising the university," in *Beyond the Corporate University*, p. 23.
47. Michael A. Peters, "The university in the knowledge economy," in *Scholars and Entrepreneurs*, p. 148.
48. Zygmunt Bauman (1998). *Globalization: The Human Consequence* (New York: Columbia University Press), p. 81.
49. Sharp, "Intellectual and after," 275.
50. See Sharp, "Intellectual and after," and John Hinkson, "Perspectives on the crisis of the university," in *Scholars and Entrepreneurs,* pp. 233–267.
51. Sharp, "Intellectual and after," pp. 284–285.
52. Nick Couldry (2001). "Dialogue in an age of enclosure: Exploring the values of cultural studies." *The Review of Education/Pedagogy/Cultural Studies*, 23:1, 17.
53. Hinkson, "Perspectives on the crisis," pp. 233–267; Sharp, "Intellectual and after."
54. Hinkson, "Perspectives on the crisis," p. 259.
55. Arundhati Roy (2001). *Power Politics* (Cambridge, MA: South End Press), p. 6.
56. The ideas on public intellectuals are taken directly from Edward Said (2001). *Reflections on Exile and Other Essays* (Cambridge: Harvard University Press), pp. 502–503. For the reference to realist utopias, see Pierre Bourdieu (2000). "For a scholarship with commitment." *Profession*, 42.
57. Cornelius Castoriadis (1997). "Culture in a democratic society," in David Ames Curtis (ed.), *The Castoriadis Reader* (Malden, MA: Blackwell), p. 343.
58. Cornelius Castoriadis (1991). "The nature and value of equity," *Philosophy, Politics, Autonomy: Essays in Political Philosophy* (New York: Oxford University Press), p. 140.
59. Cornelius Castoriadis (April 1996). "The problem of democracy today." *Democracy and Nature*, 8, 24.
60. Castoriadis, "The Greek Polis and the creation of democracy," in *Philosophy, Politics, Autonomy*, p. 112.
61. Roy, *Power Politics*, p. 3.
62. Christopher Newfield (2003). "Democratic passions: Reconstructing individual agency," in Russ Castronovo and Dana Nelson (eds), *Materializing Democracy* (Durham: Duke University Press), p. 314.
63. Derrida, "The future of the profession," p. 243.
64. Samin Amin has captured this sentiment in his comment: "Neither modernity nor democracy has reached the end of its potential development. That is why I prefer the term 'democratization,' which stresses the dynamic aspect of a still-unfinished process, to the term 'democracy,' which reinforces the illusion that we can give a definitive formula for it." See Samir Amin (June 2001). "Imperialization and globalization." *Monthly Review*, 12.
65. Alain Badiou (2001). *Ethics: An Essay on the Understanding of Evil* (London: Verso), p. 96.
66. Ron Aronson (summer 1999). "Hope after Hope?" *Social Research*, 66:2, 489.

67. Roger Simon (April 1987). "Empowerment as a pedagogy of possibility." *Language Arts*, 64: 4, 371.
68. Cited in Gary A. Olson and Lynn Worsham (2000). "Changing the subject: Judith Butler's politics of radical resignification." *JAC*, 20:4, 765.
69. Derrida, "The future of the profession," p. 235.
70. Lawrence Grossberg (1994). "Introduction: Bringing it all back home—pedagogy and cultural studies," in Henry A. Giroux and Peter McLaren (eds), *Between Borders: Pedagogy and the Politics of Cultural Studies* (New York: Routledge), p. 14.

CHAPTER FIVE

War, Crimes against Humanity, and the New Humanities: Derrida and the Promise of Europe

MICHAEL A. PETERS

[The] new Humanities would treat the history of man, the idea, the figure, and the notion of "what is proper to man". . . The most urgent guiding thread here would be the problematisation . . . of these powerful juridical performatives that have given shape to the modern history of this humanity of man . . . *on the one hand*, the Declarations of the Rights of *Man*—and of woman . . . and *on the other hand*, the concept of "crime against humanity," which since the end of the Second World War has modified the geopolitical field of international law . . . .

Derrida

Introduction

The history of the concept of "crimes against humanity" is of recent origin dating from the immediate aftermath of World War II and the so-called London Agreement of August 8 1945, which served to establish a uniform legal basis in Germany for the prosecution of war criminals and other similar offenders, other than those dealt with by the International Military Tribunal. It was adopted thereafter as the basis for Principle VI of the Charter of the Nuremberg Tribunal in 1950, which provided substantial definitions in international law, for the first time, of crimes against peace, war crimes, and crimes against humanity.[1] The principles of the Charter were affirmed by the General Assembly and adopted by the International Law Commission (ILC), which was also invited to consider the drafting of a proposal for an international body or tribunal—the International Criminal Court that became established over 50 years later, without ratification by the United States. The notion of genocide is also a recent concept, which was first defined in an addendum to the Geneva Convention in 1977, also a convention that the United States refused to sign.[2]

The United States has refused to sign a whole raft of international treaties, conventions, and protocols, including the American Convention on Human Rights (1965) and Convention on Rights of the Child (1989). Since the end of World War II the United States, in its national interests, has prosecuted or supported major wars against 7 countries and bombed 23 nations. This chapter, first, taking a leaf from Derrida's program for "new humanities" and the necessity for histories of concepts, discusses the emergence of the concepts of war crimes, war against peace, and crimes against humanity, and provides a brief analysis of the emergence of the International Criminal Court. Second it contemplates the U.S. record of war crimes since World War II raising the question of its legal culpability under an international law that it does not recognize. Third the chapter entertains emerging differences in the strategic cultures of the United States and the European Union (EU), which may signal a break up of the unity of "the West." Finally it examines what Derrida calls the "promise of Europe" in terms of his examination of the history of the concepts of man and humanity, and their contemporary definition shaped by juridical performatives of the "rights of man (and women)" and crimes against humanity.

The Concept of War Crimes and the Emergence of the International Criminal Court

For nearly half a century—almost as long as the United Nations has been in existence—the General Assembly has recognized the need to establish such a court to prosecute and punish persons responsible for crimes such as genocide. Many thought . . . that the horrors of the Second World War—the camps, the cruelty, the exterminations, the Holocaust—could never happen again. And yet they have. In Cambodia, in Bosnia and Herzegovina, in Rwanda.

Our time—this decade even—has shown us that man's capacity for evil knows no limits. Genocide . . . is now a word of our time, too, a heinous reality that calls for a historic response.

Kofi Annan

Various treaties and conventions were struck in medieval times restricting the use of weapons against Christian peoples and even during the days of the Roman Empire the rights of plunder and pillage for barbarian soldiers was restricted to three days; sometimes such rights were suspended altogether, especially when the local population belonged to territory considered originally part of the empire. Indeed just war theory on one influential conception dates from Thomas Aquinas' influential "Of War."[3]

The modern concept of "war crime" surfaced at the Versailles Conference after World War I, but did not receive a comprehensive definition until the end of World War II in the form of the 1950 Charter of the Nuremberg Tribunal, which was among the first international conventions to address war crimes.[4] The principles of international law recognized in the Charter of the Nuremberg Tribunal and in the judgment of the Tribunal were affirmed by the General Assembly and formulated and adopted by the ILC of the United Nations (UN) in 1950, although the Commission did not express any appreciation of the principles as principles of international law. Their task was merely to formulate them. The Nuremburg Principles comprise seven major principles, which assert the priority of international law over "internal law" in any case where a person, including a head of state or someone acting under orders, commits an act that constitutes a crime that falls under its principles. The priority of international law (Principles I–V) is based on concepts of individual "responsibility," "moral choice," and "fair trial," which transcend national law and include complicity in the commission of such a crime (Principle VI). The substance of crimes punishable as crimes under international law are laid out in Principle VI as:

a. Crimes against peace:
    (i) Planning, preparation, initiation or waging of a war of aggression or a war in violation of international treaties, agreements or assurances;
    (ii) Participation in a common plan or conspiracy for the accomplishment of any of the acts mentioned under (i).

b. War crimes:
   Violations of the laws or customs of war which include, but are not
   limited to, murder, ill-treatment or deportation to slave-labor or for
   any other purpose of civilian population of or in occupied territory,
   murder or ill treatment of prisoners of war, of persons on the seas,
   killing of hostages, plunder of public or private property, wanton
   destruction of cities, towns, or villages, or devastation not justified
   by military necessity.
c. Crimes against humanity:
   Murder, extermination, enslavement, deportation and other inhuman
   acts done against any civilian population, or persecutions on political, racial or religious grounds, when such acts are done or such
   persecutions are carried on in execution of or in connection with
   any crime against peace or any war crime.

The Geneva Convention of 1949 embodied these principles and
recognized how new weapon technologies exposed civilians to even
greater danger. An addendum added in 1977, which the United States
refused to sign, emphasized the right of civilians to protection against
military activity, including genocide, defined as killing or causing serious
bodily harm to individuals based on their nationality, ethnic, racial, or
religious groups and with the intent to destroy that group.

The Rome Statute of The International Criminal Court begins its
overview by recognizing that the UN has recognized and sought for over
50 years to establish an international criminal court, in order to prosecute
those involved in crimes such as genocide. In 1948 the General Assembly
adopted the Convention on the Prevention and Punishment of the Crime
of Genocide, which both defined the crime and indicated that anyone
found guilty of it would be charged and tried either by a competent tribunal of the State in the territory of which the act was committed or by
an international penal tribunal. In the same resolution (260) the General
Assembly asked the ILC to study the possibilities of establishing such an
international judicial institution. A draft statute was prepared in 1951 and
revised in 1953, although the proposal was postponed pending a definition
of aggression. In 1989 the General Assembly asked the ILC to reconsider
the proposal with jurisdiction to include drug trafficking. With the spur of
"ethnic cleansing" during conflicts in Yugoslavia erupting in 1993, the ILC
completed its draft statute and submitted it to the General Assembly in
1994. After further discussion and revision the General Assembly held a
diplomatic conference in 1998 "to finalize and adopt a convention on the
establishment of an international criminal court."

The Rome Statute for the International Criminal Court summarizes the case for the court in terms of the following reasons:

- To achieve justice for all
- To end impunity
- To help end conflicts
- To remedy the deficiencies of ad hoc tribunals
- To take over when national criminal justice institutions are unwilling or unable to act
- To deter future war criminals

As the overview states:

An international criminal court has been called the missing link in the international legal system. The International Court of Justice at The Hague handles only cases between States, not individuals. Without an international criminal court for dealing with individual responsibility as an enforcement mechanism, acts of genocide and egregious violations of human rights often go unpunished. In the last 50 years, there have been many instances of crimes against humanity and war crimes for which no individuals have been held accountable. In Cambodia in the 1970s, an estimated 2 million people were killed by the Khmer Rouge. In armed conflicts in Mozambique, Liberia, El Salvador and other countries, there has been tremendous loss of civilian life, including horrifying numbers of unarmed women and children. Massacres of civilians continue in Algeria and the Great Lakes region of Africa.

The United States of America, War Crimes, and the Iraq War

Imagine a book with the following chapters: Tribal Genocide—The Ameri-Indians; The Southern Black Slave Economy; Atomic Incineration—Hiroshima and Nagasaki (Excursus: U.S. Plans to Bomb Berlin); The Killing of Korea, 1943–1953; Indonesia, 1958–1963—Aiding Genocide; Vietnamese Ecocide, 1954–1965; First Gulf War: Iraq, 1991–2001; Ethnic Cleansing: Yugoslavia, 1991–1999; The War against Afghanistan, 1979–2001; Second Gulf War: Iraq, 2003–2004. What would we call it and how much of an accurate picture would it give of the rise of the United States to the status of the world's sole superpower? To what extent would it support or criticize the role of America in the struggle for global justice in an age of genocide?

Geoffrey Robertson (2002) begins his history of crimes against humanity by tracking the cumulative impact of a set of unprecedented events, all occurring in the last 18 months of the twentieth century, that exemplified the Nuremberg legacy: the statute to establish an International Criminal Court (ratified on April 11, 2002); the arrest of General Pinochet; the NATO war against Yugoslavia; freedom for East Timor; the Hague Tribunal; and the Lockerbie agreement. He suggests that "quite literally out of a clear blue sky" came an unprecedented attack on the twin towers—symbols of American hegemony—in an atrocity that qualified as a crime against humanity. While the story of human rights is Robertson's subject he is not sanguine about the legitimacy either of the U.S. war against Afghanistan or of the treatment of alleged terrorists at Guantanamo Bay. He documents the way the Pentagon organized a global campaign to undermine the International Criminal Court and comments that "American exceptionalism might be understandable if its domestic human rights record were irreproachable" (Robertson, 2002, p. 534). Further he singles out for special attention the U.S. treatment of prisoners and aliens, noting that death penalties are inflicted without regard to international standards, that female convicts are forced to work in chain-gangs, and that the provision for legal representation for the poor in the richest of countries are less than adequate. As many as 3,500 of its own citizens are on death row, including 70 juveniles, and the United States in theory is committed to their "disappearance," He remarks: "America stands alongside Somalia as the only country to refuse to ratify the Convention of the Rights of the Child—for no better reason than its insistence on its sovereign right to execute juveniles and to recruit seventeen-year-olds into its armed forces" (Robertson, 2002, p. 535).

Where Robertson is critical of the United States, Samantha Power (2003, p. xv) provides a devastating critique of the its inaction during the post-war period. She writes: "The United States had never in its history intervened to stop genocide and had in fact rarely even made a point of condemning it as it occurred." Power examines the history of the United States' involvement in the major genocidal attacks that have taken place since the Holocaust, including Cambodia, Iraq, Bosnia, Rwanda, Srebrenica, and Kosovo. She concludes:

For most of the second half of the twentieth century, the existence of the genocide convention appeared to achieve little. The United States

did not ratify the treaty for forty years. Those countries that did ratify it never invoked it to stop or punish genocide. And instead of
finally making U.S. policymakers more inclined to stop genocide,
the belated U.S. ratification seemed only to make them more
reluctant to use the "g-word" (Power, 2003, p. 514).

Neither Power nor Robertson are concerned with the United States'
involvement in war since the end of World War II nor have they much to
say about the so-called war on terror or the U.S.-led war on Afghanistan
and Iraq. And yet these recent wars provide a set of insights into the war-
orientation of American foreign policy, especially under the Bush regime.

Iraq has had a short and turbulent history as a modern nation-state,
punctuated with periods of rebellions and conflicts, which reflect both
imperial interventions and local tribal hierarchies. The oil question can
be traced to the setting up of the modern Iraqi state in 1920 by the
British, who, acting under a League of Nations' mandate, suppressed
Sunni and Shi'ite resistance to install Amir Faisal as the Hashemite ruler
of the new kingdom. Oil concessions that greatly benefited the
Europeans at the expense of the Iraqis were granted to the Anglo Persian
Oil Company (BP) soon after. The development of modern Iraq's political
system from an externally imposed monarchy to an internally driven dic-
tatorship under Saddam Hussein is, of course, a complex history that
resists easy description, but the question of oil—its exploration, production, and ownership—is never far from the interventions of the home
governments of the multinational oil corporations in the United States,
the United Kingdom, and France (BP, Exxon, Shell, Texaco, Gulf, etc.).
Alnasrawi (2001) has documented the close relationship between the
U.S.-based oil MNCs and the U.S. government. The White House has
consistently denied that its involvement and renewed focus on Iraq
has been oil-related. The president's spokesman Ari Fleischer is reported
as saying "The only interest the United States has in the region is furthering the cause of peace and stability, not [Iraq's] ability to generate oil."
Yet the United States had to be persuaded not to intervene when in 1958
the pro-Western British-installed monarchy was overturned. Baghdad
turned to Moscow in the early 1970s for help in deterring any U.S.
reprisals against Iraq for nationalizing the Iraq Petroleum Company
(IPC), which had been owned by Royal Dutch-Shell, BP, Exxon, Mobil,
and the French company CFP. Iraq was the first Gulf country to success-
fully nationalize its oil industry. When Saddam Hussein finally took over
in 1979 as president he increasingly he steered a pro-Western course. The
United States during the 1980s, eager to lure Iraq away from its Soviet

leaning, supplied Baghdad with the in~ chemical, and nuclear weapons. Inde~ ~an a~ removed Iraq from the list of nations t~ as supporter~ ~ rorism and Donald Rumsfeld, in h~ ~th Hussein in 1983, paved the way for the restoration o~ ~matic relations with the United States in the following y~ ~e 17 years of hostilities. Installing a U.S. client regime in Bagh~ ~ld give the U.S. and British interests direct access to Iraqi oil fields for t~e first time in 30 years, even if the official story is to hold oil revenues in trust for the Iraqi people and to use funds for reconstruction.

Under these circumstances, to speak solely of international terrorism, weapons of mass destruction and regime change aimed at democracy and world peace is more than disingenuous. To speak of a "just war" and "preemptive first strike" while denying the oil stakes is plain nonsense. We must not forget also that under Saddam Hussein's reign the Iraqi people have suffered greatly and the economy, following the impact of the Iran–Iraq War, the Gulf and UN sanctions, degenerated into one full of poverty and despair. Hussein has relentlessly persecuted Kurdish peoples. His relations with Shi'ite groups both within Iraq and in Iran had deteriorated, and he had embarked on a foreign policy with chilling effects on Middle-East politics. If I begin with reference to Iraq and the ongoing crisis it is because it demonstrates so well the intricacies, nuances, and ambiguities that accompany accounts of empire and "new world order." In the context of this new world order we face a series of conceptual slippages: From "Al-Qaeda terrorists," to the Iraqi rogue state, to Islam or the Muslim world per se and all within the space of a few months in the U.S. war rhetoric of Bush hawks.

The question of postcoloniality in respect of the Palestinians has, of course, been explored by Edward Said; yet its present and unfolding formations in the imperial war against Afghanistan, the "war on terrorism," and the war against Iraq, require a revisiting of the question of postcoloniality not only in terms of so-called world security and developments of the world system of states but also in light of the call for a "new imperialism" by the likes of Robert Cooper, one-time foreign policy advisor to Tony Blair, and Robert Kagan (see Peters, 2003a, b). How heavily the colonial past weighs on the present, demonstrating that simple histories and historiographies do not admit the complex skein of events in models that periodize the past into easy categories.

The new logic of Empire operates, in part, by reviving the old imperialist dualisms —"we/they," Christian/Muslim, White/Black, good/evil in a quasi-theological rhetoric designed to legitimate the so-called regime

change in Iraq. Since the carpet-bombing of Afghanistan and the ousting
of the Taliban U.S. attention has shifted away from rebuilding the Afghan
state to focus on the "war against terrorism," Al-Qaeda, and the rise of
Islamism. Without evidence Bush's neoconservative administration
changed the lens of American foreign policy to focus on Al-Qaeda as an
Iraqi state-sponsored terrorist organization and on "weapons of mass
destruction" (WMD) said to be horded and ready for use by the Iraqi
regime.

The U.K. prime minister Tony Blair has been strident in his support of
the United States and in publicly maintaining the imminent danger to
the "civilized world" of a rogue state with WMD. In defending these
foreign policy objectives Bush, in particular, has adopted a religious language characteristic of Christian fundamentalism, which revives all the
historical we–they prejudices characterizing the worst aspects of relations
between the West and the Islamic and Muslim worlds, with the serious
potential to severely damage relations for years to come, perhaps, even
irreparably. Meanwhile thousands of American (136,000), British (20,000),
and Australian troops still operate as the joint occupying powers under
U.S. leadership and control. The joke reported to be circulating in
Whitehall and the Pentagon is "we know that Iraq has WMD because we
supplied them."

And yet after intensive weapons searches and document investigations,
so far—and we are now many months into occupation (February
2004)—no WMD have been found. It seems as if the weapons inspec-
tions carried out by Hans Blix's team had been successful and that
Saddam Hussein's government, if unwillingly and under duress, were
responding to the UN decommissioning weapons program. In terms of
just war theory, if it is assumed to apply in these novel conditions, none
of the criteria (just cause, legitimate authority, right intentions, likeli-
hood of success, last resort, proportionality) have been satisfied.[5] Indeed
both in the United States and in the United Kingdom, questions concerning the legitimacy under international law of the war against Iraq
persistently remain. Blix himself is on record as saying, once the war was
over, that the United Sates and the United Kingdom had exaggerated, or
"over-interpreted" the case for war. He expressed skepticism about the
U.K. government's statement that Saddam Hussein could deploy chemical and biological weapons within 45 minutes and he has also spoken of
the culture of spin and hype surrounding the United States' and the
United Kingdom's attempt to make a case for war, likening their joint
conviction that Iraq had WMD and interpretation and search for WMD
to a witch hunt.

In the United States the grounds for going to war proffered by the U.S. administration have shifted from a focus on WMD to "liberating the Iraqi people"—a claim that is beginning to look absurd in face of continued attacks against U.S. and U.K. occupying troops. By August 27 as many U.S. soldiers had died since Bush declared the end of the war (May 1) as had died during the war (138) and every day thereafter the figure keeps growing topping 500 by February 2004. This has severely punctured the illusion that the campaign in Iraq involved liberation. Television images of the UN headquarters in rubble, photographs of the oil pipelines ablaze, and reports of the continued assassination of U.S.–U.K. soldiers and sympathizers reinforce this picture of failure in the Western imagination. While Rumsfield insisted that there is no need to send more U.S. troops, other top U.S. officials supported a seemingly foreign policy about-turn to seek an explicit UN mandate for a greater international contribution, including some 40,000 troops from India, Turkey, and Bangladesh. In the United Kingdom, the Hutton Inquiry into the death of Dr. Kelly, the senior public servant and Iraq weapons expert, who allegedly killed himself under duress of government questioning and the media gaze, has not been accepted by the BBC and in terms of popular opinion it is seen to be more of a "whitewash." Certainly, in both the United States and in the United Kingdom, Bush and Blair have set up independent committees of inquiry, although in both instances the terms do not seem to be wide enough to address the question of wrongful judgment.

The fact is that the United States of America has been and is involved in war crimes going by accepted definitions of international law and yet somehow it manages to keep this from the "American people." We do not know how many Ameri-Indians or Afro-Black people were killed in the violent colonization and settlement of the United States; 340,000 Japanese died as a result of the bombing of Hiroshima and Nagasaki or from its aftereffects; President Sukarno, with the support and cooperation of the United States, killed between 100,000 and 1,000,000 members of the Indonesian communist party; more than 3 million Vietnamese were killed in the Vietnam War in which the United States dropped over 8 million tons of bombs (four times the amount used by the United States in all of World War II); many more died in the secret bombing of Cambodia; some 113,000 civilians died in the First Gulf War and child mortality rates soared to 380 percent; the United States covertly provided arms, training, advisors, satellite intelligence, and air power to the Croats in "Operation Storm" directed against the helpless Serbs in Krajina where approximately 250,000 Serbs were thus ethnically cleansed; estimates for the number of civilians killed in Afghanistan and Iraq are difficult to verify; in the recent cases the United States has used chemical, biological, and depleted uranium (DU) weapons.[6] Lenora Foerstel and Brian Willson (2002) make the following observation:

> Among the treaties that the United States has refused to sign are the International Convention on Civil and Political Rights (1966); the Convention on Economic, Social and Cultural Rights (1966); the Convention on the Elimination of all forms of Racial Discrimination (1966), and the American Convention on Human Rights (1965).
>
> The United States has been particularly reluctant to sign treaties addressing the "laws of war." It has refused to sign The Declaration on the Prohibition of the Use of Thermo-Nuclear Weapons (1961); The Resolution on the Non-Use of Force in International Relations and Permanent Ban on the Use of Nuclear Weapons (1972); The Resolution on the Definition of Aggression (1974); Protocols Additional to the 1949 Geneva Convention (1977); and the Declaration on the Prohibition of Chemical Weapons (1989). Equally disturbing was the U.S. refusal to sign the Convention on Rights of the Child, introduced into the United Nations General assembly on November 20, 1989 and subsequently ratified by 191 countries.[7]

And they conclude:

> An examination of the American conduct of its wars since World War II shows the U.S. to be in violation of the Nuremberg Principles, the 1949 Geneva Convention relating to protection of civilian prisoners of war, the wounded and sick, and the amended Nuremberg Principles as formulated by the International Law Commission in 1950 proscribing war crimes and crimes against humanity. The massive murder and destruction of civilian infrastructure through the use of biological, chemical and depleted uranium weapons violates not only international laws but the moral and humanitarian standards expected in modern civilization.

In the case of the Iraq War it is clear that the model for the National Security Strategy was a blueprint for U.S. global domination written well before President Bush took power in January 2001. The document, entitled *Rebuilding America's Defenses: Strategies, Forces and Resources for a New Century*, was written in September 2000 by the neoconservative think-tank Project for the New American Century (PNAC), and it reveals that President Bush and his cabinet were planning a premeditated attack on Iraq to secure "regime change" well before he was elected. The blueprint, posted on the PNAC website (http://www.newamericancentury.org/), for the creation of a "global Pax Americana" was drawn up for Dick Cheney (now vice-president), Donald Rumsfeld (defense secretary), Paul Wolfowitz (Rumsfeld's deputy), George W. Bush's younger brother Jeb, and Lewis Libby (Cheney's chief of staff). The document clearly indicates that Bush's cabinet intended to take military control of the Gulf region whether or not Saddam Hussein was in power.[8]

Break up of "the West"?

Under the impact of a set of events tied to the experience of the war prosecuted against Iraq, Robert Kagan (2003) has questioned whether Europeans and Americans still share a common view of the world and charts the divergence of these two perspectives on the question of power—its efficacy, morality, and desirability.[9]

Kagan, a senior associate at the Carnegie Endowment for International Peace and a columnist for the Washington Post, served in the U.S. State Department from 1984 to 1988. His book *Of Passion and Power* is an expansion of an essay that originally appeared in *Policy Review*. Kagan's thesis can be summed up briefly in his own words:

> Europe is turning away from power, or to put it a little differently, it is moving beyond power into a self-contained world of laws and rules and transnational negotiation and cooperation. It is entering a post-historical paradise of peace and relative prosperity, the realization of Immanuel Kant's "perpetual peace." Meanwhile, the United States remains mired in history, exercising power in an anarchic Hobbesian world where international laws and rules are unreliable, and where true security and the defense and promotion of a liberal order still depend on the possession and use of military might (p. 3).

He suggests that this state of affairs is not simply the product of the Bush presidency or change of administration dominated by neoconservatives, but rather that the differences are long-lived and likely to endure. Europe and American no longer share a common "strategic culture." As he depicts the differences, "Americans generally see the world divided between good and evil, between friends and enemies . . ." They favor coercion over persuasion, "seek finality in international affairs" (p. 4), tending toward unilateralism. They are less inclined to act through the UN or other international institutions and more skeptical of international law.[10] By contrast, Europeans "see a more complex picture." They are both more tolerant of failure and more patient, preferring peaceful solutions, "negotiation, diplomacy, and persuasion to coercion" (p. 5). Kagan admits this caricature tends to oversimplify and obscure differences, especially that between Britain and the rest of Western Europe (principally, France and Germany), which favors the "special relationship" and tends to adopt an "American" view of power. He admits also the country and regional differences—between France and Germany on the one hand and Eastern and Western Europe on the other, as well as differences between Democrats (who are more "European") and Republicans. These differences, he argues, should not disguise the essential truth that "The United States and Europe are fundamentally different today." These differences are the new desideratum of important divergences in strategic culture. "Foreign policy intellectuals and policymakers on both sides of the Atlantic," he argues, "have denied the existence of genuine differences or sought to make light of present disagreements . . ." (p. 7). The differences are contingent and of recent origin: "An evolution away from a different strategic culture that dominated Europe for hundreds of years."

He suggests that the American founding generation was not genuinely utopian but rather "well versed in the realities of international power relations" (p. 9). They only emphasized the repulsiveness of power politics and claimed an aversion to war and military power, emphasizing the soft power of commerce and international economic competition, because they were far inferior to the great European powers. He argues for a reversal, a diametric shift or opposition of attitudes, on the basis of increased military power:

> Two centuries later, Americans and Europeans have traded places—and perspectives. This is partly because in those two hundred years, and especially in recent decades, the power equation has shifted dramatically: When the United States was weak, it practiced the strategies of indirection, the strategies of weakness; now that the United states is powerful, it behaves as powerful nations do. When the European great powers were strong, they believed in strength and martial glory. Now they see the world through the eyes of weaker powers (p. 11).

Kagan qualifies his deterministic thesis on the relation between the growth of military power and corresponding behavior in foreign affairs somewhat by adding that an ideological gap as well as a power gap has opened up between the two blocs. The ideological gap, he suggests, is based on the unique historical experience of the past century, "culminating in the creation of the European Union" (p. 11), such that Europe and the United States have developed different ideals and principles concerning the morality and utility of power. He concludes that the "strategic chasm" is growing because "material and ideological differences reinforce one another" and may be impossible to reverse.

In the course of putting his case and at the end of his analysis Kagan is driven to make a series of dramatic claims concerning the concept of the West. He suggests that the need to preserve and strengthen the cohesion and unity of the West disappeared after the end of the Cold War. While it was a necessary and convenient strategic, ideological, and psychological fiction during the Cold War, which "meant something" in relation to Communism, "the very success of the transatlantic project" embodied in NATO and the settlement of a divided Germany and the Balkan conflicts "had the inevitable effect of diminishing the significance of 'the West' " (p. 80). As he explains further:

> With less need to preserve and demonstrate the existence of a cohesive "West," it was inevitable that the generosity that had characterised American foreign policy for fifty years would diminish after the Cold War ended (p. 81).

The West no longer functions as an organizing principle of American foreign policy. Clinton could not escape this new reality and the death-knell was sounded when Bush came to office in January 2001. The declining significance of the West was evident not only in American foreign policy, it was also clear (for all presumably, except Blair) to Europe for which the central issue had become "Europe." "A European 'nationalism' mirrored the American nationalism" (p. 84) and while the Europeans revered the EU and the UN as the West, for the United States "Only NATO was 'the West,' and now Europeans were building an alternative to NATO" (p. 84).

Kagan's "solution" is to advise Europeans to adjust to American hegemony. As he asserts "it is reasonable to assume that we have only just entered a long era of American hegemony" (p. 88), and as he informs us "If America's relative power will not diminish, neither are Americans likely to change their views of how that power is to be used" (p. 89). It is a position he puts with some speculative force when he searches for an explanation:

> One of the things that most clearly divides Europeans and Americans today is a philosophical, even metaphysical disagreement over where exactly mankind stands on the continuum between the laws of the jungles and the laws of reason. Americans do not believe we are close to the realization of the Kantian dream as do Europeans (p. 91).

There is nothing else to be done other than "to readjust to the new reality of American hegemony" (p. 97). Europe might follow Cooper's advice and build its military but the central problem is that the United States "must sometimes play by the rules of a Hobbesian world, even though in doing so it violates Europe's postmodern norms." He continues: "It must refuse to abide by certain international conventions that may constrain its ability to fight effectively in Robert Cooper's jungle" (p. 99).

Kagan's analysis has caused something of a stir on both sides of the Atlantic. While his analysis indicates a divergence in strategic culture between the United States and the EU it may well also prefigure future trade and culture wars as EU consolidation and expansion continue apace. The expansion of the EU with 10 new countries joining it in 2004, adding some 200 million people, has the potential to change the dynamics of European identity formation and especially its easy identification with the West, particularly as East European countries assert their own cultural identities and national priorities.[11] This picture become even more complex with the changing agenda and Russia's membership of NATO and the prospect of Turkey joining the EU in the years ahead. Turkey's membership of the EU, postponed until the next membership round, is especially interesting for a future EU not only because of its east/west positioning but also because of its large Muslim population. (What then of Western Christendom?)

The Promise of Europe and the New Humanities

Derrida provides us with a different picture to Kagan and the neoconservatives— one that asserts the promise of Europe by inquiring into the strata and archaeology of the concept of man and the European culture of humanism that nurtures it. He projects this analysis and understanding into a programmatic description of the new Humanities based on the history of the humanity of man and focused on two powerful juridical performatives, which delivered rights of man and crimes against humanity. There is little doubt that for Europe much hinges on its legacy of humanism and Enlightenment culture, not just in the clear sense of equipping the Union with its historical concepts and motivating values, but also in terms of its future and growing role in world affairs, including its moral and political vision of the "governance of globalization" strongly profiled in the Laekin Declaration. Beyond the simple reassertion of rights and its restatement in law, the notion of European humanism, oddly, seems ossified, as though the story of human rights has reached its apex and has come to an end. It also seems that humanism serves as the basis for proto-institutions of world civic society.[12] While humanism—the very singularization belies its status as a historical complex—is held to provide the historical ground for these roles, there is little in the way of ongoing reflection on its nature or, indeed, what is required to foster its development.

In this context we cannot help but be reminded of Heidegger's (1996, orig. 1946) "Letter on Humanism" where he responds to Jean Beaufret's question, "How can we restore meaning to the word 'humanism' " by questioning whether it is necessary to retain the word given the damage it has caused. Heidegger questions what it means for "man" to become "human" and suggests that *humanitas* remains the concern of an originary thinking: "For this is humanism: Meditating and caring, that man be human and not inhumane, 'inhuman,' that is, outside his essence. But in what does the humanity of man consists? It lies in his essence" (p. 224). He then takes us through a genealogy of the concept "humanism" beginning with the *first* humanism that is in essence Roman:

> *Humanitas*, explicitly so called, was first considered and striven for in the age of the Roman Republic. *Homo humanas* was opposed to *homo barbarus*. *Homo humanas* here means the Romans, who exalted and honored Roman *virtus* through the "embodiment" of the *paideia* [education] taken over from the Greeks. These were the Greeks of the Hellenistic age, whose culture was acquired in the schools of philosophy. It was concerned with *erditio et institutio in bonas artes* [scholarship and training in good conduct]. *Paideia* thus understood was translated as humanities. The genuine *romanitas* of *homo romanus* consisted in such *humanitas*. We encounter the first humanism in Rome: It therefore remains in essence a specifically Roman phenomenon, which emerges from the encounter of Roman

civilization with the culture of late Greek civilization (Heidegger, 1996, p. 224).

This is not the place to rehearse the full answer Heidegger provides to Beaufret's question but simply to indicate a thread connecting Derrida to the task of reimagining the new Humanities.[13]

In "Structure, Sign and Play" Derrida (1978, pp. 279–280) questioned the "structurality of structure" or notion of "center," which, he argued, has served to limit the play of structure by substituting one concept for another. Indeed, he argues the history of metaphysics "like the history of the West, is the history of these metaphors and metonymies." The determination of being as *presence* is the "matrix" for a succession of terms "*eidos, arche, telos, energeia, ousia* (essence, existence, substance, subject) *aletheia*, transcendentality, consciousness, God, man, and so forth."

In this essay Derrida called into question the previous decade of French structuralism and intimated his own intellectual ambitions. The "decentering" of structure, of the transcendental signified, and of the *sovereign* subject can be found in the Nietzschean critique of metaphysics and, especially, of the concepts of Being and truth, in the Freudian critique of self-presence, as he says, "the critique of consciousness, of the subject, of self-identity and of self-proximity or self-possession" (Derrida, 1978, p. 280), and, more radically, in the Heideggerean destruction of metaphysics, "of the determination of Being as presence." He concludes this important essay by distinguishing two interpretations of structure: One Hegelian in origin and exemplified in Lévi-Strauss' work "dreams of deciphering a truth or an origin which escapes play and the order of the sign" and seeks the "inspiration of a new humanism"; the other, "which is no longer turned toward the origin, affirms play and tries to pass beyond man and humanism . . ." (Derrida, 1978, p. 292).

In "The Ends of Man," given as a lecture at an international colloquium in New York two years later (i.e., 1968), Derrida (1982, p. 114) returns to the question "Where is France, as concerns man?" and provides an account that interprets the dominant motif of post-war French philosophy as a *philosophical humanism* authorized by anthropologistic readings of Hegel, Marx, and Heidegger. Sartre's "monstrous translation" (p. 115) of Heidegger's *Dasein* legitimated an existentialist humanism, and even the critique of humanism, itself a major current of French thought in the post-war era, and presented itself more as an amalgamation of Hegel, Husserl, and Heidegger with the old metaphysical humanism. In this movement Derrida argues: "The history of the concept man is never examined. Everything occurs as if the sign 'man' had no origin, no historical, cultural, or linguistic limit" (p. 116). Derrida's own trajectory has been toward an ever-clearer specification of the subject in historical, cultural, and linguistic terms, and an excavation of the history of philosophy of the subject, through its historical concepts and motifs.[14]

Derrida reconsiders the *relève* of man in the thought of Hegel, Husserl, and Heidegger to demonstrate that in each case there is a clear critique of anthropologism. In particular Heidegger's thought is guided by the double motif of being as presence and of the proximity of being to the essence of man (p. 128). Derrida suggests that if we are not simply to restore the ordering of the system by recourse to humanist concepts or to destroy meaning, we face two strategic choices: "To attempt an exit and a deconstruction without changing terrain, by repeating what is implicit in the founding concepts and the original problematic . . .," and "To decide to change terrain, in a discontinuous and irruptive fashion, brutally placing oneself outside, and by affirming an absolute break and difference" (p. 135). Both motifs must be interlaced in a new writing. We must "change the terrain"; we must "speak several languages and produce several texts at once" (p. 135); above all, what we need "is a change of 'style'; and if there is style, Nietzsche reminded us it must be *plural*" (p. 135).[15]

Building on these early motifs and themes Derrida suggests, "The Humanities of tomorrow, in all their departments, will have to study their history, the history of the concepts that, by constructing them, instituted the disciplines and were coextensive with them." These new Humanities, he suggests, would treat the history of man and the notion of "what is proper to man," focusing on the problematization of the two powerful juridical performatives that have given shape to the modern history of this humanity of man, by which he means the Declarations of the Rights of *Man* (and of woman) and the concept of crime against humanity, and that since the end of World War II have changed the geopolitical field of international law. Derrida has woven together a set of programmatic tasks for the new Humanities based on critical and deconstructive histories of its foundational concepts—rights, Man, humanity (law), democracy, sovereignty, nation-state (politics), profession and work (sociology), literature and fiction, professoriat and professionalization. Here is Derrida's renewal; in part the philosophical apparatus for delivering on the "promise of Europe."

The new figure of Europe is a theme Derrida has addressed in a number of texts, including *Of Spirit: Heidegger and the Question* (1991) and *The Other Heading* (1992)—a new figure that speaks to an international institution of law and an international court of justice; that constitutes universal sovereignty of absolute law, together with an autonomous force, without being state-related. It is this promise that Europe represents and which highlights its potential difference with the United States. Let me refer to a rather large excerpt from Derrida (2003) that I find both interesting from a historical viewpoint and encouraging from a political perspective:

> Without forsaking its own memory, by drawing upon it, in fact, as an indispensable resource, Europe could make an essential contribution to the future of international law . . . I hope that there will be, "in Europe" "philosophers" able to measure up to the task . . . But I persist in using this name "Europe," even if in quotation marks, because, in the long and patient deconstruction required for the transformation today, the experience Europe inaugurated at the time of the Enlightenment (*Lumières, Aufklärung, Illuminismo*) in the relationship between the political and the theological or, rather, the religious, though still uneven, unfulfilled, relative and complex, will have left in European political space absolutely original marks with regard to religious doctrine . . . Such marks can be found neither in the Arab world nor in the Muslim world, nor in the Far East, nor even, and here's the most sensitive point, in American democracy, in what *in fact* governs not the principles but the predominant reality of American political culture (pp. 116–117).

In short, the promise of Europe is bound up with international law that is divorced from the presupposition of a world superstate, a world citizenship without world government, a Kantian cosmopolitanism signaling democracy to come.

Notes

1. The Nuremberg Charter did not include reference to "genocide" despite Raphael Lemkin's best efforts to have it included, although the first official mention of genocide in an international setting occurred in October 1945 in the Nuremberg indictment against all 24 defendants stating they "conducted deliberate and systematic genocide, viz., the extermination of racial and national groups, against civilian populations of certain occupied territories." But as Samantha Power (2003, p. 30) makes clear "Nineteen Nazi defendants were convicted of crimes against peace, war crimes, and crimes against humanity. No mention was made of genocide."
2. For an account of how Lemkin's concept of genocide entered into international law, see Power (2003), especially chapters 2, 3, and 4.
3. See Aquinas, "Of War," *The Summa Theologica*, http://ethics.acusd.edu/Books/Texts/Aquinas/JustWar.html.
4. Earlier drafts were contained in Control Council Law No. 10, Punishment of Persons Guilty of War Crimes, Crimes against Peace and against Humanity, December 20, 1945, 3 Official Gazette

Control Council for Germany, 50–55 (1946) based on the so-called London Agreement of August 8, 1945.

5. For an account of "war as globalization" and an examination of the U.S. National Security Strategy and reconstruction in post-war Iraq, see Peters (2004); for an account of the conditions of "postmodern terrorism" and an investigation of the U.S. "war against terrorism" compared to the U.N.'s response, see Peters (2003b).

6. All data and figures come from Foerstel and Willson (2002).

7. Most recently the United States has refused to be a signatory of the International Criminal Court.

8. The Project for the New American Century was established in 1997 as part of the New Citizenship Project by William Kristol (chairman) and Gary Schmitt (president). Its stated goal is to promote American global leadership and it originated as a set of conversative criticisms of American foreign and defense policy under the Clinton administration. It aims to provide a vision for post–Cold War global politics:

> As the 20th century draws to a close, the United States stands as the world's preeminent power. Having led the West to victory in the Cold War, America faces an opportunity and a challenge: Does the United States have the vision to build upon the achievements of past decades? Does the United States have the resolve to shape a new century favorable to American principles and interests? (http://www.newamericancentury.org/statementofprinciples.htm).

9. This section on Kagan is drawn from Peters (2003b).

10. Jagdish Bhagwati, professor of economics at the University of Columbia in New York, accused the United States of undermining the World Trade Organization, making it act like a "Mafia protection racket." Jason Nissé of *The Independent* (Sunday, May 4, 2003, p. 1, Business section) reports that Bhagwati suggests that U.S. policy of striking bilateral deals was undermining the Doha trade negotiations. Two hundred such deals had already been agreed and they generally impose strict conditions "often to do with changes to intellectual property (IP) law and the liberalisation of financial markets." Nissé reports, "The U.S. then used the WTO to police these agreements, while often ignoring the trade rules itself, as it did last year with steel tariffs." He quotes Steve Tibbet, head of campaigns and policy at War on Want, as saying "Negotiations over intellectual property rights, export subsidies and capital flows are the true spoils of war in a global economy."

11. American strategy has already shifted to focus on East Europe and East Asia. In the U.S. National Security Strategy (http://www.whitehouse.gov/nsc/nssall.html) where he articulates the doctrine of "regime change" George W. Bush emphasizes democracy, economic development, and free markets are an integral part of the strategy against terrorism. While he also states the way in which the United States is committed to "lasting institutions" like the UN, the WTO, the Coalition of American States, and NATO, it is clear that the United States has refused to sign world protocols, conventions, and agreements, including, most recently, The International Criminal Court. It is evident from events surrounding the Iraq War that the United States is less committed to the UN than its European counterparts, and, perhaps, less committed to any European-inspired proto-world organization.

12. We might also mention besides the Treaty of Rome and the Treaty on Conventional Forces in Europe (the CFE treaty), the Organization for Security and Cooperation in Europe (OSCE), the Chemical Weapons Convention (CWC), the Ottawa Convention banning antipersonnel mines, the Strasbourg Court of Human Rights, the Convention on Torture, the IMP and OECD, which operate systems of economic surveillance, the Non-Proliferation Treaty (NPT), and the International Atomic Energy Agency (IAEA).

13. The few paragraphs on Derrida's questioning of humanism are drawn from Peters (2001). See also Peters (2003e), Trifonas and Peters (2003).

14. Judith Butler's (1987, p. 175) comment is entirely apposite here: "The twentieth-century history of Hegelianism in France can be understood in terms of two constitutive moments: (1) the specification of the subject in terms of finitude, corporeal boundaries, and temporality and (2) the 'splitting' (lacan), 'displacement' (derrida), and eventual death (Foucault, Deleuze) of the hegelian subject."

15. For an account on the importance of Nietzsche to poststructuralist thought and to Derrida, see Behler (1991), Large (1993), and Schrift(1995).

References

Behler, E. (1991). *Confrontations: Derrida, Heidegger, Nietzsche.* Translated by S. Taubeneck (Stanford: Stanford University Press).

Butler, J. (1987). *Subjects of Desire: Hegelian Reflections in Twentieth-Century France* (New York: Columbia University Press).

Commission of Inquiry for the International War Crimes Tribunal. The (n.d.) "Principles of the Nuremberg Tribunal, 1950," at http://deoxy.org/wc-nurem.htm. Authentic text: English Text published in *Report of the International Law Commission Covering its Second Session, June 5–July 29, 1950*, Document A/1316, pp. 11–14.

Cooper, R. (2000, orig. 1996). *The Postmodern State and the World Order* (London: Demos, The Foreign Policy Centre).

Derrida, J. (1978). "Structure, sign and play in the discourses of the human sciences," in A. Bass (trans.), *Writing and Difference* (Chicago: University of Chicago Press).

Derrida, J. (1982). "The ends of man," in A. Bass (trans.), *Margins of Philosophy* (Chicago: University of Chicago Press), pp. 109–136.

Derrida, J. (1991). *Of Spirit: Heidegger and the Question.* Translated by G. Bennington and R. Bowlby (Chicago: University of Chicago Press).

Derrida, J. (1992). *The Other Heading.* Translated by P.-A. Brault and M. Naas (Indianapolis: Indiana University Press).

Derrida, J. (2003). "Autoimmunity: Real and symbolic suicides. A dialogue with Jacques Derrida," in Giovanna Borradori (ed.), *Philosophy in a Time of Terror: Dialogues with Jürgen Habermas and Jacques Derrida* (Chicago and London: University of Chicago Press).

Foerstel, L. and Willson, B. (2002). "United States war crimes," Centre for Research on Globalization (CRG), *globalresearch.ca*, January 26, 2002.

Heidegger, M. (1996). "Letter on humanism," in David Farrell Krell(ed.), *Basic Writings* (London: Routledge).

Kagan, R. (2003). *Of Passion and Power: American and Europe in the New World Order* (New York: Alfred A. Knopf).

Large, D. (1993). "Translator's introduction" to Sarah Kofman, *Nietzsche and Metaphor* (London: The Athlone Press), pp. vii–xl.

Peters, M. A. (2000). "Politics and deconstruction: Derrida, neo-liberalism and democracy to come," in L. Simons and H. Worth (eds), *Derrida Downunder* (Palmerston North: Dunmore Press).

Peters, M. A. (2001). "Education and humanism: Heidegger, Derrida, and the new Humanities," in G. Biesta and D. Egea-Kuehne (eds), *Derrida and Education* (London: Routledge).

Peters, M. A. (2003a). "The postmodern state, security and world order." A version of this paper was originally given as an invited public lecture at Beijing Normal University, China, Thursday, October 10, 2002. *Globalization*, 2: 2 at http://globalization.icaap.org/currentissue.html.

Peters, M. A. (2003b). "Deconstructing 'the West'? Competing visions of new world order." *Globalization*, 3: 2 at http://globalization.icaap.org/content/v3.2/01_peters.html.

Peters, M. A. (2004). "The university and the new Humanities: Professing with Derrida." *Arts and Humanities in Higher Education*, 3: 1, 41–58.

Power, S. (2003). *"A Problem from Hell": America and the Age of Genocides* (London: HarperCollins).

Robertson, G. (2002). *Crimes against Humanity: The Struggle for Global Justice* (London: Penguin Books).

Schrift, A. (1995). *Nietzsche's French Legacy: A Genealogy of Poststructuralism* (New York and London: Routledge).

Trifonas, P. and Peters, M. A. (eds) (2003). *Derrida and Philosophy of Education* (Oxford: Blackwell).

CHAPTER SIX

Higher Education and Everyday Life

STANLEY ARONOWITZ

Several Years Ago

The twentieth century history of American higher education was periodically punctuated by allegations that its institutions had been seriously compromised by corporate and state influence in the conduct of academic inquiry, and by administrative infractions against the traditional aspiration of shared governance. Thorstein Veblen's *Higher Learning in America* (1918) and Robert Lynd's *Knowledge for What?* (1939) were prescient indictments of a not yet mature corporate university. Asking whether higher learning should serve the public good or private gain, Veblen's and Lynd's rants were regarded with considerable skepticism even as the authors were accorded the status of respected cranks. At the moment of their interventions mainstream America was preoccupied with each of the two world wars and was seriously considering mobilizing its intellectual resources, including the universities. Under these circumstances appeals to academic freedom and autonomy tended to fall on deaf ears. Indeed in contrast to some European countries where scientific and technological research was conducted by independent institutes rather than universities, President Franklin D. Roosevelt's science advisors recommended that a handful of elite public and private schools such as Berkeley and Princeton be charged with the responsibilities associated with the scientific and technological aspects of the war effort. Although the decision was made to outsource the bulk of weaponry production to private firms rather than producing most materiel in government-owned plants (the components of the atomic bomb was a major exception), the government remained the client of nearly all research products. Still war and the Cold War that followed generated not only a massive arms industry but resulted in the vast expansion and diversification of the chemical, electronics, and transportation industries which were, collectively, the engines of economic expansion until the 1970s.

By the 1950s under the hegemony of the Cold War, no less a conservative than President Dwight D. Eisenhower warned against the "military–industrial complex," already discussed at great length by C. Wright Mills in his magisterial *The Power Elite* (1956) four years earlier. Veblen went so far as to argue that since the Morrell Act in 1863 by which Congress for the first time committed the Federal government to support public higher education, primarily with land grants, the business of the university was to provide knowledge and a trained cadre for private industry, especially science and technology of agricultural production. The burden of his claim is that the concept of an autonomous university, revered since the Enlightenment, remained an ideal that was far from the existing situation. More than two years before the entrance of the United States into World War II changed the landscape of the relation of higher education to the Federal government, Lynd raised the disturbing question: Should the university serve the public rather than the private interest.

These were chiefly works of social criticism, which pointed to corporatist tendencies within universities, even as most institutions of higher education promulgated the fiction that their faculty were dedicated to the disinterested pursuit of knowledge. Of course the decision of the Roosevelt administration, in the context of preparations for World War, to invest its primary war research in a handful of leading universities had already raised doubts that scientists could remain free to perform their work independent of the influence of the military or the imperatives of the Cold War. Throughout the Cold War era. these doubts occupied the work of social critics and scholars such as I. F. Stone, Michael Klare, Noam Chomsky, and Edward Herman, among others. But the argument that the national security interests of the United States overrode the concerns about their autonomy persuaded many scientists to collaborate with the Federal government's military program, especially because the Department of Defense provided significant support to basic research not directly linked to the war effort. One of the most important functions of the defense contracts was to support the university-based liberal arts, especially the humanities and social sciences. In fact, absent alternative sources of funds, national defense contracts were frequently the vehicle by means of which natural and social scientists were able to do theoretical research or do work not directly connected to the war imperatives.

By the 1980s writers like Martin Kenney discovered the "University–Corporate complex," focused not on government contracts but university/business partnerships: In *Academic Capitalism* (1997) Sheila Slaughter and Gary Rhoades drew similar conclusions: the pursuit of knowledge as a public good, let alone for its own sake, were no longer shared values of the academic community, if they ever were. The collapse of the Soviet Union and the demise of its successor states as military superpowers and political rivals to the United States raised profound issues for the scientific establishment. How to sustain the high level of research within American universities in the post–Cold War era? The meticulous empirical research of Slaughter and Rhoades demonstrated that in the wake of stagnation of federal financing in the 1980s and 1990s of basic and applied research in the sciences, leading research universities added to their dependency by entering into "partnerships" with large pharmaceutical, chemical, and electronic corporations. A 1992 conference attended by the presidents and other key officials of leading research universities was dedicated to responding to the challenge. According to conference organizer Jonathan Cole, Columbia University's provost, they had only one main option—turning to private industry for support. Under these arrangements corporations provided significant funds to the university in exchange for joint patents, and "early access and review of all proposed publications and presentations by faculty members whose work the company supported." (CHE by Sharon Walsh "Berkeley denies tenure to scientist who criticized ties to industry.") While research in the so-called policy sciences associated with branches of sociology and especially political science have not been as subject to direct corporate control and influence, these sub-disciplines have long been adjuncts of the state (Donald Fisher: *Fundamental Development of the Social Sciences*). These relationships have prompted critics to ask whether the decline in terms of real dollars of the federal government's allocations to basic, disinterested research was primarily a reflection of the conservative program of privatization of knowledge rather than budgetary constraints. Or put another way are the decades of "budget" crisis an ideological and political mask for an attack against public goods framed in purely fiscal terms?

Moreover the privatization of scientific knowledge has led to widespread secrecy. Scientists who otherwise would have unswervingly accepted the doctrine that it is in the nature of their work to share knowledge were now, by contract, sworn to discretion. The emergence of partnerships has had a chilling effect on the tradition of scientific transparency, shared knowledge, and open debate about scientific discoveries. It is not uncommon for presenters at scientific meetings to purge their papers of information, which might violate the patent rights of their corporate sponsors. And, since the reward system of research universities is results-driven and, in a fiercely competitive global market, corporate partners demand that researchers keep ahead of the competition, the erosion of the ethic of honesty has led to frequent instances of fraud in reporting evidence. Moreover some scientists have invested, or received lucrative consulting contracts, in the corporations that support their research, often reaping substantial dividends. That such practices are condemned as unethical by leading spokespersons for the American Association for the Advancement of Science and other institutions is a measure of how widespread they are within scientific circles.

But there is barely a murmur about the underlying fact of the commodification of knowledge, which has become the main conse-quence of the end of the bipolar world created by the Cold War. If knowledge is subject to market forces, that is, it can be bought and sold like any other commodity, what follows is that scientific knowledge has become private property and that the research university is sustained by its ability to sell its wares to the highest bidder, in which case it itself becomes a corporate entity. Holding trade secrets is a common practice among corporate competitors. But contradicting one of the first princi-ples of the seventeenth-century scientific Enlightenment—that in the interest of encouraging criticism and revision scientific knowledge be widely shared—commodification signifies the reverse: To the degree that the university remains a key producer of scientific knowledge it may no longer be a bastion of open inquiry. Whether we determine that the subordination of knowledge to the commodity form is in the public interest is a complex question. If the fund of fundamental knowledge upon which technological innovation depends is deemed adequate for a multiplicity of applications, many corporations decide that a high vol-ume of basic research is not only unnecessary but unproductive. Federal agencies such as the National Science Foundation may allocate some funds for these projects but, absent a compelling case such as was provided by the race to develop a nuclear weapon during World War II or during the Cold War, policy makers have concurred with drug and electronics firms that new science must take a backseat to product development, which can facilitate the investment, circulation, and the profitability of capital. In short as long as knowledge is viewed as a commodity the concept of "disinterest" in research is bound to suffer eclipse.

But perhaps the most serious challenge to the independence of the academic system of American society is the effect of these practices upon the most fundamental right still possessed by the professoriate: Academic freedom. The fact that Federal agencies such as the National Science Foundation and the National Institutes of Health charged with dispensing research funds have increasing privileged proposals "dedicated" to producing knowledge that can be readily translated into products is by now almost commonplace. Since the Clinton administration Federal science policy is to encourage dedicated rather than basic research. The relative decline of funding for theoretical physics, for example, may be attributed to the long time period of transition between basic science and practical consequences. Since the transformation of biology into a technoscience—where the fundamental molecular paradigm is intimately linked to applications— funds have become scarce for those who persist in working in the field of evolutionary science or in the old functionalist perspective. Today if the university is not prepared to support such research, and private foundations, whose scientific sensibility is not far from the mainstream consensus, are not favorably inclined, the evolutionist as well as practitioners of some older biological disciplines find themselves without the laboratory facilities, travel funds, and assistants to facilitate their work. Money is available virtually exclusively for research in molecular biology and biophysics, whose knowledge can be rapidly transformed in commercial biotechnological applications, especially for genetically modified organisms in food and pharmaceuticals. These deprivations do not appear as a violation of academic freedom because no authority is telling biologists they cannot engage in the fascinating work associated with finding the origin of our species or of any other any more than physicists are prohibited from addressing the building blocks of matter or the history of the universe. However if money is no longer available save for a tiny corps of investigators, the priorities themselves are tantamount to refusing such projects and scientists who wish to stay "relevant" are well advised to fall into line.

Of course during the period of war emergency (not yet ended) the Federal government, in the interest of national security, claims the right to establish priorities in scientific research and deploys fiscal incentives to enforce its position. This approach is particularly effective at a time when the costs of scientific research, specifically in technology needed to perform experiments, have led to the distinction between "big" science and "little" science. The exemplars of big science are well known: Groups engaged in applications of physics and engineering to space travel; the huge accelerators needed for experiments in high-energy particle physics; the massive biophysics programs at MIT and at various University of California campuses, especially Berkeley, Davis, San Diego, Irvine, and Santa Barbara. But even at centers of so-called little science such as New York's Mount Sinai School of Medicine where, during the 1980s, the focus was sharply limited to finding molecular biological solutions to problems of brain research, funding opportunities drove the research program of the entire school and there is no reason to believe that any significant research institution today would take a different approach. Under such circumstances leading theoretical physicists such as the late Richard Feynman or Steven Weinberg or evolutionists and biologists Stephen J. Gould and Richard Lewontin are important to the university as ornaments signifying their commitment to intellectual excellence. Meanwhile in the knowledge factories of lucrative research most of the work that the university needs for its financial sustenance gets done.

But with rewards go punishments. Immediately after 9/11, among the many reconfigurations of civil liberties and academic freedom, the Bush administration launched a program of harassment of professors, mainly of Middle-Eastern background, who were not U.S. citizens. Some state universities collaborated with the Justice Department by dismissing them or permitting the government to implement a program of surveillance. As serious as were these acts of political repression the government justified them on National Security grounds and as a result, save for the objections registered by human rights and civil liberties organizations, went largely unchallenged. More recently, again on national security justification, the administration is floating a proposal to enable the Federal government to intervene more directly in monitoring curricula offered by American universities to foreign students But a recent case at the prestigious University of California, Berkeley, raises far more serious issues for our conceptions of the core mission of higher education. In Fall 2003 the university administration denied tenure to Ignacio H. Chapela, an assistant professor of ecology, overriding his department's unanimous recommendation and that of the faculty senate to grant him tenure. In November 2001 Chapela, and a graduate student, David Quist, published an article in the British scientific journal *Nature* that "claimed that native corn in Mexico had been contaminated by material from genetically modified corn. . . ." Six months later the journal received a number of letters contesting the research and the journal issued an editorial note acknowledging the evidence as not "sufficient to justify the original paper." As the controversy brewed Chapela said that he suspected the journal had been pressured by scientists working with the biotechnology industry and noted that he had been a critic of a 1998 deal between UC, Berkeley, and Norvartis, a Swiss biotechnology company, by which the university received $5 million each year for five years.

The Chapela affair is only one of the more blatant instances where the administration of a leading research university is strongly suspected of invoking nonacademic criteria for turning down a candidate for tenure. During the 1960s academic dissent was frequently met by university authorities with retributive contempt. While some stood up to government pressure to discipline recalcitrant professors, Columbia University's administration took pains to create an inhospitable environment so that even some prominent tenured professors felt obliged to leave; at the same time it became an open secret that after 1968, when the entire campus was rife with student demonstrations, the administration, which held the right to grant tenure tightly in its hands, routinely denied that status to radicals, even as it claimed that it was free of prejudice since most assistant professors were denied tenure. Of course the principle and practice of academic freedom is at the heart of the matter. But alongside the capacity of the institution to tolerate criticism, especially of its own corporate relationships, lurks the long-contested issue of the role of the faculty in academic governance at a time when higher education is increasingly privatized. During the past 15 years the professoriate has stood by as the allegiances of administration have, with the encouragement of state governments, shifted from their commitment to higher education as a "public good" to becoming contract players in the theater of capitalist hegemony. With the exception of a few relatively privileged departments and elite institutions the humanities and social sciences have suffered near-crippling cuts or stagnation even as the science and technology programs are funded in order to prepare them to seek private money.

The Chapela tenure case was hardly controversial either in his own department or at the level of the faculty as a whole. That the administration made the decision to override the consensual judgment of Chapela's peers in his favor, underscores a problem that has bedeviled advocates for decades of what has been termed "shared governance." Although they have acknowledged the governing role of university administration—mistakenly I would argue—they have insisted on the equal role of the faculty, especially on academic matters such as tenure and promotion. Indeed the establishment of promotion and tenure committees, which, in most instances, are composed exclusively of peers, perpetuates the perception of shared governance. Yet in all public universities and colleges and in the large majority of private institutions, decisions of promotion and tenure committees and deans have the standing of being recommendations to a sovereign administration, which, according to its own lights, may, with impunity, turn down the recommendations of lower bodies. In fact the arbitrary authority of the president and his office is frequently challenged by candidates, faculty senates, and unions. Many schools have established appeals tribunals, which hear cases of faculty discharge, discrimination in salary issues, refusal of tenure and of promotion. In some schools where unions have bargaining rights, the case is subject to a formal grievance procedure. But in many instances candidates are obliged to go to court in order to obtain restitution and, in general, courts are extremely reluctant to intervene in what they believe are purely academic decisions.

If the broad application of tenure, won after decades of agitation and struggle, signifies that the faculty is free to pursue channels of inquiry that may be unpopular and unprofitable for the university and its partners, then there is reason to believe that its short 60-year reign is under siege. That both public and private universities and colleges have, in the wake of budget constraints and their own priorities, adopted the practice of employing adjuncts and graduate students to teach the bulk of introductory courses is fairly known. Many adjuncts are superb teachers. In any case they are no worse than the full-time faculty. In pedagogical terms the difference resides primarily in the fact that the part-timer is rarely paid for the time required for student academic advisement, nor for class preparation. Beyond these egregious conditions, the spread of a vast, contingent workforce in academe threatens both tenure and academic freedom: It undermines tenure because the overwhelming majority of part-time adjuncts are hired by semester or by the academic year; the condition of their reappointment militates against their participation in free intellectual inquiry. Unfreedom may be ascribed not so much to policy as to their uncertain situation. Any conflict with a department chair—personal, intellectual, or political—can be, and often is, an occasion for termination of even a long-standing relationship to the institution. And, recently, many schools have hired faculty on one–five year non-tenure track contracts, some of which are renewable at the discretion of the administration, others not. At Harvard, Yale, and other elite institutions these appointments may become stepping-stones to permanent jobs elsewhere. However in ordinary third-tier four-year colleges and universities, after finishing their stint, faculty members often migrate to another temporary assignment.

We are at the beginning of an era where tenure is rapidly becoming a privileged status reserved for a minority of faculty. When this or the next generation of tenured faculty retires from active service, unless the professoriate as a collectivity is better organized and mobilized than at present, we may experience a return to the situation that prevailed from the nineteenth century to the first four decades of the twentieth century. Then tenure was only rarely granted by boards of trustees at private institutions and the situation was no better at public colleges and universities For example, Lionel Trilling, one of the leading literary scholars and critics of the post–World War II period, received tenure at Columbia after more than ten years on one-year contracts during which he held the rank of instructor, despite having earned a PhD and published a major biography of Matthew Arnold and innumerable articles in leading cultural journals. Similarly although one or two professors at Columbia's anthropology department were tenured, important figures such as Ruth Benedict and Margaret Mead never held a permanent position.

The presumption of tenure for qualified scholars and intellectuals was achieved by determined and dogged advocacy by the small, but prominent, American Association of University Professors (AAUP). Founded in 1915 as a national organization dedicated to academic freedom at a moment when presidents—most of whom were politically conservative—wielded almost unlimited power, AAUP placed the institution of tenure for all qualified faculty alongside its dedication to the ability of faculty to engage in free inquiry and speak and write dissenting opinions without facing discharge and other forms of discrimination, and shared governance as its three key objectives. While the Association's efforts were crucial in the post–World War II adoption and routinization of tenure by most schools, fears of a post–World War II recession must be awarded equal credit. From an academy attended by some one-and-a-half million students in 1941, nine years later the number had doubled, largely due to the enactment by Congress in 1944 of the Servicemens Readjustment Act (popularly known as the GI Bill), which sanctioned tuition-free school attendance for returning veterans and provided them with financial support and housing during the transition between service in the armed forces and paid work. It was, next to social security, the most comprehensive New Deal reform.

But the Cold War was no less beneficial to higher education. The dramatic increase of enrollments combined with Federal funding through the Department of Defense for student loans as well as graduate assistantships continued almost unabated for 25 years until the end of the Vietnam War. From the Depression era, when the relatively small number of teachers with PhDs constituted a glut on the academic market, to the first 20 years after the war, during which time graduate programs expanded as fast as they had public funds to do so but were still woefully behind the demand, according to the popular saying all one needed to get an academic teaching job was a PhD and a heartbeat, many academic institutions hastened to institute tenure, chiefly as a motivation to attract qualified applicants. While pay was modest, at least in comparison to other opportunities for educated workers in the rapidly expanding service and industrial sectors, the prospect of lifetime job security was attractive to many who still had vivid memories of Depression hardships and may have experienced the effects of the post-war recessions of 1954, 1958, and 1960–1961.

Only the rise of academic unionism from the late 1960s through the 1980s, which witnessed the organization of more than 30 percent of faculty and staff in colleges and universities, and growing enrollments, which increased by a factor of 500 percent from 1950 to 2000, temporarily saved tenure from a powerful counterattack. Yet as many institutions, beleaguered by fiscal constraints and shifting priorities, met their curricular and pedagogical needs in the human sciences with part-time and contingent labor the routine practice among nonelite institutions of granting tenure to faculty who met certain informal publication, teaching and service requirements came under scrutiny. Of course the claim of some educational economists and leaders of academic disciplines that graduate schools had saturated the "market" by overproducing PhDs was a fallacy born of their naive acceptance of administrative claims. For if the various constituents of the higher education industry had insisted that colleges and universities replace retirees, the deceased, and others who left university employment on a one-to-one basis, indexed the number of full-time hires to enrollments, and enforced limits on faculty/student ratios, we might still suffer from a continuing shortage in some fields. In any case the concept of "glut" is an corporate ideological construct whose success is attributable not to natural market causes but to the prevailing relationship of political forces within the academy. If the "handwriting is on the wall" it is not fated to come to pass. As long as professors refuse to deconstruct the ideology of overproduction they are likely to transfer blame from the institution to themselves. Or, as in the beleaguered disciplines of language study, emulating the building trades prominent professors began to call for limiting the supply of PhDs by raising admissions standards or, as two progressives argued, institutionalizing a two-tier professoriate by establishing a special "teaching" credential (Berube and Nelson, *Higher Education under Fire*).

Why has the collective higher education administration been so compliant? After all most middle-level administrators and a considerable fraction of top officials were and remain recruited from the professorial ranks despite a powerful push from a variety of sources to install high-level corporate bureaucrats into leading academic administrative position. The common explanation for the capacity of administrators to adjust to the new market-driven realities of their "industry" relies heavily on two detours from the historical experience of expanded public funding. Under the weight of federal and state tax cuts and recessionary conditions that combined to reduce state revenues, state legislatures throughout the 1980s and 1990s (which were decades of official prosperity) have sharply reduced funding for education as a whole but, particularly in the Northeast and the West Coast, they have been harsh on state colleges and universities. In the past three years even some Southern and historic Midwest land grant universities, which were previously protected by the fact that many legislators are their graduates, have suffered some funding cuts. According to this wisdom higher education got a bad name because of student and faculty dissent from the 1960s to the present, but began to suffer when many state governments were captured by the right. Under these conditions, it is argued, administration, is after all a professional bureaucracy and not a political party, has little choice but to adjust its strategies to the new realities—privatization of the sciences and technologies, outsourcing of many services such as building maintenance, food and bookstores, and unrelieved cost-cutting in the least economically viable branches: The arts, humanities, and the "soft" social sciences such as anthropology, which do not raise outside money.

To these I would add a third transformation, which helps explain why we have seen so little resistance within the top echelon administrators. Historically presidents, provosts, and deans were, and still are, mainly recruited from faculty ranks and they accepted these posts as an entailment of academic citizenship. After six or at most nine or ten years they looked forward to returning to the ranks of the professoriate. If they were serious intellectuals—scholar, social critic, or scientist—administration was considered a "duty," like the armed services, not a career. However with the advent of the corporate university teaching and research are now regarded by many as a prelude to a much more lucrative career as administrator. The corporatization of the academy requires the formation of a cadre whose loyalty is no longer to their erstwhile colleagues, whose main duties are teaching, research, and writing, but to the new institutional mission of making the university relevant to the dominant forces within the political economy. The measure of a successful administrative career is no longer academic leadership—indeed many deans and presidents seem curiously indifferent to what goes on in the classroom or in the public life of the college or university. What counts is the size of the endowment, the quantity of research funds, and, in the public universities, success in holding the line against legislative budget cuts. How to consolidate a "team" at the top of the corporate university whose loyalty is firmly ensconced in the institution and its corporate partners?

The major requirement is to reconfigure the institution on the model of the American corporation. The corporate hierarchy has a chain of command where, in contrast to the old collegial university or even the small, family firm, the boundaries between executives and line employees is fairly rigid and the division between intellectual and manual labor is strictly enforced. In the private corporation these tiers are rarely porous. Executives are rarely recruited from the professional ranks and manual workers may rise only to the level of line supervision. As previously mentioned the trend in colleges and universities is to recruit presidents and vice-presidents for finance, administration, and other posts from the ranks of corporate chief executives, financial and operating officers, and top military commanders. In the old regime, residents who come from these ranks may earn as much as 50 percent over their base pay, but search committees cannot offer such pittances to CEOs, CFOs, and generals. The solution, gradually put in place over the past decade or so, is the Executive Pay Plan.

This plan replaces the former practice of offering a 50 percent stipend and 10–25 percent stipends to vice-presidents, deans, and provosts over their professorial pay, which terminates when they return to academic ranks. Now the president is considered to be a CEO and, as university executives and corporate executives have become increasingly interchangeable, their salaries tend to become more competitive, although by no means identical. In 2003 some presidents of leading universities were earning $500,000–750,000 a year plus stipends for housing, a car and driver, and unlimited travel funds. In addition many of them sit as paid directors of corporate boards, even those with whom the university has relationships. The sticky position is that of the academic affairs vice-president or provost for which tradition still demands a genuine academic. But the executive pay plan for the top academic officer tends to separate them from the professorial ranks. It is not uncommon for provosts and academic vice-presidents in private universities to earn twice the top rate of the elite professoriate or three times the median rate of the full-time faculty. At most public universities the ratio of provosts' to top professors' pay has risen to one-and-a-half to one. It is not likely that these individuals would appreciate term limits or, more to the point, look forward to returning to the classroom.

What has resulted from the adoption of the corporate model to higher education is that the interests of the institution are now everywhere separate from those of the collegium and we have seen the formation of a professional/managerial class whose relationship to the intellectual life of the institution is increasingly remote or, to be more exact, tends to reduce faculty and staff to employees in both the private and public sectors. The administration is charged with "management," not merely of buildings and grounds, services and finances, but also of its core activities: Teaching and learning. In many of the 3,200 institutions of post-secondary education, provosts, under presidential direction, no longer depend on faculty initiatives to undertake innovative programs, or devise new curriculum. "Academic planning" has become the province of the administration and, under the rubric of "service to the university," faculty are invited—or assigned—to do the basic work needed to put their ideas into practice. At the community colleges, which enroll half of all students in postsecondary learning, mandates from above ordinarily entail prescription of certain textbooks and even pedagogies. Since many two- and four-year degree programs are undertaken in partnership with private corporations, the curriculum may be packaged by the company, in which case, the faculty is relegated to being transmitter of received knowledge and this is no longer a symbolic act, but becomes a literal mandate.

What are the Implications for the Future of the Higher Learning?

Jacques Derrida has issued a strong but gentle plea to protect and defend academic freedom and the autonomy of the university against the nefarious consequences of corporate takeover and the consequent subordination of academic knowledge to private interests. To this we have added the dangers of the formation of a distinct administrative class whose economic and ideological interests are tied to the corporate order, and of an increasingly intrusive state in everyday academic affairs, especially abrogating faculty's control over hiring, tenure and promotion, curricular matters, and its own production of knowledge. But we have learned that the American system of higher education has been, for almost a 150 years, partially integrated into the state and, as if to belie its image of an ivory tower, a practical adjunct to the scientific and technological basis of both the production and administration of things as well as people.

If these theses are true—and one's evaluation will depend almost entirely on her or his standpoint—the task of preservation, let alone restoration, of what remains of academic freedom is nothing less than monumental. Plainly the starting point must be to challenge the professoriate to recognize the assault upon free inquiry, the autonomy of the faculty as a collectivity, and on its most powerful weapons, especially tenure. Those who would defend academic freedom are obliged to recognize that a substantial portion of the faculty has been so bludgeoned by recent developments that it has lost hope. Another, much smaller segment may be afflicted with unease at the measure of how much they have become complicit with corporate and government funders who dictate the nature and direction of much scientific research, including most of the social scientific disciplines and education. A third group lacks all reflexivity because it has been formed in the era when the concept of partnership—read faculty subordination to corporate control—seems a thing of nature and, more to the point, the royal road to academic and financial reward.

Who is left? Philosophers, social theorists, "humanists," unrepentant liberals and radicals, and a tiny fraction of libertarians who bridle at corporatization because they realize that it has little to do with the free market. Many are to be found in faculty senates and councils, among academic union activists, and public intellectuals. Needless to say, in the main, their voices remain muted in the avalanche of crises that have afflicted higher education. If Derrida's call to arms is to be heeded his interlocutors will require strategic acumen to enter the fray. Where to start will depend on what issues arouse a powerful minority to focused outrage.

The experience of social movements, especially the labor movement, tells us that the grievances that will induce a group to take action is, from the standpoint of analysis, often not the most consequential. At a time of war mobilization, faculty may not pay heed to the blatant violations of the rights of alien professors, and under pressure of fiscal constraint, may shrug off the evidence of creeping privatization. But will they rationalize administrative refusal to heed faculty recommendations for tenure and promotion? They might take umbrage at administrators, who never tire of invoking the doctrine of sacrifice in a time of emergency, treating themselves to huge salaries while imposing a salary freeze on the faculty and staff. Or at public universities and colleges they might bridle against the state's effort to subvert the faculty's prerogatives by imposing mandates—funded as well as unfunded—on the curriculum. In short what gets the professoriate to act is indeterminate in advance. But one thing we do know. The more abstract the appeal, the least likely it is to provoke practical activity. Phrases like academic freedom, corporate university, and shared governance retain ideological resonance. It is more difficult to find the concrete instances by which these ideals are violated. Such is the task of a good organizer.

CHAPTER SEVEN

Altering the Material Conditions of Access to the Humanities

JOHN WILLINSKY

Mankind thus inevitably sets itself only such tasks as it is able to solve, since closer examination will always show that the problem itself arises only when the material conditions for its solution are already present or at least in the course of formation.

Karl Marx, *Contribution to the Critique of Political Economy*

This chapter enters this book through a side door, parenthetically left ajar by Derrida in his contribution to this collection—"(Although I must leave this aside . . .)"—as if space and time did not permit him to open the issue more than a crack, even as he names it "one of the most serious questions that is posed, and posed here, between the university and the politico-economic outside of its public space" (p. 234). This questionable space is, for Derrida, "the marketplace in publishing and the role it plays in archivisation, evaluation, legitimation of academic research," and it lies for him, in this case at least, entirely within closed brackets (pp. 234–235).

Here it will be otherwise. The main and open body of this chapter is concerned with the rude mechanics and marketplace of journal publishing, as a prominent channel of production in the scholarly mills of academic work. It is about current efforts "to find the best access to a new public space," as Derrida puts it just prior to his parenthetically setting this question aside as that public space is "transformed by new techniques of communication, information, and archivisation and knowledge production" (p. 234). This chapter supplements Derrida's aside. It appends a means of finding at least a better, if not the best, form of access to a new public space, in the name of a Humanities unconditional in its resistance and persistence. It is concerned with improving one aspect in the material conditions of access to the work of the university, for those conditions determine the *relation* that Derrida asks us to consider, between university and the politico-economic world.[1] That aspect is access to scholarly journals. For his part Derrida has worked on the material conditions of teaching in the Humanities, most notably through his contribution to the founding of GREPH (*Groupe de recherches sur l'enseignement philosophique*) in 1975, which has sought to further the teaching of philosophy (Derrida, 2002a). For my part I have been among those who have been working for the last few years on developing an alternative model for journal publishing, as the journal system persists within a particular state of economic crisis, that is, in effect, reducing access to knowledge for a growing number of faculty and students, especially those who work outside of the privileged sphere of well-endowed research libraries (Willinsky, in press).

Now I realize that it may seem utterly perverse to speak, at this time, of a declining access to research and scholarship. Isn't this rather a time of instant access to too much information, from home and office, if not from airport lounge and hotel room? Yet it seems fair to claim that access to scholarship and research is declining as long as university libraries are forced to cancel journal subscriptions, even as increasing journal prices erode the library's book acquisition budgets. Meanwhile the number of journals increases. If the best research libraries have been forced to cut just over five percent of their journal titles, less fortunate libraries, especially those in developing countries, have decimated their already minimal serial collections (with some reversal of this through special free e-journal programs), and virtually eliminated book purchases.[2] While university populations continue to grow on a global scale, journals are pricing themselves into an ever-narrowing market of well-endowed research libraries, exchanging the reach of a wider circulation (of knowledge) for stable profitability.

In searching for an explanation of this economic condition, what stands out is the increasing degree of commercialization within scholarly publishing. It began in earnest after World War II. An upsurge in state support for research in the West in the midst of the Cold War led to increased supply and demand for published studies, and when the scholarly societies proved slow to respond, the commercial publishers stepped in to create new journal titles. The growth of this corporate involvement, especially in science, technology, and medicine, has led to the same sort of corporate concentration that has taken place in rest of the media.[3] In scholarly publishing the result has been often exorbitant price increases for scientific journals, which affects, in turn, access to journals in all disciplinary areas.

With print journals a publisher's services are something of a necessity. That is not as obviously the case with this new digital medium of e-journals, and this dependence on the publisher has been called into question. Unlike the scholarly book, which has not found much of a home online, the journal has been drawn to the computer screen like a moth to a candle flame.[4] The great journal migration to this online medium, however, altered the crisis state of this knowledge economy, as most journals persist in charging much the same subscription fees, if not more, for print-plus-online access. Still more than a few journals are using these new technologies to reduce their costs sufficiently so that they are able to provide different forms of open access to their contents.

Well-known titles, such as *British Medical Journal* and the *New England Journal of Medicine* (NEJM), run by professional associations, continue to sell print subscriptions, while offering readers open access to their contents (if six months after initial publication, in the case of NEJM). BioMed Central represents the corporate model of open access, supporting 90 free-to-read journals in the life sciences by charging authors a fee for accepted articles. Then there are the independent open access journals, such as *Postcolonial Text*, which is a newly launched e-journal that utilizes Open Journal Systems, an online journal management and publishing package, and an open source piece of software, which is distributed for free, that I have been involved in developing.[5] This open source (free) system allows operation on a zero budget (with volunteer copyediting and proofreading), as well as having its principal editors located in Cameroon, India, South Africa, Sri Lanka, and the West Indies, as well as Canada. And yet it is fair to say that the open access model has had the same impact on the journals in this field as it has in the sciences or social sciences.[6]

On one level this is perfectly understandable, given that those working in the Humanities are not so technologically inclined as those in the sciences, nor have their journals suffered the same drastic escalation of subscription prices, well into the thousands of dollars, nor do they place the same critical emphasis on journal publication as they do in the sciences. Yet journals in the Humanities do play a vital role in the intellectual life of this area, whether in giving ideas a trial run prior to book-length treatments, in sustaining debate and exchange, and in creating a critical context for the analysis of major developments. Where the Humanities have gone some distance in increasing access to scholarly resources has been through projects such as the Rossetti Archive at the University of Virginia (with the complete writings and pictures of Dante Gabriel Rossetti), the still-in-progress *Stanford Encyclopedia of Philosophy*, or Project Gutenberg (which offers many complete works of literature for which the copyright has expired and a smattering of the major philosophical texts, from Plato's *Republic* to Dewey's *Democracy and Education*).

Yet greater access to journals in the Humanities would seem both a critical and practical step toward the unconditional university imagined by Derrida. Converting journals to some form of open access would give, by far, more people a chance to experience what is current and critical, as well as tentative and open in the work of the Humanities. And access to research and scholarship has begun to be, at least among a certain class of readers, a real issue, judging by a recent *New York Times* editorial in praise of "Open access to scientific research," which complained that scholarly publishing today "looks less like dissemination than restriction, especially if it is measured against the potential access offered by the Internet" (2003, p. A27). Not surprisingly the *Times* sees the issue largely in terms of increasing public access to medical research: "Most of us, admittedly, will not have much use for free access to new discoveries in, say, particle physics. But it is a different matter when it comes to medical research. Popular nostrums abound on the Web, but it can be very hard, if not impossible, to find the results of properly vetted, taxpayer-financed science—and in some cases it can be hard for your doctor to find them, too." The very right of access to any of this knowledge, whether on particle physics, cancer treatments, or human rights, seems to me more fundamental than whether "most of us," as the *Times* puts it, will "have much use" for it. This is why the Humanities need to be part of this struggle over the political economy of knowledge.

Now I recognize that to pin any form of hope on a shift from print to electronic publishing may seem to reinforce the very real digital divide that separates those who have access to the Internet and those who do not, a divide which will continue to condition access to knowledge as surely and for as long as any of the other divides by which we live. But in the case of access to scholarship we need to first recognize that print journals have been contributing to an economic divide that has contin-ued to grow over the last two decades, to the point where to walk into a university library in Nairobi is to find that there are no longer any print subscriptions or to visit the Kenyan Medical Research Institute is to find it hanging onto its final five subscriptions. I do not think it too much of an exaggeration to say that, in this particular knowledge economy of scholarly publishing, print reached its limits decades ago in the circulation of knowledge on a global scale, and is now contributing to an increasing gap between who has access to this knowledge, and thus the right to participate in its production.

On the other hand the very machinery of contemporary scholarly production and transmission—the computer and the Internet—is slowly being distributed among universities around the world. The conditions of access to the technology can amount to no more than five computers in an African university library or no student access, except through a librarian (Muthayan and Muinde, 2003). Yet even then these inadequate technologies, by our standards, have already begun to make it possible for faculty and students in disadvantaged institutions to access a much greater part of this academic world of knowledge than they had been able to through print, and this increase has, in turn, improved their opportunities for contributing to this knowledge (Willinsky, in press). The capacity of these new technologies to reduce dissemination costs have made it possible for the World Health Organization (WHO) and the International Network for the Availability of Scientific Publications to convince donors and sponsors (including commercial publishers) to provide faculty and students in developing countries with open access to electronic editions of thousands of titles. It costs the journal publishers little enough to grant this open access to their journals in developing countries, but it has already altered, but by no means alleviated, the devastating conditions of access that are the result of our current journal economy.

If the university is to be without condition any time soon, and if we mean by university a global pursuit of higher learning, and if the university is to possess, in Derrida's words, "an *unconditional* freedom to question and assert, or even the right to say publicly all that is required by research, knowledge, and thought concerning the truth" (Derrida, p. 233), then access to that questioning and saying, and access to the scholarly apparatus that determines what is asserted publicly, is a critical first step. After all does the "right to say everything" mean anything at all, if the "right to say it publicly, to publish it" does not allow for some experience of how others are saying and publishing it through their scholarly work? This is only to say that scholarly work, especially as it is supported by public or publicly spirited institutions, should be made as available as economically possible, and thus this need to explore and test the new economics of electronic journal publishing to see what it could make of a greater access to this particular knowledge work that goes on in universities.

To speak of improving the material conditions of access to journals is to speak of a human right to know what is known. This right is not just about being able to read of others exercising an unconditional freedom to question and assert, but to see that it is within one's reach as a member of that global community, to participate in that freedom, to see the possibilities of exchange and circulation to this knowing, to acquire the means of contributing to this knowledge. Nor is open access only about the circulation of this knowledge within a global university community. To move journals into an open access model means that they are also available in public libraries, community centers, colleges, and high schools, where with print journals there has rarely even been a question of access to this knowledge.

The journal is also a natural point of interest for increasing open access because of how it emerges out of the special, if not-quite-unconditional, contribution made by authors, editors, and reviewers to journals, which is not typically the case with scholarly books. The freely given quality of the journal has its own way of rooting this knowledge as a public good. It provides the basis for faculty members reasserting their property rights over their work, rights that they otherwise sign away to journal publishers, who perversely insist that the journal cannot be published unless they own the work outright (as opposed to being granted a limited right of first publication). The journal is the perfect site for a practical reassertion of scholarship's place within the public domain.

A good number of scholars already use the journal to exercise, as Derrida advocates, the right to speak and to resist unconditionally "everything that concerns the question and the history of truth, in its relation to the question of man, of what is proper to man, of human rights, of crimes against humanity and so forth . . . above all *in* the Humanities" (2002b, p. 113). Yet it makes something of a mockery of this independence to have the resulting knowledge, otherwise safely placed out of harm's way, hidden behind passwords and research library doors. How do those who are interested in seeing the university resist the powers of state or economy imagine this can happen when they are so little interested in making the basis of that resistance—the knowledge and substance that makes resistance necessary, sound comprehensible and reasonable—available to anyone who lives and works outside of the relatively small circle of well-endowed universities? So along comes this moment when it might just be possible to speak the truth to power on a larger scale, to marshal evidence and argument on behalf of those who cannot otherwise muster such resources in a more open fashion. If the university is to profess an "unlimited commitment to the truth," as

Derrida puts it, it must at some point be concerned with the right of access to that truth (p. 234).

In this sense the incipient open access movement in journal publishing has something to offer to the "right to philosophy" that Derrida addresses in his work with the philosophy teaching group, GREPH, with its goal of organizing "a body of research in the connections that exist between philosophy and its teachings" (Derrida, 2002b, p. 97). He speaks of this right to philosophy in three important senses. It is for him a fundamental *right* to *philosophy*; it is about *going right to* philosophy; and it is a question of *who has the right* to philosophy (2002a, p. 3). And yet for Derrida, it is a right that is achieved in the very spirit of philosophy: "Philosophy is the most easily shared thing in the world. No one can forbid access to it. The moment one has the desire or will for it, one has the right to it. The right is inscribed itself" (p. 23).

As for how to go about this right to philosophy, and to the Humanities more generally, Derrida calls for a "necessary 'delocalization' to the teaching body" (2002a, p. 113). I take this delocalization to be about opening access to the very court of this philosophy, taking the back-and-forth quality of philosophy out of doors, beyond the cloistered quad, and into the piazza, much as the Royal Society of London, which formed in the seventeenth century, grew out of coffee-house discussions, giving rise, in the process, to a pamphlet publication of miscellaneous experiments and natural history findings for a wider public, with the *Philosophical Transactions* being first published in 1665—now regarded as the first scientific journal in English—by its secretary Henry Oldenburg. Only this time the public sphere is delocalized in a global, virtual sense.

Derrida recognizes this universal right to philosophy is not without some risk. It does make philosophy "more accessible to ideological misappropriations or to its dissolution in nonphilosophical disciplines," and he stands up for what is unique about philosophy's contribution, defending its need to "train" students in "critical vigilance" against what philosophy might otherwise become among the human sciences (2002a p.112). The available means for recognizing that right, for philosophers to fulfill the one human right that is entirely up to them to acknowledge or withhold, is through training and teaching. So while Derrida speaks of philosophy as that which is most easily shared, as if it were simply part of the language freely spoken, he is just as quick to acknowledge that it depends, in fact, on structured and deliberate efforts to support this undeniable access, namely through training, in his case:

> To have access *effectively*, in effect, to these discursive procedures and thus to have the right to the *philosophical such as it is spoken*, for

philosophical democracy, democracy in philosophy, to be possible (and there is no democracy in general without that, and democracy, the democracy that remains still to come, is also a philosophical concept), one must be trained in the these procedures (2002a, p. 29, original emphasis).

GREPH was dedicated to increasing access to the teaching of philosophy, not just at the university level but in the schools and elsewhere, and this clearly distinguishes it from my project, which is all about opening the pages of philosophy and other journals to those who might find their way to them. Derrida was, some 30 years ago, working with others to uphold the "the right to teaching," which bears a connection to the movement for open admissions, perhaps most notably with the founding of Britain's Open University in 1969 (p. 36). This "right of access (to whatever, teaching, philosophy, and so forth) assumes the access to right, which assumes the capacity to read and interpret, in short, instruction" (p. 36).

I do not want to undermine the value of being able to study philosophy with a good teacher in my efforts to open access to the journals. Much of what scholarly journals contain is given to technical minutiae and hair-splitting debate, which will remain inaccessible to the common reader, even with the very best teaching. But not all of it. And access to teaching and to the literature can go hand in hand in extending this right to philosophy. Derrida holds to the idea that this ability to reach a wider audience is itself a test of philosophy, and quotes, to that effect, Kant's insistence "that every philosophical teaching be capable of being made *popular* (that is, of being made sufficiently clear to the sense to be communicated to everyone), if the teacher is not to be suspected of being muddled in his own concepts" (cited by Derrida, 2002a, pp. 44–45). Kant felt that going public and "being made popular" is part of what philosophy should do, as a philosophy is often referred to as *a teaching*. Kant also set out implicit limits to that teaching in answering the question of what Enlightenment is in the pages of the newspaper *Berlinische Monatsschrift* in 1784. His response to the question was to invoke Horace and declare that "the motto of enlightenment is therefore: *Sapere aude!* Have the courage to use your *own* understanding!" (1970, p. 54, original emphasis). In this op-ed piece, he called for a "freedom to make *public use* of one's reason in all matters" and "without outside guidance" (pp. 55, 58, original emphasis). This teaching is aimed at moving people out from under the tutelage of others. It can be supported by increasing people's access to resources that would support this public reasoning and freedom.

Certainly these new machines are increasing access to university instruction. The open universities have been among the first to use new technologies to improve distance education. MIT has an Open Knowledge Initiative, which is setting standards for learning technologies, and its OpenCourseWare is designed to "provide free, searchable, coherent access to MIT's course materials for educators in the non-profit sector, students, and individual learners around the world," as the website puts it, and it does so "to advance knowledge and education to best serve the nation and the world," with the support of Hewlett Packard and the Andrew Mellon Foundation. This does not mean that you can take the courses for free, at least not for credit, although some of the texts being studied are through open access sites.[7]

MIT's efforts to open the material basis of learning, to support teachers and learners through access to its course materials is consonant with the drive for open access to journals. Each journal that moves to open access offers teachers and students resources that could add to the learning experiences of both, especially in universities where such resources are otherwise scarce. It could also make all the difference for the high school teacher or student seeking to take a step beyond the standard curriculum.

Still, increasing access to scholarly journals is about a right to philosophy and the Humanities, which goes beyond supporting instruction. This philosophical *training*, to use Derrida's word, with its reading regimen and exercises, is bound within pedagogy's inevitable power relations, as he also notes.[8] The broader sense of philosophy, as inherently a form of teaching, is something that persists outside of the classroom, as does the right to this philosophy, whether on an ongoing or occasional basis, whether for the policy analyst trying to frame a common social issue in a new way, as well as for the common reader, who, having enjoyed the work of Stephen Hawking, might happen upon Hélène Mialet's article in *Critical Inquiry* on the mind–body dilemmas of scientific "genius," which arise in her interview of him (2003), while a fan of David Cronenberg's films might find, in the same issue of *Critical Inquiry*, Teresa de Lauretis' analysis of his 1999 film, *eXistenZ*, which she treats as "a reflection of the new technologies of postmodernity—information, communication, and biotechnologies and the new interactive media" (2003, p. 547).

This right to philosophy should not require that citizens be enrolled, registered, assigned, and taught in order to qualify for this right to knowledge. If the Humanities is going to increase its presence in that relation between university and the politico-economic world, if it is going to play a more integral role in the *democracy to come*, as Derrida emphasizes (2002b, p. 13), then the door to this knowledge, as public and published good, should be opened, no less than the classroom door.

The specter of learning in the Humanities at issue here, then, is more about what is *self-taught*. This autodidactism accounts for so much of what we know and has always been the working person's tutor, the lifelong learner's best instructor. For teachers the best moments of teaching often arise from just being there, in the presence of a student who is figuring it out for herself or himself. And much learning takes place without a teacher in sight. Such is my case for scholars to open the fields of their own best learning to this larger body of students and readers by taking advantage of these new publishing technologies to reconstruct the journal publishing economy. It could expand the potential universe of learning, following on the tradition of the public library movement and other efforts at popular self-education. It could assist Derrida in pursuing the lofty ideal of "ensuring each citizen the chance of encountering one of three things that are called philosophy at least once in his or her life"; then we need to open more that access to teaching (2002a, p. 39).

Yet in introducing this public right to philosophy into the argument for open access, I am not asking scholars to redirect their efforts toward catering to this expanded audience. Certainly money is being made in writing quickie guides, from *Plato for Beginners* to *Kant in 90 Minutes*, judging by the number of these series, covering the same hoary figures, found in bookstores these days. The apparent success of these series only adds to the argument that open access to the journal literature, where the same ideas are fully alive and critically engaged, may attract a greater audience than anticipated; even the size of that audience matters little if this is indeed a right to know. Yet the value of this literature remains in its scholarly achievements, and it owes that wider public and professional audience (e.g., policy makers, teachers, etc.) no more than the right to know what is known, especially when that right is realizable on a much greater scale—although by no means on a universal basis—through new journal publishing technologies.

Now it may happen that opening scholarly literature to this larger audience gradually alters its own tone and tenor, as writers find their work unconsciously affected over time by the light of day shining in on it. The writing may be altered as well, as it takes shape in the knowledge that it must now work its sense and sensibility for a larger world than before. Open access is not, however, about abandoning the scholarly project in any way. Rather it is about reasserting a basic principle about the nature of knowledge. I am referring to the belief that the circulation of knowledge is vital to its very claims as knowledge, and that a continuing decline in that circulation does not bode well for the future of the university or what it would make of knowledge, especially as that academic community continues to expand on a worldwide basis.

I am siding here with Helen Longino, who in her efforts to move beyond the "science wars" establishes in *The Fate of Knowledge* how "the social is not a corrupting but a validating element in knowledge" (2002, p. 122). She treats the social restrictions or material conditions that typically hamper a qualified candidate's ability to participate in research and scholarship, whether through economic disparities or through forms of discrimination, as simply a "cognitive failure," which diminishes the quality of knowledge through which we understand the world (p. 132).[9] It represents a failure on the part of the academic community to subject its ideas to the largest possible hearing, and that failure is directly attributable to a knowledge economy that may be unduly restricting access and participation in the circulation of that knowledge. Again it may seem bizarre to suggest that the current state of access to journals amounts to a cognitive failure among the "epistemic community," to use another of Longino's terms (p. 132). And while radical gains have been made in some areas in the last few years, notably in the amount of medical research available to universities in impoverished countries through the efforts of the WHO, my case is that a great deal more can be done by this community to improve access in this particular area of the journal literature.

Without addressing the material conditions of journal publishing, Longino adds to this open access argument by stressing how this community "must also take active steps to ensure that the alternative points of view are developed enough to be a source of criticism and new perspectives" (p. 132). This requires, to her mind, "publicly recognized forums for the criticism of evidence, of methods, and of assumptions and reasoning," which is what the journal literature represents already, one might argue, except that its public inaccessibility certainly hampers its public recognition as such a forum (p. 129). Without trying to tie Longino into my argument for open access to journals, this model does address her concerns over "limitation of space" as well as "the privatization of information and ideas," which "contribute to the marginalization of critical discourse" (p. 129). It also poses a relatively easy way to address the need, she identifies, to "help citizens acquire a tolerance for the provisionality, partiality, and plurality of knowledge" (2002, p. 213). For nowhere is this aspect of knowledge more readily apparent than in the give-and-take of journals.

None of this, I should state, requires that scholars alter what they make of their work in the Humanities. This is not a call for greater "relevance," or a veiled threat to academic freedom. Let scholars pursue their right of resistance or not. I only ask that some notice be taken of the material conditions of this knowledge's circulation, as it bears on the quality of that knowledge, both in an epistemological and democratic sense, and I only ask this in light of the new alternatives opened up by the wholesale move of journals to online publishing environments. But not only can those working in the Humanities continue to pursue their scholarly interests—whether or not it is concerned with unconditional forms of academic resistance—they can see their star rise by publishing their work in journals using some form of open access policy. I mean this not only in a moral sense, but in the crassest career and financial sense, as open access dramatically increases readership and levels of citation for authors whose work is freely available.[10]

Having made this case for supporting a wider audience among scholars, students, and the public, let me also make it clear that putting journals online is not simply a matter of pasting pages on a screen. The challenge is to design a new publishing environment that stays true to the scholarly article, while furthering its scholarly and public qualities. Without going into the technical details of online publishing here (yes, one aside leads to another, let me say parenthetically in turn), let me offer the example of the Public Knowledge Project with which I work. We are in the process of developing publishing systems designed to provide readers with richer context and background for approaching any given article. These systems provide the reader with a ready means to check their reading of a piece, with a click or two, against what is being said in related work, to gather background on the author, as well as view other works, and to trace the ideas presented through other forms, whether among media databases, government policies, or historical archives.[11]

We have now to test whether providing readers with this greater context extends their reach within this literature (or just confuses, distracts, and annoys them). We also want to know if making it easier to situate an article within this broader context could add to the scholarly quality of the work itself, as it supports both the writing and review process. While we do not have the answers to these questions yet, it is hoped that if we can arrive at improved designs for scholarly publishing it will add to the argument in favor of increasing access to this literature. Our very pursuit of these questions bears its own relation to the Humanities as a field that would seek to understand how texts are read and interpreted, and regards close reading its default methodology.

As this new publishing environment we are experimenting with integrates scholarship with other public domains of discourse, it has everything to do with Derrida's political agenda for the unconditional university and the right to philosophy, and for what he frames as, in a related work on this theme, the debt and duty associated with the right to philosophy (2002b, pp. 16–17).[12] For if the relation between the university and the world outside of it is about the *democracy to come*, as Derrida would have it, then the university has some responsibility for knowledge's vital role in democracies. The Internet has raised our expectations of the information that governments and other agencies make available; it has accelerated the mobilization of political alliances and informed political action, and it has led to experiments in public deliberation and policy consultation.[13] It has created a knowledge commons, one to which scholarship's contribution stands to be greatly increased in a systematic fashion. As access to knowledge is both a democratic right and a necessity, it does not seem unfair to think that Humanities scholars need to be among those who should be instrumental in establishing the public right of access to this public good otherwise known as scholarship. On the other hand to continue to demonstrate relative indifference toward the public accessibility of our own work makes it that much more difficult, surely, to call others on their philosophical shortcomings and democratic failings.[14]

Improving access to this knowledge has everything to do, as well, with the democratic quality of life among communities operating across national boundaries, such as the universities as forming a global community, and how the democratic right of representation and participation in that republic of scholarly letters might be advanced by wider rather than restricted access to the journal literature is one small but vital part of it in the global exchange and circulation of knowledge that constitutes the democratic work of the university. That quality of this democratic right depends on many factors, from being so underpaid and overworked by your institution that conducting research is not possible, to having a reliable source of electricity. But the democratic quality of this academic community surely relies, as well, on the very thing that each of us (as authors, editors, and members of scholarly associations) in the university community helps to determine, and that is the material conditions of access associated with the circulation and exchange of scholarship and research.

As I have already suggested this is not about scholarship in the Humanities having to prove its relevance to democratic life. The cases that have been made for the contributions of this work can continue to be made. Rather, the very effort to make our scholarship more open speaks to reasserting knowledge's place within the public sphere so vital to democracy. To position a greater portion of this work as a freely available public good establishes an alternative to the competitive and corporate scope of global knowledge economies. And it does so, of course, on a global rather than national basis, although not without raising questions of linguistic imperialism, which are hardly new to research and scholarship. After all if we are to deconstruct our own history, asking critical questions of "the history even of the notion of critique" (p. 235), then we are bound to confront the scope of isolation and solipsism that besets the closed circle of scholarly work, as if publishing in the best journals, with the best publishers, were a critical, deconstructive end in itself.

Our independence as scholars has rested for too long on the inaccessibility of this work, not just in what is at times the necessarily convoluted nature of language, but as a result of the relative obscurity in which it circulates. Derrida's notion, then, of the "weakness and vulnerability of the university" is as much, for me, about its own failure to recognize its responsibilities to a larger academic community, which has developed on a global basis (p. 236). How are we to protect the independence and resistance of the university if we have turned the knowledge at issue into its own source of inequality through indifference to the material conditions of access, in a vain pursuit of greater publishing glory?

The critique that Derrida calls for—"in which nothing is beyond question" (p. 235)—must begin, much like charity, at home. We need to see how readily we allow our scholarship to become subject to corporate interests in a knowledge economy of ruthless exclusion, mergers and acquisitions, surveillance and enforcement.[15] Universities may currently be at risk, Derrida warns, of "becoming a branch office of conglomerates and corporations," but the knowledge we produce is already, in too many cases, a corporate asset, whether of Blackwells, Taylor and Francis, or Cambridge University Press, as a condition of publication (p. 237).

If we are indeed to make something of the Humanities' special powers to resist, through its embrace of theory, its unrelenting questioning, then scholars working in this area need to put their words where, as it were, their mouths are. That is, they need to find ways of deconstructing a publishing system that delimits access in favor of one that creates a public and global organ open to scholarly participation and common readers, and that provides its own incentive to the spread of the Internet. The digital divide that we need to be concerned with is the divide constructed between those with access to this knowledge and those without. For it is that divide alone that is immediately and directly in our hands to control and overcome. To put it far too simply, what we give for free to publishers, we need to make free to readers and colleagues, where it can do us the most good in an intellectual, altruistic, and personal sense. The copyright over scholarship is ours, in the first instance, under the special academic exception we are afforded as part of scholarship's public trust (McSherry, 2001). It would otherwise seem that we are squandering that trust at this point out of an indifference to such economics of access, and in pursuit of the career rewards of publishing in the top journals.

How is open access to the journal literature in the Humanities to be achieved in this immediate and direct way? There are a number of routes. Certainly the easiest is to simply post a copy of their work on the Web, in addition to publishing it elsewhere, as I have done with this chapter. This can be done on one's own home page, but the best way to do it is to place the article in what is called an "eprint archive," where it is indexed and thus all the more openly available (Harnad, 2003). These archives are being set up by universities and by subject area, with the software for them being freely available, and with many journals having explicit policies allowing such a free posting.[16]

A second route to open access is to involve editors, editorial boards, and possibly scholarly associations in converting existing journals to some form of open access. Open access for existing journals can take the form of immediate and complete access to the online edition of the journal (with perhaps a print subscription system retained in place), or it can amount to delayed open access, which is offered some months after initial publication to subscribers, or it can be made geographically exclusive, with open access made available to those who register for this service from developing countries.

A third route to open access is to start a new journal that is designed from the outset to make its contents free to read, which is what we have done with *Postcolonial Text*. Such journals can take advantage of open source management software to reduce their costs, involve a wider range of editors as the journal's office is virtually located everywhere, and deploy innovative tools for providing a richer context for reading. Improving the material conditions of access to the contents of these journals augments the circulation of knowledge.

Within that part of the Humanities devoted to a resistance that exercises the right to say everything publicly, there has yet to emerge a systematic effort to open this scholarship in a regular way to the public spaces of the Internet. My supplement to Derrida's aside, then, would prompt Humanities scholars, who are otherwise taken with principles of unconditional resistance, to look up from their screens and books long enough to consider the rude mechanics of where and how their work is delivered to the world. It seems entirely consistent with their own interests in the nature and history of knowledge to attend to new and experimental efforts in publishing, in their democratic and global claims to be representing what is properly the right of humankind. To increase democratic access to knowledge in this way certainly has its risks, its trade-offs, its loss of privilege. It will mean more of the same in the journal literature, a further crowding of already crowded fields. It could well lead to greater specialization, and the reading of more about less. And then there is the inevitable loss of the fine paper, the smell of glue and ink, which have long marked the journals that arrive in the mail.

It is not that there will ever be unconditional access to the work of scholarship, any more than we will ever come to work in unconditional institutions, except in that nether world of *what could take place tomorrow*. Yet at this point, today, we may have a historic opportunity to change the material conditions of access to this knowledge that we work so hard to produce. It's true that the changes called for here are opportunely focused on that narrow band of our work that makes up the journal literature. Yet each journal that takes this step of opening itself to this larger public space serves as a demonstration of the place such knowledge can occupy within the democracy that is here now, as well as within the one to come, in part as a result of such efforts.

Notes

1. Marx:"My inquiry led me to the conclusion that neither legal relations nor political forms could be comprehended whether by themselves or on the basis of a so-called general development of the human mind, but that on the contrary they originate in the material conditions of life, the totality of which Hegel, following the example of English and French thinkers of the eighteenth century, embraces within the term 'civil society' " (1859).
2. On the serial crisis, see the Association of Research Libraries website (http://www.arl.org), which demonstrates how the best libraries in North America cut six percent, on average, of their journal subscriptions between 1989 and 2000, and see Willinsky (in press) for a summary of far more drastic cuts among the minimal libraries of developing countries. On the monograph crisis and the related university press crisis, see Regier (2003).
3. As a result of mergers over the last few years, Elsevier, Springer, and Taylor and Francis control 60 percent of the journals in the leading citation index, ISI Web of Science (Merger Mania, 2003).
4. A recent survey conducted by the Association of Learned and Professional Society Publishers reports that 72 percent of journals in the Humanities and Social Sciences, compared to 83 percent in the sciences, now have online editions (Cox and Cox, 2003, p. 5).
5. Open Journal Systems, developed through the Public Knowledge Project (http://pkp.ubc.ca), automates many of the management and clerical tasks of journal publishing, improving record-keeping while reducing management time, as well as eliminating photocopying, postage, and stationery costs, not to mention printing, distribution, and subscription-management expenses.
6. The Directory of Open Access Journals at the University of Lund lists seven journals in philosophy at this point, including *Animus* and the *African Journal of Philosophy* and nine in language and literature, including *Agora* and *Romanticism on the Net*. The variations include *Postmodern Culture*, which offers open access only to its current issue, while *College English* offers access only

to back issues. The *Stanford Encyclopedia of Philosophy*, while obviously not a journal, deserves notice as a wonderful open access resource.

7. For example, Sally Haslanger at MIT has placed her first-year Problems of Philosophy course in OpenCourseWare, and it includes her lecture notes for 2001, beginning with the Ontology Argument and the list of readings, from Dostoevsky to Nietzsche, as well as a practice exam, which asks whether Bill Gates, should he give all of his money to famine relief in order to achieve a Nobel Prize, is still praiseworthy and morally permissible: "Explain and justify your answer in light of the moral theories we've considered."

8. Derrida would not have "us think or dream of teaching without power, free from teaching's own power effects or liberated from all power outside of or higher than itself" (2002, p. 79).

9. Longino: "The exclusion of women and members of certain racial minorities from scientific education and the scientific professions constitutes not only a social injustice but a cognitive failing. Similarly, the automatic devaluation in Europe and North America of science from elsewhere constitutes a cognitive failing" (2002, p. 132).

10. The empirical basis is admittedly thin for this claim, but Steven Lawrence compared citations levels for comparable sets of print and open access computer science papers, and found the open access papers were cited four times as often (2001). Gene Glass reports on how the two leading articles in the open access *Education Policy Analysis Archives* journal, which he edits, have received over 50,000 hits with the frequency of visits continuing to grow, and with the daily visits from "unique visits" to the journal in the area of 2,500 (2003).

11. For example, with the publishing system we have developed, a Research Support Tool offers readers links to open access resources related to the article that they are considering, on the assumption that they do not have access to a research library or may not know how to use one effectively. The readers' search through these resources is further directed by the key concepts the author has identified for their work, thereby providing a much richer context supporting the reader's understanding and interpretation of the work. See the Research Support Tool demonstration on the Public Knowledge Project (http://pkp/ubc.ca).

12. Peter Pericles Trifonas goes some distance toward connecting the democracy to come to public education in his commentary on Derrida, when he analyzes how " 'the right to philosophy' is also a question of democracy and of the right to all to participate in the curricular orientation of a public education" (2002, p. 89).

13. For a discussion of the limits of the U.S. government's handling of the post-Bhopal Right-to-Know legislation around environmental issues, within the context of "empowerment as access," see Wyatt Galusky (2003). On the use of the Internet for the mobilization of resistance through the Zapatista Movement, see Maria Garrido and Alexander Halavais (2003).

14. While the right to this knowledge is obviously not based on a person's qualifications, the question of whether deliberative democracy (which I see open access to scholarship supporting) favors those who already possess the capacity to deliberate (and read research) is addressed by Cohen and Rogers, who point to examples of wide participation in deliberation, based on interest and opportunity, as well as to the use of training programs on deliberative planning processes (2002, pp. 244–246).

15. A recent agreement with Elsevier Science in India forces librarians to forbid those who "walk in" to the library (as opposed to being members of the library)—never mind that they traveled for two days to do their research at that library—to print out or otherwise "save" a copy of the journal article they are reading online in the subscribing library.

16. See Project Romeo (Rights Metadata for Open Archiving) for journal policies on eprint archiving (http://www.lboro.ac.uk/departments/ls/disresearch/romeo/). The arXiv.org Eprint Service, to which high-energy physicists have been contributing papers for the past decade, is the best example in this field, thanks to the pioneering work of Paul Ginsparg (2001). The paper is placed there before it is published (in what was known as a "preprint"), and it is thereafter published in one of the physics journals. Unfortunately, arXiv.org has little affected the need for

libraries to subscribe to physics journals (which conduct the reviews), with average subscription prices well over $1,000 annually for this discipline, even as most faculty access the literature through the free arXiv.org Eprint Service.

References

Cohen, J. and Rogers, J. (2003). "Power and reason," in Archon Funga and Erik Olin Wright (eds), *Deepening Democracy: Institutional Innovations in Empowered Participatory Governance* (London: Verso), pp. 237–255.

Cox, J. and Cox, L. (2003). *Scholarly Publishing Practice: The ALPSP Report on Academic Journal Publishers' Policies and Practices in Online Publishing* (Worthing, UK: Association of Learned and Professional Society Publishers).

de Lauretis, Teresa. (2003). "Becoming inorganic." *Critical Inquiry* 29:4, 547–570.

Derrida, J. (2002). "The future of the profession or the unconditional university (Thanks to the 'Humanities' what could take place tomorrow)."

Derrida, J. (2002a). *Who's Afraid of Philosophy: Right to Philosophy I.* Translated by Jan Plug (Stanford, CA: Stanford University Press).

Derrida, J. (2002b). *Ethics, Institutions and the Right to Philosophy.* Edited and translated by Peter Pericles Trifonas (Lanham, MA: Rowman and Littlefield).

Galusky, W. (2003). "Identifying with information: Citizen empowerment, the Internet, and the Environmental Anti-Toxins Movement," in Martha McCaughey and Michael D. Ayers (eds), *Cyberactivism: Online Activism in Theory and Practice.* (New York: Routledge), pp. 185–205.

Garrido, M. and Halavais, A. (2003). "Mapping networks of support for the Zapatista movement: Applying social-networks analysis to study contemporary social movements," in Martha McCaughey and Michael D. Ayers (eds), *Cyberactivism: Online Activism in Theory and Practice* (New York: Routledge), pp. 165–184.

Ginsparg, P. (2001). *Creating a Global Knowledge Network.* A paper presented at Second Joint ICSU Press-UNESCO Expert Conference on Electronic Publishing in Science, Paris. http://arxiv.org/blurb/pg01unesco.html.

Glass, G. (2003). *Education Policy Analysis Archives Activity.* Paper given at American Educational Research Association Conference, Chicago.

Harnad, S. (2003). "Electronic preprints and postprints," *Encyclopedia of Library and Information Science,* Marcel Dekker, Inc., http://www.ecs.soton.ac.uk/~harnad/Temp/eprints.htm.

Kant, Immanuel. (1970). "An answer to the question. What is enlightenment?" In Kant, *Political Writings.* Edited by Hans Reiss, translated by H. B. Nisbett. (Cambridge, U.K.: Cambridge University Press), pp. 54–60.

Lawrence, S. (2001). "Online or invisible?" *Nature,* 411(6837), 521. Retrieved April 30, 2002, from http://www.neci.nec.com/~lawrence/papers/online-nature01/

Longino, H. (2002). *The Fate of Knowledge* (Princeton, NJ: University of Princeton Press).

Marx, K. (1859). Preface to *A Contribution to the Critique of Political Economy.* Translated by W. Ryazanskaya (Moscow: Progress Publishers). http://www.marxists.org/archive/marx/works/1859/critique-pol-economy/

McSherry, C. (2001). *Who Owns Academic Work: Battling for Control of Intellectual Property* (Cambridge, MA: Harvard University Press).

Merger Mania (2003). *Scholarly Communication Reports,* 7(5), 2.

Mialet, Helene. (2003). "Reading Hawking's presence: an interview with a self-effacing man." *Critical Inquiry,* 29:4, 571–599.

Muthayan, Sal and Florence Muinde. (2003). "The public knowledge project's open journal systems: african perspective from Kenya and South Africa." Paper presented at the International Symposium on Open Access and the public Domain in Digital Data Information for Science, NESCO, Paris, France.

"Open access to scientific research" (August 7, 2003). *New York Times*, p. A27.

Regier, W. S. (June 13, 2003). "Five problems and 9 solutions for university presses." *Chronicle of Higher Education*, B7–B9.

Trifonas, P. P. (2002). "What comes next? Or after difference: Meditations on the debt and duty to the right of philosophy," in Jacques Derrida, *Ethics, Institutions and the Right to Philosophy*. Edited and translated by Peter Pericles Trifonas (Lanham, MA: Rowman and Littlefield), pp. 57–105.

Willinsky, J. (in press). The Access Principle: The Case for *Open Access to Research and Scholarship*. (Cambridge, MA: MIT Press).

CHAPTER EIGHT

The Grammatology of the Future

SUNG-DO KIM
(Interviews with Gregory Ulmer on Deconstruction
and the Digital Future of the Humanities)

SUNG-DO KIM[1]: An introduction of your work to a new audience (in Korea) provides an opportunity to consider your career as one possible response to the question of the future of the Humanities (the Human Sciences). This question in its largest terms concerns the future of the book, of libraries, and of school as such. The point of departure of your research was Jacques Derrida's *De la grammatologie*, which I translated into Korean. Perhaps we could begin with a reminder of how you understand "grammatology." What is your relationship to the scholarship on literacy, including such figures as Walter Ong, Jack Goody, Eric Havelock, and Marshall McLuhan?

GREGORY ULMER[2]: I first became aware of grammatology in graduate school. One of the defining stories of my career is about my visit to a bookstore in Boston in 1970, where I found a copy of Derrida's *De la grammatologie*. I was writing a dissertation on Jean-Jacques Rousseau, a figure to whom Derrida devotes a long discussion in this study. Thinking it was a conventional interpretation of Rousseau, I bought it, but reading it had the unusual effect of causing me to shift my interest from Rousseau to Derrida.

One point Derrida made was to deconstruct the binary pair speech/writing by exposing the bias in Western metaphysics in favor of the spoken word over its mere "copy" in writing. Grammatology as a field of knowledge concerns the history and theory of writing. All my research occurs within the frame of grammatology, which places all questions in the context of literacy as an apparatus (social machine). Derrida's work passes through this field, but the figures you named, such as Ong and Havelock, helped create this question by articulating the divide between orality and literacy. I read Marshall McLuhan's *Gutenberg Galaxy* when it first came out, in an undergraduate course at the University of Montana (Missoula), and perhaps that early exposure to this perspective prepared the way for my "recognition" of Derrida's argument. McLuhan wrote perhaps the first study of what I now call "electracy."

The key insight of grammatology is that literacy is an "apparatus" (the term is borrowed from media studies)—a matrix of interdependent dimensions: Technology (the Greek invention of alphabetic writing), institutional practices (Plato's Academy as the first school and his *Phaedrus* as the first discourse on method in the West). Plato is credited with the invention of Philosophy because he formulated the first "concept" when he added an ontological function to the copulative verb "to be" and asked the metaphysical question, "what IS 'justice?' " (in *The Republic*). He wanted to know not what justice could do or how it was performed, but what was its nature, its properties in the abstract, in principle, apart from any particular embodiment. Aristotle took up this project— the invention of the practices of literacy. He founded another school (the Lyceum) and extended "method" into the invention of logic, rhetoric, and poetics as formalized procedures. As one commentator put it, to appreciate the radicality of these innovations we need to realize that before Aristotle there were no "things" (no entities selected out from the flow of the world by the procedure of definition and constructed into class hierarchies).

My research relies upon the grammatologists you mentioned, who are experts on that period of ancient history, who study the documents in the original Greek. Eric Havelock, for example, demonstrated that literacy included not only a technology and its institutionalization in school, but the invention of a new subject formation arising out of the experience of reading and writing—the self. To experience one's identity or subjectivization in terms of "selfhood" is specific or native to the alphabetic apparatus. I do not read Greek myself; so I accept Havelock's authority (in Preface to Plato). To refute apparatus theory one will have to know Classical Greek.

In my research I use the history of literacy to investigate the digital apparatus, which I have named with the neologism electracy. The term alludes to "electricity" and Derrida's "trace," and is useful to signal the scope of my inquiry, which includes the relationships among the technology, institutional practices, and identity formations emerging now in our own era of new media. The invention of photography in the 1830s is a convenient date to demarcate the beginning of electracy. The technology of the alphabet allowed the Greeks to record and then manipulate the spoken word. The new recording technologies of digital imaging (whose features continue to undergo a rapid evolution) capture the whole scene—the sight, sound, and motion—of human activity. The difficulty of studying our own moment, is that we are immersed in it, and everything is in flux. Grammatology uses the history of literacy as an analogy with our own moment, to map this history onto our own situation in order to locate the sites open to invention. We forget sometimes that every feature of writing was invented. We may assume that many of the events of this history will repeat themselves, although there is no technological determinism in this process, no automatic outcome, as a certain reading of McLuhan might lead some to believe.

The analogy provides a template for noticing the relationship of inventions to specific historical circumstances, covering the entire evolution of writing through the manuscript era, the printing press, the separation of science from the Church in the Renaissance, up to our own time. Thus I read the scholars not only to become informed about the relativity of literacy to its historical conditions, but also to get ideas about what institutional practices need to be invented in order to facilitate the best possible adjustment of education to electracy. For example, in his study of Peter Ramus, Walter Ong describes how Ramus transformed logic by adapting Aristotle's topical logic to the space of the printed page. The result was the invention of the practice of the topical outline, one ramification of which was the replacement of the complexities of Scholastic logic with a much simpler logic based on what had been a primer for middle school students. A research assignment in this context is: Invent a practice that adapts topical logic to the space of the computer or video screen.

SUNG-DO KIM: In this pedagogical context your theory of heuretics and chorography are absolutely original. Say something about your trilogy, *Applied Grammatology* (1985), *Teletheory* (1989), and *Heuretics* (1994). How would you explain the unity or continuity of these three works? I would love to have your auto-critique of these studies.

GREGORY ULMER: Several coincidences made possible my career as a theorist. First was the fact that my graduate work was in Comparative Literature, which already was organized not by the histories of the national literatures but by theories of narrative and the like, and which provided the gateway (or Trojan horse) that brought critical theory into American universities. Second was that my first job at the University of Florida was in the Humanities Department, where I taught a survey of the "Western Tradition" from the Ancient Greeks to the present covering the arts, architecture, literature, philosophy, and music. This experience moved me from being a trained specialist to being an educated person. The combination of theory and a review of the entire tradition gave me a grasp of the "big picture," at least from a certain Eurocentric vantage point.

When I transferred from the Humanities Department to the English Department I taught, in addition to the theory course, courses in Film Studies and in Composition. These practical circumstances helped me make the connection between my research on grammatology and my teaching. I came to understand that I was more or less in the same position in relation to our new media that Plato and Aristotle were to the new media of their day. You could say that I wanted to be the Aristotle of electracy. I integrated my teaching and research around the issue of bootstrapping from literacy to electracy by inventing in my classes the institutional practices of the new media apparatus.

The insight motivating *Applied Grammatology: Poste-Pedagogy from Jacques Derrida to Joseph Beuys* (AG) concerned pedagogy itself. A commonplace of Film Studies is the invisibility or transparency of the Hollywood style of realism. I could see that something similar was going on in teaching, that there was an invisible style of university education. Pedagogy is a system of representation, the means by which learners are brought into contact with disciplinary knowledge. This representation was not only realist, but invisible. This invisibility or transparency had permitted pedagogy to escape the revolution in representation, which overturned nearly every other discourse in the arts and sciences beginning in the late nineteenth century. In the context of grammatology this revolution could be read as a symptom of apparatus shift. My assumption was that electracy (I did not yet have this term) could be found by bringing together the historical stream of new recording technologies with the avant-garde experiments in the arts. These experiments I understood as a laboratory inventing a host of new rhetorics and logics. My job was to provide a service through this reading of recent history, to demonstrate the fit between the features of the technologies and the poetics and aesthetics of the avant-garde, the two dimensions together thus constituting a repertoire that only needed to be adapted to schooling, in order to educate the next generation in the reading and writing of our own time.

Part of the challenge of AG was to lay down the foundations of a research program, to establish first of all my understanding of pedagogy as a representational system. The point of departure was Derrida's critique of Western metaphysics, which I approached by asking what pedagogy was implicit in Derrida's philosophy. I started working on this book right after I got tenure (1977), when I no longer had to worry about whether or not my research was immediately publishable. It was an exciting moment, to contemplate the possibilities of a "modernist" pedagogy, a teaching that treated disciplinary knowledge the way cubist collage treated painting, or dadaist poetics treated literature. This prospect was summarized in "The object of post-criticism," an essay published in *The Anti-Aesthetic* (1983), edited by Hal Foster. While the deconstructionists were defending Derrida's status as a conventional philosopher, I was more interested in the boldness of his decision to base his inquiry on the linguistics of James Joyce's *Finnegans Wake*, which elevates the macaronic pun to an epic scale, and could be said to be authored in Indo-European itself. The effect is to set philosophy off in a new direction, abandoning the drive toward univocality and total control of meaning, to commit instead to the exploitation of the full ambiguity of meaning of which language is capable, or should we just say: Poetry.

The second book of the trilogy, *Teletheory: Grammatology in the Age of Video* (1989), continues the project of a post-realist or modernist pedagogy by proposing the poetics of a genre in which to conduct electrate learning. The purpose of this poetics was to bring learning into contact with imaging, with the understanding that the institutionalization of electracy has taken place most fully in Entertainment (organizing the mediated society within the frame of corporate capitalism). Literate critique treats this condition negatively as "the society of the spectacle." The "spectacle" is a condition of simulacrum in which reality and the image merge, producing a radical disruption in the established cosmology, so to speak. The spectacle is the "Things-Fall-Apart" (Achebe) of literacy. A film such as *The Matrix* is electracy represented from the literate point of view (as an apocalyptic nightmare). Seen from the point of view of apparatus theory, however, the entertainment industry in all its forms is inventing the practices of electracy. The challenge for educators is to recognize, appropriate, and redesign these practices into an electrate equivalent of logic, rhetoric, and poetics. Nor are we talking about adapting advertising formats to the writing of books. The point is not to write books about media, but to perform learning and inquiry using media technology. Here is the lasting importance of a filmmaker such as Jean-Luc Godard, who began his career as a film critic, and soon decided that, to be adequate to its object of study, criticism would itself have to be a film. There was supposed to be a chapter on Godard in AG, but instead I wrote about Sergei Eisenstein and his attempt to make a film version of Karl Marx's *Das Kapital*. The Godard chapter was postponed to *Teletheory*, but still was not included and to this day I have done nothing more than to point at this extraordinary relay (a "relay" is an example that does not serve as a model but orients a poetics in the right direction).

The question organizing *Teletheory* was taken from Hayden White's *Metahistory*. White wondered what historiography would be if it had been invented in the twentieth century rather than in the nineteenth, which would mean that its science would have the stance not of positivism but of the uncertainty principle, and its narrative form would not be realist naturalism but surrealist experiment. Although White speculated that this post-realist historiography was impossible (unsustainable as knowledge), I adopted White's proposal as the answer to education in a society of the spectacle. The result was a genre I called "mystory" (after history and herstory). Mystory has no form or medium of its own, but is a practice. It extends the feminist insight that the personal is political, that ideology must be approached holistically as an ecology, and formalizes into a method Nietzsche's insight that in every career there is a secret point at which the aphorism of thought intersects with the anecdote of life. The third dimension of the apparatus—subject formation—is brought into play, to be made as open to invention as are technology and the institutional practices.

The subject of identity is changing in electracy. The observer is part of the observation, as the physicists pointed out. The electrate learner is not in the objective stance of the positivist scientist, nor in the subjective stance of the individualist Romantic, or in the alienated stance of the existentialist. The subject of electracy is not "one," but is a group subject, an effect of a relational network whose behaviors may be observed at the individual level in the lives of celebrities, and at the collective level in the machinations of corporations. Gilles Deleuze and Felix Guattari have done the most to theorize this identity condition. We should keep in mind that this group subject does not replace but supplements the tribal and national identities that persist in the strata of oral and literate experience. Mystory is a mapping strategy, which brings this group positioning into the awareness and grasp of a literate individual. It does for the "self" of a person what global positioning satellites do for the body—locate one's personhood in an ideological cultural field. Mystory maps the default coordinates of one's interpellation or hailing (to use the terminology of Louis Althusser) into the identity formations of a specific historical time and space.

A mystory is a means to communicate with oneself, which is to say it brings to completion in a certain way the humanistic tradition, the commitment to self-knowledge, which goes back to Socrates and the legend of his encounter with the oracle at Delphi. *Teletheory* concludes with a demonstration of the genre, with my version of a mystory, entitled "Derrida at the Little Bighorn." The effect of making a mystory is that of having a conversation with one's superego. Freud described the superego as an interior monument, to represent how the external social and cultural conditions of the lifeworld become internalized through introjection or incorporation in the identity of particular citizens. I imagined the superego as an internalized Mount Rushmore, referring to the national monument in the Black Hills of South Dakota where the heads of four American presidents, 60 feet high—Washington, Jefferson, Lincoln, and Teddy Roosevelt—are carved into a granite cliff. Originally conceived as a tourist attraction, Rushmore is now a national shrine. If the Taliban ever take over America, the first thing they will do is blow up this monument (the way the blew up the Great Buddha statues carved in the cliffs of Afghanistan). Mystory is a way to find out whose heads are on the "Rushmore" of your internal monument, to learn whose values and behaviors have set the rules of your personal order. There is one head for each of the discourse institutions into whose language you have entered: Family, School (community history), Entertainment, Career (profession, specialized knowledge). The experiment is composed as an assemblage, juxtaposing documentation of my association with each of these discourses. My internal monument consisted of Walter Ulmer (my father), George Custer (famous for being massacred at the Little Bighorn River during the Indian wars, after whom my county in the state of Montana was named), Gary Cooper (a favorite film star), and Jacques Derrida (to whom I apprenticed myself when learning how to be a theorist).

SUNG-DO KIM: This assemblage anticipates your work with hypermedia, about which you say a scholar does not provide a line of argument but constructs a paradigm of possibilities and interactivity. You have used the term "rhetoric" repeatedly, including in Heuretics with a reference to a rhetoric of hypermedia. How can a discipline so ancient (and so specific to literacy), be related to the newest media?

GREGORY ULMER: By way of answer I should move on to the third book of the trilogy, *Heuretics: The Logic of Invention* (1994). In *Heuretics* I finally was able to make explicit the invention or generative process that I had been using implicitly and partly intuitively in the previous books. "Heuretics" is not a neologism, but the dictionary labels it as obsolete. It has the same root as "Eureka" and "heuristics," and is paired with hermeneutics (the logic of interpretation). I am using heuretics to invent the educational practices of electracy. It is one thing to say that new media require new practices (many people have said as much), but another to actually design such practices. One needs a way to generate ideas. Heuretics is that way. The purpose of the book is to share this "way," to invite my colleagues and students into the process of invention.

I discovered the method during the many years I taught a course in the history of theory. In teaching undergraduates how to read a series of discourses on method, from Plato through Machiavelli to Marx and up to the manifestoes of the avant-garde, I noticed a basic recipe running through all of the writings, which I adopted first as a hermeneutics. The formula for inventing a new language practice includes a contrast (C) with an established practice, which needs to be replaced; an analogy (A) with some other existing practice in some unrelated area that one admires; a theory (T) of language; a target (T) institution, which needs a new or a different functionality. The method is to inventory the practical features of each of these domains, and then synthesize them into a hybrid set of operating rules. These rules must be embodied in turn in some form, some means of communication, the tale (t) of the CATT. In *Heuretics* I explained this CATTt poetics for generating a new method.

To demonstrate and test the CATTt I proposed a practice for hyper-media (digital) rhetoric (understood in the sense of a set of principles guiding the production of a composition). Rhetoric is a convenient term to legitimate the introduction of media production courses into English departments. Literary studies have always been concerned not only with hermeneutics, scholarship, and criticism (the study of existing works), but also with the production or making of new texts. When our students have to live and work in a society of the spectacle, it is our responsibility to teach them electracy, that is, to educate them not only to be able to read but also to write (design) images. In my CATTt the Contrast was the conventional argumentative (literate) essay; Analogy was American Method acting used by many Hollywood actors. As for Theory, the key ingredient was Derrida's collaboration with the architect Peter Eisenman on the design of an architectural "folly" (folie) for the Parc de la Villette in Paris (a project involving many such teams, overseen by Bernard Tschumi). Derrida proposed to Eisenman that the design be based on the notion of space (chora), which Plato introduced in his dialogue *Timaeus* to solve the metaphysical problem of how Being and Becoming interact.

Using the grammatological analogy I noticed that when Aristotle invented literate rhetoric (this phrase is redundant) he replaced Plato's space (chora)—in which chaos was sorted into the order of the four elements of Greek cosmology—Earth, Air, Fire, Water. Plato's metaphor for this sorting was the winnowing basket, which had also been an important symbol in the Eleusinian mystery ritual. Aristotle preferred a different notion of space also available in the culture—topos—a more restricted "place," an abstract container of a "thing." Aristotle promoted his physics of place (topos) into his metaphysics, his study or invention of literate categories. He proposed the metaphor of the "topic" to explain how the memory operations of writing could be used to store and retrieve arguments—the well-known "places of invention." You may recognize the heuretic strategy already: I proposed an electrate inventio (invention) in which digital information would be stored and retrieved not as topics (places) but as chora (space, region). Hence the name "choragraphy" (choral writing). You can see why I needed to retain the reference to rhetoric, which I am using analogically to generate the practices of electracy.

For those familiar with theory, a shorthand way to explain how choral invention works is to point to the deconstruction of literate metaphysics underway in modernist and postmodern arts and letters. As a pedagogy choragraphy formalizes and makes available for mass distribution through schooling of operations that originated intuitively or for different reasons in the post-realist revolutions of the twentieth century. The negative or deconstructive phase necessary for the realization of electracy involves the dissolution of literate metaphysics, that is, literate category formation—reality represented and organized as concepts. The notion of the "bachelor machine" gathers neatly this process, whether (to name only a few examples) in the literature of Kafka and Rousell, the art of Duchamp and Tanguy, or in the theory of Bataille and Deleuze/Guattari. In a bachelor machine (a radical work of art or theory using an impossible machine as an allegory or catechresis for an unthinkable logic) conceptual categories and topics dissolve into one another, staining and mixing and blurring all borderings and edges—psychological, logical, political, social.

This deconstructive phase is only part of the story—the necessary breakdown of the metaphysics of one apparatus, and its replacement by a new category formation. I am insisting on the term "metaphysics" to clarify that the philosophical "closure of metaphysics" is not the end of category formation, any more than the "death of the novel" is the end of narrative or the notorious "death of the author" is the end of agency. On the positive side choragraphy is the method of category construction—specifically for the category native to digital imaging. Reflecting my deconstructive and postmodernist sensibility, choragraphy is a neologism, generated from the original "chorography" (with an "o"), which is an ancient mapping practice that dates back to Ptolemy. Chorography was significant from Renaissance townscapes through nineteenth-century panoramas. It is a hybrid form mixing the geometric measurements of cartography with the perspective representation of the plastic arts.

Choragraphy (with an "a") advances the mystory by shifting from the documentation of superego figures to the registration of one's "cognitive map." Frederic Jameson borrowed cognitive map from architecture, where it was used to refer to the mental image that citizens have of their city or environs. This map is now refunctioned in terms of chora, such that the material field of one's lifeworld serves when put into digital form as the spaces of invention (in every sense of the word). The grammatological analogy guiding the evolution of this practice through the entire trilogy is the pedagogy of the memory palace. Students in the manuscript era, whose performance of learning took the form of impromptu or improvised oratory, often in competitive debates, managed information by means of a memory palace. The palace was unique to its maker; no two were alike. This is a key feature of the analogy, suggesting that the interface bringing together learners with global information will be a "homepage" in the sense suggested by the memory palace: It will be singular, specific to its user, customized, rather than the universal encyclopedic one-size-fits-all of the print encyclopedia.

To memorize the quantities of information stored in manuscripts the student first rehearsed the familiar features of his/her hometown—its main street or plaza with its public buildings—ending perhaps at the family house. At regular intervals along this familiar path (way) "active images" were placed (often violent or sexual figures derived from popular lore or mythology, or personal experience). Associated with these images were quantities of text (the works of Cicero, collected sermons), whose trigger often was some visual or verbal pun. The exercises of Saint Ignatius Loyola were based on this tradition, and assured the survival of mnemonics in the Jesuit order. Mnemotechniques continue to be practiced today wherever information has to be committed to living memory: By students preparing for exams; by actors learning a role. Choragraphy proposes to adapt this mnemonics to memory management in digital media, as the basis for creating categorical images, an image metaphysics. One's homepage in this practice becomes a virtual memory palace in which the mystory, reconfigured as a composite diegesis of a life narrative in progress, becomes the prosthesis of reasoning about all matters—personal, professional, political. To the feminist slogan of herstory—that the personal is political—choragraphy now adds, "the personal is political and professional." Knowing in electracy is fundamentally emotional as well as intellectual, in other words; the body joins the mind in the activity of reason.

The point to emphasize is that *Heuretics* is not only about choragraphy, but is to be used by anyone to generate a method or practice relevant to any CATTt, however one might want to fill in those heuristic inventories. Heuretics—not the book but the approach to theory—is as encompassing as hermeneutics, in principle, and as an operation at a high level of abstraction should be able to support a library (or database) of further work. My research, meanwhile, continues along the way of choragraphy.

SUNG-DO KIM: Let us put this review more explicitly into the context of the Internet or World Wide Web. How do you explain the success of this medium? What are its real effects on university knowledge, or more specifically on pedagogy in general? My question concerns the relations among media, culture, and the human sciences. Despite their obvious importance in the universities, the professors often ignore (in every sense of the term) the impingement of the media on their domain, an importance that can only increase with the continuing evolution of digital equipment. What arguments do you use with these tenaciously resistant colleagues to convince them of the relevance and value of new media for academic culture and discourses themselves?

GREGORY ULMER: The success of the Web may be explained by an analogy with the success of print (millions of books manufactured in the first decade of the existence of the press), or with the success of film (the hundred-year history of cinema), and the global dissemination of television. It is part of the lore of the equipment that the first personal computer, which had an interface of only a few switches and could be made to add two plus two only with considerable effort, sold several thousand units. As Marshall McLuhan among others pointed out, the media (and perhaps all technologies) are extensions of our senses, a reading continued in such notions as terminal identity, the cyborg, and the post-human, alluding to the merger or hybridizing of organic and machinic "life" forms. Aristotle said that learning is the greatest pleasure, acknowledging the sensory and sensual (aesthetic) dimension of interacting with our world. If learning is not pleasurable, we could say, we are probably doing it wrong. Or, to be fair, we should say that literacy, because of its abstractive nature, its necessary removal from immediate experience and hence from the aesthetic realm altogether, is inherently difficult for human beings, who nonetheless have adapted to its gyrations and institutional contortions with considerable success. It is hard to see, after 2,500 years, that literacy is a contortionist's paradise.

The story of the personal computer is continuing evidence that information processing internally and externally (taking in and sending out messages, participating in the circulation of meaning) is to the mind what breathing is to the lungs or eating is to the stomach (shall we just call it "love" for short, to include Plato's original sexual metaphor?). Philosophy: The love of wisdom. This is what is meant by referring to the apparatus as a "social machine": The equipment is in dialogue with desire. The "hackers' dream" of total information instantly available is as old as humankind. A shaman is a cosmological hacker. We will not be satisfied until we have simulated omnipotence, telepathy, teleportation, and all the other fantasies of information dominance. Wisdom was loved in oral civilization, and will continue to be loved in electracy, even if there is no wisdom without stupidity, just as we could say, after Virilio, there is no train without the train wreck, or no space shuttle without the disintegration of the Challenger and the Columbia, no television without atom bombs (the latter two grew out of the same physics). The specialists who invented UNIVAC during World War II thought that the world would need no more than five or six machines. It is possible that they overestimated, in that it will turn out we only need one computer, but it will be a global wireless network that anyone may access from anywhere; but I don't want to get into science fiction scenarios, neither utopian nor dystopian. Virilio, to stick with just his example for a moment, suggested that the Internet makes possible the general accident, the disaster that happens simultaneously everywhere, whose speed eliminates space and time and the civic or public spheres of the polis along with them, making it impossible for humanity to defend against this catastrophe. The general accident is a possibility, he insists, not a necessity. It depends on what we do, on our ability to invent.

So one easy response to reluctant colleagues is the negative one, inviting them to bring to bear their disciplinary knowledge on the problems produced by this new paradigm. To my colleagues in the humanities, and even more specifically in the language arts, I point to the history of writing as an apparatus relative to a certain history. The motto for an appropriate attitude I borrow from the Japanese poet, Basho, who wrote that one should not follow in the footsteps of the masters, but seek what they sought. What the masters of the humanities sought were the practices of literacy. Those of us working in research universities are expected to address the real problems of our community. The spectacle is the name of a problem: What to do with the image? How to fashion it as a means of survival and of well-being? We could leave the invention of electracy to entertainment, the military, or business. But to embrace the research project of chorography does not take anything away from the other kinds of projects we consider important—scholarship, critique, hermeneutics, and the general promotion of literacy. To borrow a page from entrepreneurial wisdom, we must understand that we are not in the book business, but in the language business; not in the novel and essay business, but in the business of narrative and reasoning. We may serve at once as a museum or archive and a site of innovation.

SUNG-DO KIM: Does the book still have a place, then?

GREGORY ULMER: It has a place in the museum, along with the manuscript, the scroll, the clay tablet, the notched stick. We have to keep in mind that the book is just the most visible feature of an apparatus. It represents the institutional practices that are needed to operate it as a piece of equipment, as well as the behaviors of selfhood that it sustains. The new interfaces of voice-recognition, datagloves, eye movement will eventually make the keyboard obsolete, and a different pedagogy and curriculum are needed to teach students to think and communicate in this way. In the movie *Minority Report* the character (Tom Cruise) inter- acts with the computer in this full-body performative way. The filmmak- ers imagined this future reading–writing as being similar to practicing a martial art.

There is no denying that book culture possesses some profoundly important qualities, which are unique to it, and which will be lost in electracy, just as happened with the culture of the bards singing the epics in oral culture. It would be wonderful to be able to hear a bard sing a ver- sion of *The Iliad* from memory, but that practice of orality is now lost. Within a few generations people will say that it would be wonderful to meet someone who could author a densely argued 300-page theoretical treatise, and there still may be a few professors of "Classics" still able to do it. Meanwhile I am teaching a seminar next year on the question of how to perform theoretical inquiry in a medium of images, such as the animation program Flash. What aspects of theoretical (conceptual) "writ- ing" will be preserved in new media speculation, and what aspects will disappear as nonfunctional? That is a question we will try to sort out.

SUNG-DO KIM: And the library . . .?

GREGORY ULMER: We have to think of media history as dynamic, in continuous evolution. The new apparatus emerges at first as a gadget, a stunt, and is displayed or installed on the margins of existing dominant practices. A good example is the beginnings of cinema, with films included as a kind of side-show attached to live venues such as Vaudeville. Vaudeville was absorbed by radio, then television, and has disappeared. Most libraries today are equipped with computer terminals and networks, and this equipment will eventually usurp and absorb the entire storage and retrieval functions of society. No doubt there will still be libraries and books for a long time, serving an archival and museum function, but all new information development will be digital. There are many symptoms showing that this process is well underway. For example, many universities no longer keep paper copies of dissertations, but store them electronically. This seemingly innocent solution to the storage problems of libraries has important consequences for epistemology. Once digital media are the support for research, the way is open for the new practices of electracy to direct inquiry. The new category formation of electracy in turn will force a reform of the divisions of knowledge, since image categories are holistic and do not approach reality through the various fragmentations of literate sub-specialization. In short, an apparatus is an "ecology."

SUNG-DO KIM: You have distinguished three modes for the organization of information, regardless of medium: Narrative, exposition, and pattern. You stated that story and document in digital media are subordinated to the operations of pattern. Could you clarify what you mean by this observation? It reminds me in a way of Kate Hayles's replacement of the dichotomy of presence and absence with the opposition between pattern and randomness in order to explain electronic signs, the flickering signifiers.

GREGORY ULMER: There is a continuity of functions from one apparatus to another, related to the continuity of human faculties and their enhancement or suppression within each historical epoch. People tell stories, solve problems, make sense of the world, but they perform these functions in different ways, and the performance actually alters human reality. The novel and the essay, for example, were invented in the early 1600s, following the invention of the printing press in the 1450s. Cervantes is credited with the first novel (*Don Quijote*), and Montaigne and Bacon share credit for the first essays. Robert Scholes showed that these institutional practices organized the world in a way quite different from that of the manuscript era. In the print era narrative became reserved for fiction, fancy, imagination (the novel), and exposition was reserved for truth-telling, knowledge (essay). Each version of the language apparatus reduces the complex but unstable higher forms of the previous apparatus down to a collection of simple forms, which are then recombined and gathered into new complex higher forms. As you might expect this process is repeating itself in the transition from print to digital media.

A basic insight of this history is that within the natural languages there are really only three fundamental ways to organize the distribution of information over time. We have not yet achieved telepathic communication; so the limited capacities of the human sensorium require the time-release of signs. The three modes are narration (introduced during orality, expressed as the novel in print and the feature film in cinema); exposition (introduced in literacy, expressed as the essay in print and the documentary in film and video); and pattern (prehistoric, prehuman no doubt, expressed as poetry in literacy and advertising in media). Two more modes at least are available outside natural language—drawing (the responsibility of the Fine Arts in literacy) and numeracy (taken over from religion and magic by science). In orality all five modes are unified and are not separated out and isolated as they are in literacy. Electracy again is bringing all five modes into relationship in a new holistic metaphysics. An electrate person will be able to draw, write, and program, and the challenge not just to the university but to education as an institution is to develop a curriculum and pedagogy that brings these modes together into one practice.

Of the natural language modes, all three are present in every composition, but with one dominant and the others subordinate according to the conventions of a given discourse. Perhaps one of the reasons why the film *Citizen Kane* is considered by many to be the best American film ever made is due in part to the perfect balance of all three modes in its composition. These orders may also be approached in terms of cognitive schemas, which are developed and internalized through education. The simple but miraculous fact is that when literate people encounter a book they already know what it is and how to use it. When encountering any message literate people have a set of expectations and make assumptions about it—about how it is organized. There is a fit between the apparatus and experience. For a technology to be practical, it goes without saying, yet is sometimes ignored, there must be a practice that is internalized in the minds and bodies of users. The institution in which the message circulates, its genre conventions and the like, cue which reading strategy to use. The default sequence when other signals are ambiguous, such as when coming across an avant-garde experiment out of context, is to look for an explanatory argument (at least this is the American default). If there is no argument, then look for a story. In the absence of story, look for a center of consciousness, a biography, an authorial voice. If there is no voice look for a musical order of theme and variation. If all else fails, look finally for an image, that is, a pattern of any kind, any signifier that repeats within the collection, to produce a minimal coherence of atmosphere, an aesthetic feeling or mood resulting from the cumulative whole. I have found that many students are unaware of this default checklist, and stop after the first step to declare that the item in question "makes no sense." At the same time I have found that it only takes one session to familiarize them with the procedure, after which they have little trouble applying it to almost anything they are shown.

In electracy the institutional conventions, modes, and forms of literacy are breaking down, and the simple forms are recombining into new configurations. Our theory tells us what to expect, where to look, what kinds of conventions are needed. What may be observed at this point is that the default sequence is being inverted. In literacy narrative and exposition (argument) were ordinate, each in its respective realm of fiction and truth; pattern (image) was subordinate in both realms. The institution that is to electracy what school is to literacy is entertainment. The practices of new media are most aggressively being invented in entertainment (popular media organized within the capitalist profit motive), especially in advertising. Ironically, perhaps, the two most prolific sites of electrate invention are the commercial arts and the experimental arts, with the two becoming perhaps unwilling allies beginning with the movement of Pop Art (Andy Warhol).

The old literate conventions, which used to distinguish discourses of value from discourses of fact, are weakening. A new holistic order is forming in which truth, fiction, lie, error, and ignorance are simultaneously integrated in the economy and circulation of meaning. This is the condition of the simulacrum, the spectacle. This condition is a problem only to the extent that educational practices have yet to be designed and implemented in the schools to help people become electrate (to learn and internalize the new default sequence). Of course children are becoming electrate in a "wild" state, so to speak, through their participation in the culture of entertainment. The lesson of the apparatus is that this huge commitment of youth energy to video games, online chat, cell phones, digital file swapping, and the like is producing a new experience of identity that is transforming the human subject (again).

SUNG-DO KIM: You explain the phenomena of advertising, MTV, GUI, and so forth by analogy with pidgin and creole languages. But these visual media are severely criticized by many who say that they constitute barriers to logical and conceptual reasoning necessary for the disciplinary knowledge of the university. Yet you seem to be optimistic about the critical and ethical values of these hybrid and heterogeneous visual images. In this same context you have shown an interest in Freud for his revelation of a new inferential dimension of narrative and analytical invention. You used the word "conduction" to distinguish this inference from Peirce's notion of abduction, which is still not fully understood in the scientific milieu. Do these two thinkers furnish a common ground for the development of a theory of invention? Perhaps I am asking about the importance to your work of a whole set of theories from Freud to Deleuze and Guattari.

GREGORY ULMER: As I keep saying the research task of the arts and letters disciplines today is to do for the digital image what Classical Greeks did for the alphabetic word. The Greeks invented a metaphysics—understood in the sense of a classification system, a new way to categorize the world, different from the more or less totemistic order used in oral civilization. The vantage point of the history of writing reveals a secret history—the emergence of electracy—seen in the developments in philosophy, arts, and recording technologies through the nineteenth and twentieth centuries. The technology story is the most obvious, beginning with the invention of photography, which is why this history sometimes takes on the appearance of a technological determinism (as if the alphabet "caused" logic, or the printing press caused the Protestant Reformation). No the apparatus shift is not a story of cause and effect but a clustering of interrelated events. To appreciate this point requires a brief detour through the intellectual history of "fetishism."

Grammatology with its interest in institutional practices brings out the importance of the story of colonialism and the postcolonial to the emergence of electracy. Electracy as an apparatus implies a new metaphysics (category system), which does not arise automatically by itself but has to be invented. Electracy must be invented from within literacy, just as it was oral peoples who invented literacy. Here the CATTt heuristic shows that it has hermeneutic value as well. The new metaphysics is thought first by contrast, negatively, in the writings and observations of Enlightenment Europeans describing the practices of the Africans and other peoples encountered in the colonizing process. The negative discovery may be summarized with one word—"fetish. " The thing and its institutional setting in African civilization was a violation of the values and ideologies of the Greco-Roman-Judeo-Christian worldview. This hostility toward fetish culture is codified in the theories of Marx and Freud. However, as

Freud himself noted in describing the paradoxes of unconscious thought, negation is a defense that allows unacceptable thoughts to be entertained under the sign of "no." The no is a primordial abstraction, which separates readily from a proposition, leaving the unwelcome idea fully internalized. We see this event of incorporation at the collective level in the rebellion of the arts against the repressive bourgeois "Victorian" culture of Europe, and the turn to non-Western societies and their arts and behaviors as sources for alternative practices and attitudes. Gauguin in Tahiti is an emblem of this turn. The contrast now becomes positive. Fetish is admired with the same intensity with which it was at first despised.

In our context it is not difficult to understand why theorists condemned fetish while artists embraced it, since fetish embodies a metaphysics of the image. The philosophers condemned the artists' embrace of fetish by applying the term "primitivism," which carries an association of "racism." From the point of view of grammatology, primitivism is similar to spectacle in that both these terms are literate defenses against the apparatus shift to an image metaphysics. The grammatological reading of primitivism is as another chapter in the continuing history of syncretism between and among different civilizations. The European civilization that colonized Africa and the New World was formed from the syncretism of the Greco-Roman and Judeo-Christian civilizations. The story of colonization, enslavement of one civilization by another, and the eventual conversion of the master culture to the way of the slave culture (and vice versa) to form a powerful new hybrid describes both the history of the Roman encounter with Christianity, and the European colonial creation of the Black Atlantic. The institution of hybridization in this more recent cycle was not religion but art, with the "conversion" taking place in the new institution of entertainment and its organization of popular and vernacular cultures into a commodity form in the mass media. Marx's use of the fetish as a metaphor to describe the commodity is not the insult that he intended, but is an accurate identification of an adaptive syncretic process. Someone needs to update Max Weber's *Protestantism* and the *Spirit of Capital* for our postcolonial moment, to show the new nexus of Christianity, capitalism, and Voodoo. The new worldview is Jew-Greek-Creole.

Some key moments in this story of the becoming-fetish of Western metaphysics would include Pablo Picasso's painting *Demoiselles d'Avignon* and Elvis Presley's *Blue Suede Shoes*. It is important to note that this hybridization extends beyond the history of the Black Atlantic to include what Derrida calls mondialization, a certain globalization, to take into account, for example, Western exchanges with Asia, with Japan and China (and Korea). The importing of Zen Buddhism to America in the Beat movement, or Richard Wilhelm's translation of the *I Ching* into German in the 1920s, not to mention the spread of Elvis impersonation around the world, are important moments in this process. One way to understand what is happening in the world today is to juxtapose the civilizations of Japan and of Islam to see the range of possible attitudes to syncretism: Japan after World War II embraced this creolization, while parts of the Islamic world are rejecting it (violently).

The relevance to my research of mondialization is that the rhetoric, logic, and poetics of image metaphysics were being invented independently and for different reasons in the arts. That this should be the case is due to the fundamentally aesthetic nature of image reason. The readymade is such an important event in this invention—from Duchamp through Warhol's Pop icons to Cindy Sherman's film stills—as an image equivalent to Aristotle's invention of "definition"—creating conceptual categories by sorting out essences from accidents to produce hierarchies of classes. The general rebellion against the abstractness of Western analytical (alphabetic) reason manifested in philosophy and the arts (the names of Nietzsche and Ezra Pound may stand in as prototypes)—is a symptom of the emergence of electracy and the need for a metaphysics of the image (for which the oral metaphysics of fetishism is a relay). The interest in non-Western civilizations—which may be redescribed as any civilization not based on alphabetic writing, whether still within the oral apparatus as in the case of Africa and the Americas, or operating with an ideogrammatic writing as in Asia—is due not just to their alternative values and forms, but as analogies (CATTt) for generating an electrate categorization.

What happens to "critical thinking" in this apparatus shift? "Criticism" is not an absolute value but is a feature of the analytical (dialectic) powers of literacy. The university as such, as the heir of Plato's *Academy*, is the social machine of analysis. The institutionalization of analysis in the bureaucracy of divisions of knowledge (natural science, social science, humanities, professions) and departments (English, mathematics, and the like) is not dictated by the nature of reality, but by the strengths and weaknesses of the apparatus. People still need to learn in electracy, but the university may not be the best institutional arrangement, just as the Church (the institution by means of which oral religion adapted to literacy) was not the best institutional setting for the practice of science (a practice native to literacy). There will still be universities in electrate civilization, just as there are still churches in literate societies. But universities and churches will both have to make room for the new institutions of electracy.

Which brings me at last to your question about Freud and Peirce. Literate method invented and codified three principal modes of inference, distinct but interdependent, guiding the movement of thought from the known to the unknown: Abduction, deduction, and induction. Anyone familiar with a Sherlock Holmes mystory knows how these operations work together in the solution of a crime. Walter Ong noted that the detective story is the prototype of the literate narrative, just as the Homeric epic is the prototype of the oral narrative. The difference between quotidian and scientific inference is that the latter has to invent the rules and conventions that control the process of inferential movement, whereas the detective relies upon the semiotics of cultural common sense (the kind of reason currently absorbing the attention of cognitive science and the field of artificial intelligence).

The special place of Freud in the emergence of electracy (and the continuing importance of psychoanalysis in post-structural theory) is due not to his clinical observations, but to his description of a new mode of inference, which he called the unconscious. Jacques Lacan discerned the rhetorical and logical background of Freud's discovery when he declared that the unconscious was structured like a language. Noting Freud's frequent use of metaphors based on electricity, I named this forth kind of inference "conduction." Picasso is credited with introducing the first innovation in the representation of three-dimensional space in the plastic arts when he borrowed collage from the crafts to make a still-life. Freud's unconscious could similarly be appreciated as the first innovation in inference since the Hellenic period. Collage and the unconscious are both relevant to conduction as an inferential imaging. Conduction does not replace literate inference but adds to it a further practice, which is needed to integrate text–image compositions in hypermedia. Conduction, distilled and separated out from the dream work of unconscious thought, needs to be taught as part of the introduction of image classification in schooling.

To move from the known to the unknown in conduction is to follow an aesthetic order, moving directly from one image to another in an associational series. A number of theorists have described and even applied conduction (if not by that name), such as Georges Bataille in his pornosophic novella, *The Story of the Eye*. Roland Barthes analyzed the logic of Bataille's narrative in an important essay. Gilles Deleuze's and Felix Guattari's schizoanalysis extends conduction into a profoundly new territory with their notions of plateaus, machinic assemblages, and bachelor machines. From a narrow or defensive point of view it may seem that critical thinking is destroyed by the spectacle. Indeed that is a risk and the history of colonialism shows that the encounter of civilizations bearing different apparatuses may be horrendously violent. My interest in poststructual theory is that it is a major site in which literacy is attempting to bootstrap into electracy. In *What is Philosophy?* Deleuze and Guattari, showing that despite everything they are still the heirs of Plato, admit that the work of philosophy continues to be the invention of concepts. In the context of grammatology we may see that they are using literate practice to fashion the principles of image reason (conduction). Education in general, and the university in particular, should follow their lead and take up the heuretic challenge of apparatus shift, in order not to repeat an equivalence of the attempt by the Christian Church to suppress natural science.

SUNG-DO KIM: Perhaps you could say more about mondialization. Globalization threatens the reason for being of cultures in their diversity. For you globalization includes the creation of an electronic apparatus, which displaces the nation-state. This also threatened the autonomy of a culture of print literacy. What are the true political stakes of globalization in the sectors of culture and media?

GREGORY ULMER: Benedict Anderson's *Imagined Community* is a work of grammatology in that it shows the necessary relationship of print literacy to the practical existence of the nation-state. Grammatology assumes a kind of correspondence interrelating the registers of an apparatus. The third dimension of an apparatus—subject formation, identity behaviors—functions at both the individual and collective levels. Oral peoples experienced subject as spirit and organize politically in tribes. Literate people experience the subject as self and organize, in the print era, as nation-states. Of course peoples with different historical experience, once this political order was introduced, could reproduce it, just as any language may be adapted to alphabetic representation.

The theory suggests that electate people will experience subject in a way different from both spirit and self, and will organize politically in some way other than tribe or nation. These changes may be observed now. At the collective level the key operating features that define a nation-state—geographic borders, economic self-interest, and symbolic culture—are breaking down. The quarrels between the Church and State, which undermined the Holy Roman Empire and made possible the rise of independent nations, are analogous to the tendencies gradually separating nations from corporations today. The mass migrations and genocides of our time show the fragility and complexity of all inside/outside relationships. The global attraction and repulsion in response to American popular culture show the leakage and porosity of symbolic capital. What form will an electrate political order take? I don't know. The theory shows the need and opportunity here for invention. Perhaps the forces of dissipative structures, chaos theory, will work at this institutional level to produce some kind of self-organizing system of order. I assume the Internet will play a role in the practicalities of such an order, just as print in the form of literature and journalism supported the formation of national identities.

At the level of the individual the history of literacy shows that the experience of self arose from immersion in a culture of reading and writing, leading to the behaviors we associate with individualism. The collective effect of this individual experience was the transformation of the Greeks from groups of tribes gathered in a particular region to citizens of city states. Today immersion in image culture (the spectacle) is producing a different experience of identity, manifested in all the disruptions and interferences affecting identity politics. People experience themselves increasingly as an image, that is, as a body, rather than as a mind or idea, which happened to reside in a body. All the disorders related to body-image (anorexia, bulimia, steroid abuse, and everything related to what some condemn as the decline of character and morality) are symptoms of the emergence of a new subject formation. Kate Hayles calls this the post-human but in my terms it is the post-self. A good place to study the emergence of the post-self is in the lives of celebrities, who live in their daily lives the consequences of having an image that circulates apart from their presence and control.

SUNG-DO KIM: Personally I was inspired by your work *Applied Grammatology* in an important phase of my intellectual career. Specifically I was in the process of constructing an epistemology of the concept of an applied human sciences. Traditionally the human sciences were assumed by definition and by nature to be pure, or they took a negative stance toward the pragmatic application of their theories and concepts, in a word, to the utility of reason submitted to economic interests and the logic of reality. According to you the human sciences are capable of making real contact with society, culture, and ordinary people. It is here that I note my interest in your expression, "the new consultancy," which is unfamiliar to Korean readers. Could you please give a definition and explication of this phrase, and its relation to a grammatology of applied knowledge?

GREGORY ULMER: My first trilogy of books produced ultimately the poetics of choragraphy. My goal now is to explore the possibilities of choragraphy as a practice for electracy. There is nothing original about my predictions of apparatus shift: Such futurology is a commonplace of McLuhanism. My contribution is the project to design and test specific practices of electracy (to produce the working operations of a new media pedagogy). I am working on a second trilogy whose organizing theme is a proposal for an Internet consulting agency called the EmerAgency ("emergency" with a capital "A" added). The A alludes to a number of theoretical contexts: Derrida's differance, Lacan's autre, Levinas's autrui, Brecht's alienation effect. This conceptual agency serves as a frame of reference in my networked classes, in which assignments are posed as consulting projects. Consulting is an existing institution, a collective pedagogy, the means by which specialized disciplinary knowledge is communicated to sites of need in the community, related to public policy formation and to problem solving in all sectors of society—business, government, nonprofit concerns. You will recognize the strategy of deconstruction in this idea: The EmerAgency is a deconstruction of the institution of consulting.

In terms of the apparatus, the Internet is approached as an institution-alization native to digital technology, a potential equivalent within electracy of what school was in literacy. When he founded his Academy, could Plato imagine the modern university? When he proposed his dialectical method (first break a problem down into its basic parts; then recombine the parts in their logical order), could he foresee quantum physics? We have to imagine 2,500 years into the future to compare the fruits of the Internet with those of the Academy (which produced what we think of today as academic knowledge). The theory suggests that what is coming is "Internet knowledge," perhaps as different from academic knowledge as academic knowledge is different from the Eleusinian mysteries that predominated in Plato's world.

The immediate task is to invent a specific practice for the Internet, a hybrid of some features of literacy with some of the new possibilities supported by digital media. For example, the Internet opens a new chan-nel of communication above and beyond the existing networks of oral and literate institutions, which are by now fixed, conventionalized, and closed to alternative knowledge. The Internet bypasses these fixed chan-nels and creates opportunities for contacts across institutional and disci-plinary discourses. The EmerAgency proposes to bring classroom experimentation into direct contact with policy issues in the community through what might be called "direct consulting," after the idea of "direct democracy." This "choral" approach to consulting deconstructs all the oppositions organizing conventional consulting, such as the opposition between pure and applied research that you mentioned. "Inventional" consulting especially circumvents the cognitive jurisdictions now controlling the distribution of problems to disciplines. There are utilitarian preconceptions governing which knowledge is most relevant to which troubles and difficulties experienced in the community (crime, pollution, health, abuse of all kinds, corruption, war). The history of invention shows that innovations in fields of knowledge nearly always come from outside that field, by experts in some related or even some unrelated domain. The goal of the EmerAgency is not to compete with conventional consulting or to replace the procedures of empirical science, but to supplement them, especially in settings in which the best instrumental research has not been able to solve the troubles of the community. The EmerAgency, like the Internet itself, and electracy in general, does not replace existing practices, but opens new dimensions and possibilities for work and education. Specifically the goal is to bring knowledge of arts and letters to bear on community problems and policy issues.

The point of access of choragraphy to the conditions of policy formation is the fact that what counts as a problem or solution is dependent upon the category system (the metaphysics) of a society. The EmerAgency intervenes at this level, which appears in conventional terms to be a question of pure research—the project to design or discover the classificational powers of electracy: The categorical image. In addition to using the EmerAgency as a frame for using the Internet in my teaching, I have explored its research potential with colleagues in a creative group called the Florida Research Ensemble (FRE). The first book of the second trilogy is coauthored with this group. It is a report on our application of choragraphy to a consultation on the Miami River (Miami, Florida), a "zone" that is the site of nearly every policy problem facing American (and world) cities today. Our method was to treat this zone as an "image," to translate it into a "chora," which, as I explained earlier, is the electrate equivalent of "topic" in digital memory. Chora as a categorical image treats a zone not by breaking it down into its constituent problems, into its elements (that is the method of literacy). Rather, a chora is a holistic category, something like a quantum field, whose specific nature is an emergent property of the whole, which disappears under the act of analysis. What choragraphy tells us is that this river zone is itself a sorting machine, a bordering engine generating the experience of inside/outside. The coherence principle of this image category is that of aesthetic atmosphere, which is the "spirit" specific to this region (place), emergent from the mix of geography (subtropics), nationalities and ethnic groups (Cubans, Haitians, African Americans), architectures, economies, and the like. This coherence is what the French Situationists called a "situation," or Ezra Pound called a "vortex." These terms are synonyms for chora.

The FRE consultation on the policy issues affecting the Miami River is at the level of applying a new kind of category to the region, from which should follow a reassessment of the River "problem." The holistic quality of chora dictated that our methodology had to be syncretic, bringing together our post-structural epistemologies with the epistemology of the culture that proved to be the focus of our study—the Haitian immigrants and traders coming to Miami. On the Western side of the exchange we took up the implication of transforming "topos" (topic) to chora, wherever we encountered that opportunity. The bridges crossing the Miami River suggested the famous problem of the seven bridges of Koenigsberg. A kind of local game in Koenigsberg (then a part of Germany) asked whether it was possible to walk the route connected by the bridges without crossing any bridge more than once. The solution to this puzzle by Euler in the eighteenth century produced the beginnings of topological mathematics. Jacques Lacan adapted topology in its evolved forms (knot theory, four-dimensional figures such as the cross-cap) as a way to write the intersubjective, "extimate" (inside–outside) nature of the psyche. The FRE project to continue this series (from Euler to Lacan, from the geography of a city to the operations of the psyche) is to design an online Web interface such that one reasons through a policy problem by moving through an image of Miami. The title of the book recording this experiment is *Miami Miautre: Psychogeography of the Virtual City* (unpublished). The title is a macaronic pun across languages (Miami = My friend; Miautre = My other).

The non-Western part of the method is derived from the epistemology of Haitian vernacular traditions, motivated by emergence of the Haitian question at the center of our inquiry. The specific choice of practice was motivated by the pun on "consultation." Our consultation was "conducted" not only in the sense of Western science but also in the sense of consulting a diviner in Vodun (Voodoo) religion. The part of divination (a decision science native to the oral apparatus) that most attracted us was its capacity to form a cognitive map connecting the intractable problems of a particular individual with the accumulated wisdom of the community. You will recall that this integration of individual and collective experience is a goal of mystory as a pedagogical genre. What this creolizing of post-structuralism with divination meant in practice was that the consultant (called an "egent" rather than an "agent"—performed by one of the members of the group) posed a "burning question" (regarding a personal problem). The position of this individual in her mystory was juxtaposed with documentation of the conditions in the River zone to produce a correspondence that the egent ("querent" in the terminology of divination) recognized as an answer to her question. In a way that is counterintuitive from a literate perspective, this absolutely singular metaphor (what Barthes would call a structural portrait) attunes the chaotic heterogeneous circumstances of the River into an image category. This attunement is what Heidegger called "Stimmung." It is an objective mood supporting shared or collective understanding. It is also ephemeral, temporary, like a quantum measurement.

Having generated in Miami the prototype for this method of "critical divination," the FRE tested it further in two more zones—the Merrimack River in Massachusetts and Lower Manhattan (related to the 9/11 event). The long-range goal of the new consultancy is to produce a website interface that is a global American wisdom oracle. Our research on Voodoo divination revealed its origins in African Yoruban practices. The Yoruban oracle works in the same way as the Chinese I Ching. Because it is so ancient, with a tradition of commentary covering all the Chinese philosophical schools, the I Ching was chosen as the relay for our website oracle. The point is not to reproduce the wisdom of Ancient China, but to use the I Ching as a heuretic relay for generating a contemporary American (global) oracle. American decision science in any case has taken the idea of oracles as at least a metaphor for what modern knowledge desires: An ability to foresee or even manipulate the future. The Rand Corporation in the 1950s named their decision protocols the "Delphi Project." They had the right idea in alluding to the oral epistemology of divination, but they did not take this alternative tradition seriously enough. We are not using divination merely as a metaphor, but are actively syncretizing our theories with divination information processing. Nor are we confining our relay to a Western model, but looking outside the Western tradition.

The working title for this Internet oracle is the "KaCHING," evoking at once the I Ching inspiration and the onomatopoetic word for the sound of a cash register, to allude to the capitalist economy within which electracy presently operates. An important difference between the I Ching and the KaCHING is that in the latter one does not find the wisdom readymade but discovers American wisdom by helping to design the equivalent of a set of American (global) hexagrams (each hexagram is an archetypal situation). Testing this project in a recent graduate seminar the students used President Bush's foreign policy as a clue to American global wisdom. The basic insight is that to Americans everything looks like a "frontier," similar to that joke about people whose only tool is a hammer—to them everything looks like a nail. Thus American policy in the Middle East and Iraq is based on the premise that our enemies are "Indians," as the Native American was construed during the colonization of North America: As irrational savages outside the reach of negotiation, who must be eliminated with surgical strikes in what Richard Slotkin called actions of redemptive violence. The American prototype for action is the gunfighter. In other words Bush cannot be blamed very much for his policies, in that, as Slotkin shows in his book, *Gunfighter Nation*, Bush is following the "wisdom" used by nearly every American president since Teddy Roosevelt. The goal of this seminar is to use heuretics to design an alternative prototype, or myth. As Slotkin explained such myths are embodied in scenarios that are drawn upon equally by moviemakers and policy planners. For a new myth to be plausible to a given culture it must be rooted in the history and conventions of the community. Since jazz is as unique to America as is the frontier experience, we are testing the "jazz ensemble" as the new prototype for American foreign policy: Not "gunfighter nation," but "bebopper world."

Perhaps I have said enough to give you an idea of where choragraphy is taking me, my students, and my partners in the FRE. This work is in the early stages. One book of the EmerAgency trilogy just appeared from Longman Publishers: *Internet Invention: From Literacy to Electracy*. It uses the mystory as a pedagogy to help students to experience the process of creative insight (mystory as a way to simulate the Eureka experience of illumination, before one becomes habituated to the authority of normal science). Given the importance of global syncretism to electracy, perhaps you and I need to talk again, except that I will interview you about your experience of introducing French theory into Korean culture with its roots in the Asian habits of mind, ideologies, and writing systems. Your project is an important example of global creolization, I would say. That Florida and Korea are both peninsulas is all that is needed to form a conductive connection between us. After all it is not hard to hear the chora in "Korea." I am thinking of the border, the most heavily defended border in the world, they say, that divides your peninsula. Perhaps that problem could be a job for the EmerAgency.

Notes

1. Sung-Do Kim earned the Master and PhD degrees in linguistics and semiotics from the University of Paris10 (Nanterre), with a DEA from L'EHESS in oriental linguistics. He is founder and director of the Interdisciplinary Program for Visual Culture (Korea University), and

chair of the Department of Linguistics (Korea University). He translated into Korean *De la Grammatologie* by Derrida, *Du Sens* by Greimas, and the works of many semioticians, including a selection of Peircian writings (in press). He is the author of three books (in Korean): (1) *Lectures on Contemporary Semiotics*; (2) *From Logos to Mythos: New Horizons of Saussurian Thought*; (3) *From Structure to Passions: A Study on the Semiotic and Semantic Thought of Greimas.* A fourth book, *Digital Language and the Transformations of the Humanities*, is in press.

2. Gregory L. Ulmer is professor of English and Media Studies at the University of Florida. His most recent book is *Internet Invention: From Literacy to Electracy* (Longman Publishers, 2003). His website includes examples of student work produced in his classes taught in the Networked Writing Environment (web.nwe.ufl.edu/~gulmer). He is on the faculty of the European Graduate School (Saas-Fee, Switzerland).

CHAPTER NINE

Moving Devi

GAYATRI CHAKRAVORTY SPIVAK

On page 18 of Derrida's brilliant "Future of the Profession" in this
volume is a dig at Cultural Studies: "These Humanities to come will
cross disciplinary borders without dissolving the specificity of each discipline into what is called, often in a very confused way, interdisciplinarity,
or into what is lumped with another good-for-everything concept,
'cultural studies.' "This is now a common gesture among serious deconstructive Europeanist Comparative Literature academics. I think it might
be more advisable to try to mend Cultural Studies than to think that a
better model of interdisciplinarity will spring up in the general field
called Humanities at the U.S. university. The U.S. university was of
course originally based on a European model, but now it has developed
distinct twists and turns, which are in turn copied by the Europeans. In
the United States, Humanities are literature and philosophy. History is
institutionally a "social science." Philosophy is not noticeably an interdisciplinarity subject. And it is in literature departments that the suspect
interdisciplinarity of Cultural Studies finds a home. If by Humanities is
meant the French Human Sciences—Anthro, Poli Sci, History—and this
French conception provides the model for "specificity of disciplinary
borders," which Derrida wants to maintain, then Cultural Studies,
properly reconceived, brings something to the table. Cultural Studies
points vaguely in the direction of the human sciences, and if we could
whittle away at this vagueness then the CS impulse could be retrained to
go to work for the kind of thing—to come—that Derrida invokes. As for
"the natural sciences—even mathematics" that Derrida invokes, we can

hope for an impossible possibilization. But, as our list of contributors will show, at this historical moment we cannot despise Cultural Studies in the hope of an institutional sharing of Derrida's profession of faith by those constituted disciplines. At any rate I come back to the same thing. Mend Cultural Studies, don't just scorn it; it won't go away. And if it is allowed to sink to the lowest common denominator of tertiary education in the United States, it will mar all the disciplines it embraces in its enthusiastic grasp.

I am not sure what it is to "profess with," especially when the profession of faith is not of a priest but of a professor who places it within a textual abyss, which would forbid a chorus, implied by the "with."[1] Derrida is on target in the thinking of collectivity. "How many are we?" again and again, to quote *Politics of Friendship*.[2] So sharing an abyssally deferred profession of faith long-distance seems problematic. And if to profess means, as he suggests in his essay, being a professor by profession, Derrida is hardly your typical professor, and, even in the same institution, professors, even of like mind, profess wildly differently. Derrida's mode in the essay is you and I (plural), as in the classroom. I will therefore stick with "learning from Derrida," which has been my slogan for 36 years—ever since I tremblingly opened the pages of *De la grammatologie*. And it is well known that no reader ever learns quite what the book says.

For a long time now I have been trying to redo Cultural Studies, learning from deconstruction. And that's what I thought I would offer to this collection—the implications and vulnerabilities of Cultural Studies in practice, a wild piece—so that next time, my friends Tim Bahti, Jacques Derrida, and Hillis Miller will not simply say a negative thing about Cultural Studies and push off.[3]

The modern University is indeed, "the one whose European model, after a rich and complex medieval history, has become prevalent . . . over the last two centuries in states of a democratic type" (p. 233). We always hope that Cultural Studies can point toward a discontinuous outside. That is where learning from Derrida can kick in. My chapter ends with such a dedication, outside the orbit of the academy, which includes museums. Is the dedication, at least, worthy of tolerance from deconstructive thinkers? You will judge. The question of what universities are like in a nondemocratic state, as the United States is on the way to becoming, opens the way to a different set of questions.

In 1982, when Cultural Studies was not yet a popular concept in the United States, I uttered a speech entitled "Can the subaltern speak?" at a Marxist convention. There I tried to engage precolonial Indic material for the first time. It meant pushing away my allegiance to "French theory." To keep working with Derrida I had to endorse him, to make sure that my own engagement with deconstruction survived my new engagement with that new material. I saw this new engagement not as identity, but as making use of the extracurricular "knowledge" I had because of the accident of birth, a subsequent staple of general U.S. Cultural Studies methodology. I knew nothing of the Indic material in a disciplinary mode, and hence betrayed academic rigor. I proceeded with my serviceable Sanskrit and little else. I located the "subaltern" in the middle class, in which I was myself "responsible." The essay itself was a resolute suppression of the autobiographical, in more ways than I can yet reveal.

One curious thing: That essay was not so much a critique of British colonialism, as of the Hindu patriarchy with which it collaborated. Because most metropolitan readers "skip the Sanskrit part," where this criticism is contained, some readers have saddled me with presenting widow-burning as an act of resistance against colonialism, than which no more absurd position can be sustained.

In "Moving Devi," some 17 years later, the Western stuff—marked by Foucault/Deleuze in the beginning and Derrida in the end—is digested, for better or for worse. It has disappeared amorphously into the raw material of the object–being of my responsibility, I hope.[4] It does not oppress; it is not a thing to quarrel with. I am also at ease with the Indic material, not little because of the calm guidance and encouragement of my late friend, Bimal Krishna Matilal, whose name I will take again in the essay proper. I am no longer beset by the need to occlude the traces of the irreducibly autobiographical in cultural speculation of this sort. It will be harder for the reader to take sides now in the colonizer/colonized binary, although my position vis-à-vis state terrorism remains unchanged. There are many subalterns in the pages of this essay, their speech is still unheard, but not a one of them resembles me.

In 1998 I was asked to write an essay for the catalogue accompanying an exhibition on the great goddess (Devi) at the Arthur M. Sackler gallery in Washington. "Moving Devi" emerged in response. A shorter version was published in the catalogue.[5] This unwieldy hybrid essay is as much about the authority of autobiography in the problem of reading as was "Can the subaltern speak?," although the earlier essay was not yet ready to disclose this. My understanding of the autobiographical subject is a position without identity. How that computes in the writing is for you to judge.

When I revised the essay for journal publication, I had just been reading a lot of writing samples for a postcolonial position. It seems that many younger scholars now refer to metropolitan migrant writers as subaltern. Yet Gandhi and Nehru were not subalterns for the Subaltern Studies collective. (It goes without saying that the historians themselves did not claim subalternity.) Subsequently Hardt and Negri coined the absurd phrase "subaltern nationalism."[6] The term subaltern has lost its power to indicate people from the very bottom layer of society excluded even from the logic of the class structure. This may indeed be one of the reasons why I take the museum visitor from the model minority—sometimes myself—as a constituted subject, which forgets the other in its haste to claim otherness, only with reference to the metropolitan majority.

Here, now, is the essay proper, an example of the vicissitudes of Cultural Studies.

Every critical conviction persuades me that if I were representative of anything, I would not know that I was.[7] Yet, surely, I must at least represent the passage in migration, from *ethnos* to *ethnikos*—from being home to being a resident alien—as I write on the great goddess as she steps into a great U.S. museum?[8] I will allow "myself" to occupy this stereotype as I think about her. Surely it is because of this stereotype that I was asked to be part of the catalogue?

I have moved from a Hindu majority in the center of Hinduism to a Hindu minority in a new imperialist metropolis where Hinduism was, until day before yesterday, in the museum. Yesterday when the active polytheist imagination accessed the mindset of the visitor in the museum, a colloidal solution, shaken up between here and there, was surely secreted? I want to ruminate upon this transference from careless participant to uneasy observer. I speak of Devi, from somewhere upon this transference-circuit, not as an expert among experts.

I have no disciplinary access to knowledge about knowledge upon this topic. I must write of/from that frailer base—"making sense." I am an educated "native informant," the peculiar subject of metropolitan Cultural Studies. I must destabilize the constitution of the Devi as yesterday's object of investigation. I must not say what standard textbooks say: "The Great Goddess, or Maha-Devi as she is known in India, burst onto the Hindu religious stage in the middle of the first millennium of the Christian era."[9] That is yesterday's talk. I am in the history of the (globalizing) present. I must let foolish common sense interrupt the power of knowledge and declare what follows.

There is no great goddess.[10] When activated each goddess is the great goddess. That is the secret of polytheism. Intellectual Hinduism—to speak of it thus in the singular is to assume too much—seeks to emphasize its monotheist, monist, juridico-legal singular version. A certain line of Hindu thought has striven to see the polytheist moment as a more or less divine and playful allegory of the philosophico-theological. With Buddhism that moment seems to become altogether extra-orbitant, until Mahayana Buddhism brings it back in.[11]

For some of us the more interesting aspect of this impulse is its replication in varieties of the dominant—orthodox Brahminism, Puranic syncretism, or, finally, semitized reform Hinduisms reactive to the British. If today's metropolitan immigration is linked to this chain of displacements, the effort of the "Hindu-majority-model-minority" is to reconstellate this something called Hinduism as "a living heritage as ancient as it is modern,"[12] and in the current context to what amounts to a state religion fostering a general atmosphere of terrorism in India. The European-model university is either helpless or collaborative.

These displacements signify great waves of cultural politics. Does "being in a culture" bring with it a special way of feeling in thinking? Twenty-five years ago the British critic Raymond Williams thought that the way to observe culture where it is in the making is through "structures of feeling."[13] And more recently Derrida has reread Marx's thought within his own (and Marx's) Abrahamic cultural fix of messianicity—the possibility of welcome structuring the human as human.[14] Can we make some such claim for a "Hindu" way of viewing, thinking of it "culturally" rather than from within a system of belief? Common sense tells us that any such claim is necessarily behind the time of its possibility. Surrendering ourselves to that inescapable necessity—that we cannot break through into the vanishing present—let us venture a guess as to what an everyday polytheist structure of feeling might be.[15]

I am drawing now upon my conversations with the late Professor Matilal, who was one of the greatest international authorities on Hindu religious and philosophical culture. Discussing the *Mahābharata* with him I had suggested that the active polytheist imagination negotiates with the unanticipatable yet perennial possibility of the metamorphosis of the transcendental as supernatural in the natural. To my way of thinking this seemed to be the secret of the *dvaita* structure of feeling: The unanticipatable emergence of the supernatural in the natural—the tenacious dog on the mountain path is suddenly King Dharma for Yudhisthira in the last Book of the *Mahābharata*—rather unlike any sustained notion of incarnation. Perhaps this is why the Sanskrit word for "incarnation" (*avatar*)—has nothing to do with "putting on flesh." It means rather—"a come-down [being]." Everything around us is, after all, "come-down," if we assume an "up-there."

It is not too fanciful to say that a possible *dvaita* "structure of feeling," if there are such structures, would be the future anteriority of every being as potentially, unanticipatably, *avatār* in the general sense. It is within this general uneven unanticipatable possibility of *avatarana* or descent—this cathexis by the ulterior, as it were—that the "lesser" god or goddess, when fixed in devotion, is as "great" as the greatest: *ein jeder Engel ist schrecklich*. How did Rilke know? Perhaps "culture" is semi-permeable by the imagination?[16]

In Mahasweta Devi's lovely story "Statue" a passage about Manosha, a late Puranic almost-human snake-goddess, catches my drift. Manosha, although a minor goddess, is everything for her particular protégés: "The brass Manosha, with her wide-open indifferent brass pop-eyes, has been hearing the prayers of devotees for two hundred years. She hears it still."[17] For the families Manosha had devastated previous to this passage, she was the presiding goddess of the household and, when in action, was the great goddess, the goddess of everything. The dark consequences of a *dvaita avatarana*—where the moment is sustained into stabilized worship of an unfortunate, young female person—are represented in Satyajit Ray's 1960 film *Devi*.

When I first read about the Greek pantheon and its division of labor in college I, therefore, had a problem. Was not each god or goddess the god or goddess of everything when s/he was cathected in devotion or worship? I felt convinced that the commentators had got it wrong, for they did not know polytheism in cultural practice. The difference between "Greece" and "India" seemed only knowledge, unsustained by the responsibility of experience. The authority of autobiography (as well as knowledge) must remain forever problematic because that binary opposition does not hold at the limit, either way.

Our word is *dvaita* (two-ness, with the secondary meaning of doubt—in this case about the stability or constancy of the apparent), not *poly*theist. Since *each* other being is the only other being, there are always only two, not many. For the *dvaitin* or two-ness-minded radical alterity is in an impossible invagination in every instance of the other.

Invagination. When you think anything can be contaminated by the supernatural, by alterity, "[i]t is precisely [by] a principle of contamination, a law of impurity, a parasitical economy." Parasitically to the merely "real," alongside its ecology, runs this unanticipatable possibility of alteration. "A participation without belonging—a taking part in without being a part of . . . the boundary of the set comes to form, by invagination, an internal pocket larger than the whole."[18] The supernatural in the pocket of the natural, *dvaitavāda* in action, a structure of feeling folded in, again and again, to alterity.

In usual cultural explanations, classical and modern, the austere transcendentalization of radical alterity in Indic monism is made to coexist with these invaginated representations of the quick change into alterity by way of an argument from allegory. I am suggesting that the relationship is ironic rather than allegorical, if by irony is understood "the permanent parabasis of an allegory (of the *advaita*) . . . the systematic undoing, in other words, of the abstract."[19] The *dvaita* episteme or mindset, the structure of feeling that shelters the invaginated radical other as perhaps already descended in what surrounds us, interrupts *advaita*. And an *advaita* or non-dual impulse establishes itself imperfectly when a cathected god or goddess occupies the entire godspace.

"*Dvaita*" and "*advaita*," especially the latter, are here being used as common nouns. With or without the "allegorical" explanation they (especially *advaita*) have been perceived as proper names of doctrinal *ensembles* that are, at best, in a binary relationship, offering historical possibilities of openness and/or closure in response to their negotiations with the profane, at all social levels. Indeed a more dialectical vocabulary of forms of appearance [*Erscheinungsformen*] of essential structural relationships [*Verhältnisse*] would probably fit the case better. However that complex binary is perceived, the idea being advanced here is that perhaps the *dvaita* and the *advaita* are also lowercase names of a sleight of mind, a cultural mind-trick where the outlines bleed into each other in the mode of a permanent possibility of a parabasis in the future anterior. The *dvaita* will have pierced the *advaita* already, perhaps; and vice versa, asymmetrically. It is in this structure of feeling that devi(s), and deva(s) too, of course, have their being.

Thus in the structure of feeling–thinking, the attempt is not only at the transcendentalization of the figure of radical alterity, which is all that is evident if we examine comparable movements among peoples of the Book. The polytheist moment (not the same as the *dvaita/advaita* [non]relationship) is not often invoked there, except as an originary violent female prehistory, before binaries can be launched. Freud is of course the most monumental example, but other instances can be found.[20] Our suggestion has been that, in an effort to stabilize the future anterior, Hindu polytheist cultural practice attempts to *presentize* the uneven but permanent parabasis of the natural by the supernatural, thus making phenomenality resonate with its transcendent double, where the double (*dvi*) stands for an indefiniteness that is not merely the opposite of one as many. That originary indefiniteness is celebrated in the fact that the one itself is *a-dvaita*—non-dual—rather than singular.

Let us now examine an extreme and eloquent case, where the *advaita* is the abstract God of Islam:

> Let the lips utter non-stop
> *Lā ilāhā illellā* [the Islamic credo: There is no greater God than God]
> The Lord's prophet sent this law.
> But keep form and name as one
> In spirit, and say it over thus.
> If you call without form-sign
> How will you know your Lord?

This is Lalan Shah Fakir (1774–1890), chief among Bengali Sufi (a misnomer, again) lyricists. The hazy margins of South Asian Islam will yield other examples. What is important on the track of the Devi is the possibility that when the *dvaita* interrupts the abstract, the feminine enters.[21] If Lalan can interrupt his abstract and imageless Lord with the *dvaita* urge to *rūpa* (manifestation, "form" in my translation), he is a step away from suggesting, in another song, that Khadija—Muhammad's eldest wife—*is* Allah: *je khodejā shei to khodā*, that one cannot determine the coordinates of Prophet and Lady separately; *ké bā nobi ké bā bibi*, that it is a marriage of transaction between the same and the same, othered. Not formless (*nirākār*) but one-formed: *ekkārété moharānā*.

As Muhammad's chief wife, Khadija is here the chief goddess, as it were. She is chief player in the play of *advaita/dvaita* in Lalan's hymn. But this is tightly structured poetic counter-theology. The *dvaita* impulse is at work to mark out (or in) the borders of Islam. The 14 wives of the Prophet are suddenly the 14 worlds of Indic mythology, without any attempt at establishing allegoric continuity. Lalan is no blasphemer. Three of the wives were before the *kālemā*; before, that is, the Islamic revelation. And therefore it is of the 11 within Islam that Lalan the Islamic *dvaitin* sings: *egāro jon dāsya bhābé Lālan koi koré upāshona*—Lalan says that the 11 worship in the servant's way.

Lalan writes this scene of woman within the way of *bhakti* or devotion, widely recognized as a historical challenge from within to the caste-fixed inflexibility of high Hinduism.[22] *Bhakti*, creating affective links between the subject and the invaginated radical alterity of the *dvaitin* mindset, inscribes and assigns the subject's position within a taxonomy of phenomenal effect: The Sanskrit word literally invokes this taxonomic division. When Lalan iconizes the 11 wives of Muhammad as worshiping him in the servant's way, he is not guilty of *naturalistic* sexism (see note 17).

He is speaking rather of the various assigned subject-positions within the text of *bhakti*, themselves undoubtedly related to the highly detailed taxonomy of the *rasa*s (names of implied affective responses to texts) available within the general Indic aesthetic.[23] *Dāsya* or servant-ness is one of the affective roles cultivable within the script of *bhakti*. It is not a natural attitude to be developed as a virtue, and it is not gendered.

Bhakti is thus a parabasis or interruptive irony of rule-bound high Hinduism as well as of the *advaita* mindset.

Permanent parabasis. It seems to me more and more that this may be a name for the most effective and plural way of dealing, from below, with the repeated mortal experience of nonpassage to the other side.[24] The plurality in this plural way is fragile and irreducibly uneven—dependent upon an "institution" that can be as amorphous as culture (gendering plus religion? I risk a definition of culture's bottom line) of which we can speak only by begging the question. The variously and much-negotiated *dvaita/advaita* sleight of mind may be the experience of one such nonpassage.

(When *bhakti* lived in the crannies of culture where it could give the lie to caste and scripture, it did so—and does; and it opened doors for women's agency. There were woman practitioners and teachers. It must, however, be admitted that these women were exceptional. Mirabai, the fifteenth–sixteenth century aristocrat, leaves home to be *Krishnabhakta* [it seems interesting that *bhakta*—the adjectival noun from *bhakti*—{division in} devotion—admits no feminine] in the *dāsya* (servant) or *madhura/gārhasthya* (wife) mode. The maternal mode is also possible.[25] But within the Orissa–Bengal *bhakti* tradition of Sri Chaitanya (1486–1533), out of a 191 devotees listed in one reference book, only 17 are women, 5 of them members of Chaitanya's direct family. Of a 100 poets, only 1 is female.[26] The most striking characteristic of this group is the near-institutionalization of sexual indeterminacy. But the chief appearance of this phenomenon was in men affecting the feminine. The most superior *bhāva* was the *sakhi bhāva* toward Krishna—to be Krishna's girlfriend. Many of the male *bhakta*s were also called by female names. This identity crossing and troping of the sexual self did not touch gendering. The object—Krishna—remained male. When Madhavi Dasi, the only named female poet, mourns Chaitanya's death, she laments from within untroped female gendering: "Whoever sees that golden face floats in waves of love / Madhavi is now deprived by the fault of her own karma."[27] Affecting Radha, Krishna's chief girlfriend [that is what *sakhi* is, I mean no disrespect] in Rādhā *bhāva*, remains similarly drag-troped.)

Speaking of epistemo-affective specificity (structure of feeling in thinking as a presupposition) I have been denying the great goddess exclusive "greatness" in the experience of the culture. But if culture may be the name of an amorphous/polymorphous "institution," which holds us (*dhr* = to hold, gives *dharma*), it—again that question-begging—is also disclosed in institutions of a more systematic and formal structuring: Festivals are among them. And no person from Bengal—as is the present writer—can deny that in terms of goddess festivals—Durga and Kali mark the year much more flamboyantly than any other divine figure.

But that feeling of half-belief or "suspended" belief—that the metropolitan middle class in India (mostly the origin of the immigrant museum-goer who was my "implied reader" for the catalogue essay) may attach to the festivals of Durga or Kali—is not what travels to the metropolitan museum in the United States. This is not due only to the willed epistemic emphasis of eurocentric economic migration.[28] It is also because the colonial museumization of Indian culture, with its roots in German comparative religion, is an altogether more specialized affair. Its starting point may be loosely assigned to a positive evaluation of what Friedrich Hegel had called, negatively, a *verstandlose Gestaltungsgabe* (a mindless gift for morphogenesis) in his *Lectures on the Aesthetic*.[29]

If one steps upon that established scholarly terrain the blithe assertion of "Durga and Kali, of course," begins to get muddled, for we step into the enclosed garden of Art History, not to mention the history of religion. On the other hand for the educated native informant from Eastern India, Durga and Kali, Durgapuja and Kalipuja, remain distinguishable. Too much learning would here make present certainties indeterminate.

There are hyphenated and/or expatriate South Asian art historians of South Asian art, of course. How does their learning complicate the certainties of cultural competence? I cannot know. No doubt such experts negotiate the culture/discipline divide by way of some variation of the unevenly pluralist parabasis of which we have already spoken, complicated by the fact that their authority sometimes takes on extra weight by that very negotiation, a move from story to fabula, as it were.[30] "Religious" denomination and gender complicate the issue further.

Let me quote a learned passage written for British academic validation by a located female South Asian Asianist, born a Seventh Day Adventist in Calcutta, by political conviction a Communist. A labyrinth opens there . . .

TA [the Taittiriya Aranyaka] x:18 tells us of an unnamed wife of Rudra; *TA* x: I of Durgā Devi Vairācani (Virācana's daughter); *TA*

x:I: 7 of Durgi, Katyāyani and Kanyākumāri; *KU* [Kena Upanisad]
III: 12 of Umā Haimavati. *TA* x:18 has a parallel Dravidian text
which makes Rudra Umāpati (Uma's husband). *MU* [Mundaka
Upanisad] 1:2:4 mentions Kāli and Karāli among the seven tongues
of fire. The *SGS* [Sānkhāyana Grhya Sutra] II:15:14 and also *Manu*
III:89 mention Bhadrakāli. These texts, as is shown from their
vagueness, are inconclusive even if taken in their totality; the epic-
Puranic Durga did not develop from any one of them, but from all
of them and also from many other elements.[31]

Why have I gone into all this and not started comfortably with
feminist reminiscences moving inexorably toward a foregone "postcolonial" conclusion? I think because I have a strong sense of straddling a
transitional historical moment, and political correctness would arrest it.
All historical moments, whatever they may be, seem and are transitional.
Historians judge between transitions. I will account for the specific
transition I surmise. It is that soon the generations of U.S.-born Indian
Americans, descendants of the first big wave of Indian immigrants after
Lyndon Johnson relaxed the quota system in 1965, will have changed
performative into performance. The possibility of performance (citation)
inhabits the performative. Yet the two are not "the same." In this case it
involves a willing exchange of civil society. Today the dubious self-naming
"international civil society," works at obliterating this exchange, instru-
mentalizing cultural politics for capitalist globalization and the new
imperialism. I have no moral position on it, but write this for the record.

Hedged in by this framing, then, I give witness to the great goddesses,
Durga and Kali. You will work out my negotiations. " 'I' is only a
convenient term for somebody who has no real being. Lies will flow
from my lips, but there may perhaps be some truth mixed up with them;
it is for you to seek out this truth and to decide whether any part of it is
worth keeping. If not, you will of course throw the whole of it into the
wastepaper basket and forget all about it."[32]

In this mode of lying truth (fiction in the underived robust sense as the
authority of autobiography) Durga and Kali will remain different. For
Durga I will choose the story of the dismemberment of Sati. For Kali an
illustrated translation of a hymn by Ramproshad. I will give an account
of the "little mothers" of Bengal, of *vāmāchāra* and the *Chandimangal*, and
close with a hesitant dedication. To begin my fiction I caution again.

It is difficult to deny that something like a history leaves its mark on
"us"; but this mark, in a time of migration, seems a dynamic. Thus even
if there is a structure of feeling that can, vaguely, be called Hindu, it

would not be identical with the "Indian" structure of feeling, of course, whatever that might be. If we insisted we would be inhabiting *Hindutva*, the slogan of Hindu nationalism upon the subcontinent. In the United States would this be something like a dominant residual? I think more and more that a critical vocabulary for describing culture is only good for the person who puts it together.

If ever I had a *dvaita* sense of my city it came from the story of Durga. A bit of her body had fallen upon Calcutta, and made it a place of pilgrimage. I knew that the Durga who had been dismembered should be called "Sati." I knew that the 10-armed, familial, annual autumn image celebrated in the high holy days could not be called Sati. This plural naming of alterity—some minimal identity presupposed somewhere, just to hang the names on—is taken for granted by the *dvaita* mindset. Being "in a culture" is to pre-comprehend, presuppose, even suppose. The question of belief comes up in crisis, but even then perhaps in performance rather than in a strictly cognitive assent.

Here is the story told by Sukumari Bhattacharji, the source of the learned passage above, now for children:

> One day, while Sati was sitting outside her house, she saw a number of gods and goddesses passing by . . . "Where are all of you going?" They answered, "Don't you know of Daksha's magnificent sacrifice?" . . . [Sati] could not believe that they had been deliberately overlooked. . . . Sati asked her husband if he could explain her father's abnormal conduct. Shiva was sure he could. . . . Daksha intensely disliked Shiva and his unconventional way of life . . . So, Sati ran to her father, ignoring the banter and sneers directed at Shiva, and said to Daksha, "What kind of sacrifice is this, father, where the supreme god Shiva has not been invited?" The status-conscious Daksha . . . replied sarcastically, ". . . You have married beneath your social status, my child. I cannot insult these assembled dignitaries by asking that lunatic loafer to be here!" . . . Unable to bear the insults uttered against her dearly beloved husband she fell down in a swoon and died. . . . [Shiva] was mad with fury and . . . rushed to Daksha's sacrifice. . . . Shiva tore Daksha's head from his neck and threw it away. The sacrifice itself assumed the shape of a deer [lovely *dvaita* touch!] and fled. Shiva with his Pinaka bow in hand, chased and shot it. . . . Shiva now came to where his beloved Sati lay dead and an uncontrollable fit of madness seized him . . . [P]icking up Sati's body, he walked, jumped, danced and traversed long distances for many days on end, oblivious that the

mortal remains of Sati were dropping off, bit by bit, over many places. All these places, including those where parts of her jewellery fell, later became places of pilgrimage.[33]

In most Puranic accounts Sati's death is more theologized than in the intuitive popular story. In the *Kālikāpurāna* she meditates a moment upon the undivided pre-semic possibility of utterances,—*sphāta* not *mantra*—splits the top-center of her skull, and gives up her life.[34] In the *Devibhāgavata* she burns herself through the fire of her concentration (*yogāgni*) in order to satisfy the ethics of good-womanhood (*satidharma*) because her father had engaged in unseemly sexual behavior under the influence of a magic garland indirectly conferred upon him by another one of her fictive manifestations![35] In one the dismemberment is motivated by the other gods' caution rather than the husband's frenzy. In the other the gods enter the corpse, cut it up from the inside, and make the pieces fall in specific places.[36]

Classical iconic representation makes no effort to grasp the drift of a story. And indeed the stories are not starting-places. They are pluralized presentifications of the *dvaita* episteme at odds with the theological impulse. The mode of existence of the icon as meaningful, from the point of view not of the scholar but the culturally competent observer (a vast and many-tiered sprawling space of agency always "after" culture but also its condition of possibility) is something like a submerged genre-"painting." The culturally competent (in this sense) may provide some generic narrative dynamic to move the Devi and her companions along the stream of "history." It is in that assumption that a few generalizations will here be advanced.

I have cited Freud as dismisser of polytheism, defining it as prehistory and the intolerable rule of powerful women. If we take Freud as everybody's father (or anti-father) we are working with the axiomatics of imperialism: Europe gives the model of every knowledge. The University is European. On the other hand if we relax Freud's chronologic to a logic, we will see Freud's brothers, or at least male cousins, in these Puranas. There can be no doubt that the general cast of the "authorship" of the Puranas is male.[37] Women speak in them but the frame-narrator is generally masculine. There can also be no doubt, I think, that there is a degree of "relative autonomy" to the great social text of sexual difference, which overflows cultural frontiers, without losing specificity. It is therefore not surprising that, in the pores of these authorized versions of Sati's dismemberment, there are efforts at controlling the feminine as female. Relative autonomy is relative; it is not a postulation of universal deep structures of human sexual dynamics. It is in the sector of the relativity of the relatively autonomous that we look for cultural specificity.

These considerations made we see in the Puranic texts that the females empowers, but males act. At the end of the chapter previous to the dismemberment story in the *Devibhāgavata*, there is a vertiginous spiraling of such empowering and acting, which comes to a halt when the two male gods of the Puranic trinity think they act on their own and thus are cut off from empowerment through their hubris. The third calls his sons, they pray to the female fictive power, and the entire spiral starts again with this supernatural division of gendered labor intact.

Within this division in the high Puranic texts male gods are allowed elaborate courtship privileges. Brahma is represented as publicly (although transgressively) spilling his semen on earth, lusting after Sati. But the Devi celebrated in the Puranic account is the pleasureless mother. Sati punishes herself for pleasuring others.

At the beginning of this essay I suggested that the unanticipatable and irregular presentification of the slippage into *avatarana* (or descent from a transcendental semiotic) is the habit of the *dvaita* episteme. The denaturalization of the goddess, which has been tracked in the last few paragraphs, can be seen as a counterpull: To stabilize the *dvaita* episteme by reversing the *avatarana* into reminders of *arohana* or ascent. Thus the *Devibhāgavata* loosens the connection between death, mourning, dismemberment, descent of body parts, inscription of geography: "The pilgrimages created by Sati's body parts have indeed been spoken of, but also those that are famous on earth for other reasons."[38]

This loosening of connection between Sati's body parts and natural space comes at the end of a torrential list of pilgrimages, which began with the following declaration: "Wherever the cut limbs of Sati fell, in those very spots Shiva established himself, assuming various forms." The loosening of connection is accomplished through a double-barreled list of 108 items, place-name in the locative case with the accompanying body part mentioned only in the initial one: "Vishālākshi [the large-eyed one] at Vārānasi lives on Gauri's face" (p. 55). (Gauri is another name of the Devi.) The subsequent references are not necessarily to a body part. And soon the "poetic function" takes over making the repeated couplings seem dictated by sheer euphony.[39] The pairs start looking like ordinary epithet–subject couples rather than located body part couples as the formality of the verse gathers momentum, and various rhetorical moves are made. Now the subject is enclitic upon and contained in the epithet. Now the so-called subjects are themselves epithets dependent upon the location of the so-called epithets as condition, respectively qualifying and modifying an absent subject, by now fragmented by force of rhetoric, at least 108 times. Intact manifestations, belonging to other narratives, are sometimes introduced to dilute the force of the dismemberment story. Consider these two pairs, among many: "Sex-loving at the door of the Ganga [*gangādvāré ratipriyā*]" (p. 68) is clearly a riff on the woman's body as geography, but not of the Sati's body part story. The subject is an epithet entailed by the overtly metaphorical locative: The river mouth as vagina. And "Radha in Vrindaban forest [*Rādhā vrindābané bané*]" (p. 69), refers to a completely different story, thus negating the narrative and generative force of the dismemberment. The final names, inhabiting a common rhetorical move of "the best of a set," are not connected with the dismemberment story at all: "Among good women she is Arundhati, among charming women she is Tilottam. In the mind she is named Brahmakal and among all embodied [beings] she is Shakti" (p. 83). From names to attributes. There is no Devi here. As we saw in the opening verse it is Shiva who is sited in the *pitha*s.

This would be the bits of narrative and antinarrative within which the images are set. Such Puranic references are archaic rather than functionally residual in metropolitan hybridization. For the specialists they find their place in the academic subdivision of labor, unevenly divided among continents.[40]

Among the four broad "kinds" of Indian scriptures—Purana ("ancient") is a temporizing claim to antiquity, whereas Veda is "known," even "known by heart," Smriti is "remembered" and Sruti "heard as revealed." The double-structured pull of the *dvaita* is felt within the Puranas. Some are more a tabulation of the thingliness of the signifier, others more inclined toward the mindiness of the signified. The tension is generally coded as less and more Brahminical, respectively—what Raymond Williams would code as the dominant incessantly appropriating the emergent.

This is the kind of difference that is usually noted between the *Devibhāgavatapurana* and the *Mārkandeyapurāna*. The former more airy, the latter more earthy. We have just noticed how the body-part–real-space referential narrateme was unevenly sublated into a locative condition-dependent logical structure of potentially reference-undermining naming in the *Devibhāgavata*'s account of Sati's dismemberment. (This is the kind of sentence that irritates conservative Indianist scholars muscle-bound by their discipline as well as racist left conservatives of whatever color. In the meantime the dominant passes everything off as transcendent high culture.)[41]

The list in the fifth chapter of the *Devimāhātmya* section of the *Mārkandeyapurāna*—read by Birendrakrishna Bhadra on All India Radio

in the 1950s—is well known to most culturalist Hindus. It comes closest
to the always deferred possibility of a sublation of the Devi into her
attributes. But the list is here directed toward a Devi who is located in all
that is, and the reciter/reader performs his respects by enunciating that
directedness. To the goddess who, in all that is, is well-established as
consciousness, respectful greetings, goes the first line. A marvelous series
of parallel lines follows: Respectful greetings are given to her as she is
well-established as intelligence, sleep, hunger, shadow, power, thirst,
patience, birth, modesty, tranquility, faith, beauty, grace, activity, memory,
compassion, contentment, mother, and the best of all, error.[42]

Yet this powerful song of praise is narratively framed as Visnu's *Māyā*.
I propose to translate *Māyā* as "fiction," an English word philosophically
unconnected with prose. Like all translations this translation too "is a
movement . . . that transports [the] language beyond its own limits."[43]
But *Māyā* in the limited sense or translation of "illusion" has given
trouble to readers and believers through the centuries. *Māyā* as fiction
would carry the paradox of the range of power of this antonym to
"truth."

However the great goddess is made to occupy the place of power, it is
always as fiction, not as truth. It is not a question of the multiplicity of
manifestation; gods and goddesses share it; it is a *dvaita* world. It is not
even a question of doing—both do. But she does through fiction and
they—the singularity of the Puranic male *isvara* is nowhere near as grand
as the singularity of the morphogenetic multinominated Devi—through
method. If *Māyā* is understood as fiction, this is how the gendered
empowerment–activity dyad mentioned above would be re-grasped.
There is never an exception to this in all the male–female binaries strewn
through the Puranic corpus: *Prakrti/purusa* (comparable to *physis/nomos*,
matter/consciousness, *hylè\morphè*) and *prajnā/upāya* (wisdom/method)
are only two of the best-known.

The name of that fiction or *Māyā* is the apparent magic of fertility—
animate and inanimate. This is seen as unitary, even before the human-
image propriation of the supernatural. Therefore for the Hindu, whatever
that may be, it is different to be identified with the worship of different
male gods—a Shaiva is different from a Vaishnava, a Brahmavādi is loosely
an *advaitin* until the nineteenth-century reformist Brahmos took the slot.
But if you are a Shākta, Durga and Kali must be acknowledged as the
same. The acknowledgment of this always unitary female power (at the
time of first writing, the Indian film star Hema Malini was pushing her
dance drama on Durga by cluing on to a culturally conservative feminism as "the strength and power of the woman" on the New York TV

channel "Eye on Asia") is yet another way of attempting to control what Freud would call "the uncanny."[44] Such acknowledgment cannot be translated into normative social attitudes toward female human beings. And indeed women cannot feel fertility as the uncanny in quite the same way. For reverence for fiction (*Māyā*) as female to be unleashed, the *dvaita* trick must happen, and the female subject exit sociality.

More of this later. For the moment let us note that the name of the version of the great goddess who animates the section of the *Mārkandeyapurāna* that is called *Devimāhātmya* is Chandi—the "irate." Indeed, by displacement, this section of the text is also called *Chandi*. In the mode of glorification each of the "little mother" goddesses of Bengal is also a chandi. *Ein jeder Engel ist schrecklich.*

To encounter specifically female focalization in the *dvaita* presentification of the goddess in her biotic sphere, we will have to leave the great goddess, and turn to these little mothers of Eastern India, surrounded by their specific flora and fauna.[45] The high pantheon is dominantly male-focalized.

When cathected in ritual each small goddess is the great goddess. The cycle of her praise and worship is much shorter than the annual festival cycle of the great ones; daily, weekly, or by the phases of the moon. She relates not only to the house (there are male deities who bless and curse a particular foundation) but to the household as it is run by women, often by women in subordinate positions, such as a daughter-in-law or a virgin daughter. Even widows worship these little mothers, although for them the male greater gods come into social focus again.

There is no doubt that the addition of "chandi" to their names respects what I have already remarked: Each goddess, when cathected in worship, is the great goddess. But with specific reference to the minor goddess Sitala (this remark would, *mutatis mutandis*, apply unevenly to all the minor goddesses of Bengal), a commentator adds: "This Chandi is not Durga, rather she is the hunting deity of the hill-tribes of Chhotanagpur of Bihar. Purulia, as it was formerly under Bihar, hence, the Chandi of Bihar of the aboriginal groups spreads her impact in Purulia district."[46] Yet "*candi*," even as a common noun, as presumably here, is a Sanskrit word. It is not possible to separate the Aboriginal and the Indo-European on the occasion of the goddess. They share a heartbeat: "That which, from moment to moment, *from one moment to the other*, having come again from an other of the other to whom it is als__delivered up (and this can be me), this heart receives, it will *perhaps* receive in a rhythmic pulsation what is called blood, and the latter receive the force to arrive."[47] Except in stratified social practice where "Indo-European" and "Aboriginal" have been forcibly kept separate for millennia. And perhaps in the museum.

Most of the regional accounts of the historical emergence of these minor goddesses are also accounts of resistance and flexibility: Resistance to the increasingly caste-bound ritualism of high Hinduism. Scholarship tells us, of course, that even these great gods and goddesses owed a good deal to the aboriginal cultures already in place on the subcontinent when the Indo-European speakers began to settle; and that Hindu history is a history of the imperfect obliteration of traces. But the emergence of the gendered secondary pantheon as resistance is part of a cultural self-representation, which is not necessarily scholarly. I am not responsible in Hindi as I am in Bengali, my mother tongue, and English, the object of my reasoned love and a general instrument of power. I am therefore better acquainted with a portion of the considerable writings in Bengali and on Bengal about the coming into being of these gods and goddesses of field, stream, forest, hill, and household. Not as a specialist but as a "Bengali," whatever that might be.

These goddesses, who came to be worshiped in the house without a priest and in Bengali rather than Sanskrit, are seen, in a certain kind of Bengali writing, as aligned to the aboriginal descent of the Bengali, to a resistance to the great tradition, as a sign of ecumenicism. The vision of Bengali identity captured in this temporizing points to a gender-liberated, egalitarian, and humane people, domesticating Buddhism as high Buddhism moves to East Asia, coming to terms with Islam as Bengali Islam opens its doors to the oppressed outcastes, acknowledging the body as the iconic representation of the universe. The account consolidates the *dvaita* structure of feeling (if there be such a thing) by bringing it within a calculus of representation and practice, by removing from it the element of chanciness, by constituting it as the evidence of an "identity," not of Indian culture so much as of Bengali humanism. It is a tempting exercise, especially when garnished by such open-ended statements as this from the first extant text in Bengali, composed between the eighth and twelfth centuries: *jetoi boli tetavi tal / guru bo se sisa kal* (the more said the more error / guru says the student deaf).[48]

Let us now leave the labyrinthine truths of this temporization of identity, and look at a text in the history of the present, aligning it with the ones we have already assembled in these pages.

If one believes that "the synchronic" is at least a methodological possibility, a pamphlet entitled *Meyeder Brorokatha* is also part of "our" present.[49] The book was bought at a fair for the aboriginal Sabars in Rajnowagarh in West Bengal, organized by the local Sabar welfare committee. Rajnowagarh is a relatively remote place. Most of the Sabars, except for a handful of adults and schoolchildren, are illiterate. The few "regular" Indians present at that activist-organized fair were from the urban middle class. Rural Hindus and Muslims do not mingle with the Aboriginals by choice, for pleasure. In other words the itinerant bookseller on a rusty bicycle, from whose horde a celebrated activist bought me a bunch of books, had no real buyer at that particular fair. But it is conceivable that at the more usual rural fairs, organized around festival days or around the weekly or biweekly market days, men buy these books for their wives and daughters so that they may learn the religious authority behind their ritual practices. In the last decade I have touched the normality of this grassroots readership, and try always (with no guarantees, of course) to compute their distance from the New Immigrant spectator of the Devi icons in the museum, of Hema Malini at Lincoln Center, in order not to speak nonsense in the name of global feminism or hybridity.

Forty six household rituals are listed in the book—*broto*-s (from Sanskrit *vrata* = restraining practice), not *puja*-s. Women's rituals without a priest. I quote the opening lines of the poem accompanying one to give the reader a sense of the performance in it. I had read them before in a novel by Bibhutibhusan Bandyopadhyaya that Satyajit Ray translated into film in his *Apu* trilogy.

> Pond of good works, Garland of flowers
> Who worships in the morning?
> I am Sati Lilabati
> Lucky girl with seven brothers

and so on.

The text as it was used in Bandyopadhyaya's novel (as opposed to the pamphlet bought at the fair) was not real but cited in a fictional frame to signify "village girl." But if and when a village girl utters this within an appropriate performance, she is also citing fiction, in our English colloquial sense of course, but also because the performance is in the frame of the *Māyā* of the world. She acts two parts in the script—the questioner and the answerer–performer, specifically named: I am Sati Lilabati. Sati is a word in the language—meaning, presumably, a paragon of the specifically womanly virtues; and the expert will give me a list of Lilabatis; it's a common enough monikker.

What matters to us is that there is something moving in the self-bestowal of that grand theatrical appellation—Sati Lilabati—upon a young girl, even as her good fortune is carefully designated as the possession of seven brothers. O my Antigone! Behind these *broto*-s are quite often stories of women saving their men. There is indeed a degree of (the representation at least of) agency on this register, validated by traditional gendering, securing domestic loyalty.

The ostensible goal is a good husband. There is something like a relationship between this and the personal columns of newspapers, seeking partners. Chance and choice are at play here. The personal column relies on a theory of the subject of decision, only apparently ungendered. The *broto* relies on propitiating the animal world as much as anything else. The ritual begins with offerings made to snakes and frogs. The connection between such gestures and fertility remains enigmatic.

There is a *broto* listed here, for example, involving the goddess Earth. The chant commemorates the *dvaita* moment, within that structure of feeling, not just the dead metaphor in "mother earth." The Earth is a *Devi*: "Come Mother Earth, sit on a lotus leaf." The chant goes on to praise her husband, the king of the universe, in the hope of marrying a king.

These performative pieces, without need of an officiating priest, organize woman's time theatrically. The connection with the ostensible purpose—good husband or good fortune—is thin, less focused than the personal column or lottery tickets. And these temporizing stagings of the woman's being in and of the *oikos* do not produce an affective relationship with the great goddess as such. As the great goddess of the male imaginary recedes further and further into distanced and fixed visibility (as in Lacan's reading of *Antigone*), the invaginated *dvaita* episteme uses its part-containing-the-whole resources to create a space of theater for the women who sustain rural society.[50]

This sort of little mother ritual is the staging of the woman's day. The great goddess festival is a grand exceptional event. And indeed at those festivals the womenfolk are the preparers of food and the ingredients for ritual detail, not the human protagonist.

In *Meyeder Brotokatha*, the pamphlet of little mother rituals, there *are* narratives that invoke the high pantheon. They are perfunctory tales using the *dvaita* principle of quick shifts from human to other-than-human at random, to end inevitably in an injunction to perform the specific *broto*, with no noticeable logical build up. The ritual seems the remains of some other text, whose meaning is errant here. Was that textuality an indeterminate weave of aboriginality and the para-Vedic Puranas? I like best the eccentric scholar who writes: "Bengalis, like Indians in general, had their origin in Negrito or Negro-Bantoo race," and points out repeatedly that it is only in southwestern Bengal that the little mother Sitala—goddess of smallpox—is worshiped fully in the aboriginal way, and points at the sliding scale of ritual and imaging that she is offered.[51]

No "Indian culture" here. No great goddess as such. No serious ethnography either—just a traffic in regional identity in the name of women, in the household.

When the story of the dismemberment of Sati turns up in this pamphlet, it does not continue on to the establishment of *pitha*-s or places of pilgrimage. There is no account here of the limning of a sacred geography upon a place we now call South Asia. The region does not exist here, only the courtyard and the field. There is a hiatus between the end of the Sati's-death story and the injunction for the particular *broto* to which it is unaccountably attached.

As the new immigrant woman crosses the threshold of the museum she reads the images in the museum as cultural evidence or investment, even as proof of a feminist culture. "Interest in the feminine dimension of transcendence as revealed in mythologies, theologies, and cults of goddess figures throughout the world has been keen in recent years both among those concerned with 'Women Studies' and among religion scholars generally."[52] I want now to leave the rural theater, and to flesh out this viewer's look by referring to my own childhood. Autobiography is at best an example, no authority.

Indian cultural evidence is in the children's story. Professor Bhattacharji has distilled Bengali popular tradition there. The Sahitya Samsad Dictionary of the Bengali language lists the 77 places consecrated by Sati's body simply as part of the definition of the word *pith* [Sanskrit *pitha*] or "seat."

As it provides the modern place names beside the ancient, there is no hesitation in the dictionary. There can be no doubt from this lexicography that the naming was yet another way of consolidating settlement in a new land. If one follows through, one sometimes comes up with a geographical information system, which uses a woman's body to bring under one map self-contained aboriginal settlements. I feel my lack of expertise rather strongly here. But consider the place where Sati's upper lip came to rest: "Bhairavaparvata (Avantidesa near Ujjain). The country of Avanti, much of which was rich land, had been colonized or conquered by the Aryan tribes who came down the Indus valley and turned East from the Gulf of Cutch."[53]

Behind the fictive authority of autobiography, and the ecstatic celebration of the yearly Durga puja in Calcutta, there is the shadow of the first colonial conquest of India, by "my own kind":

> [A]ll over the world there was the cult of a holy family—composed
> of "mother and son" at first, but later (when the man's contribution
> in the procreative process was recognized) of father, mother and
> son. In India this family consisted of Siva, Parvati and Kartikeya.
> Later the family grew to include Ganesa, Laksmi and Sarasvati, who
> constitute the group now worshiped in India in the autumn.[54]

What did this mean in my childhood and adolescence? New clothes
for every day of the five-day festival, drinking mescalin-paste milk in the
bosom of the family on the fifth night, visiting and comparing innumerable images all over town, complaining about and loving film-soundtrack
and amateur theater blaring over loudspeakers, and going the rounds of
visiting extended family and friends, abruptly cut off when I left India in
1961. It is possible to connect to simulacra—citations within a general
metropolitan civil performative—here in the United States, but I am not
given to the expatriate staging of national origin for a culturalism that
removes the nation-state of origin from independent transnational consideration. Lest I seem to suggest that the "originary" place is without
simulation, I will relate Durga puja ("Devi Puja" in Bihar and Uttar
Pradesh)—the sanctioned worship of the great goddess—through a photograph (figure 9.1) by Kalo Baran Laha, which engages a rather different theater.

Mr. Laha is a hotel owner in the country town of Purulia in West
Bengal. He photographs, with a group of friends, for his own pleasure,
establishing a record of life, mostly of Aboriginals, in the region. This
photograph of a boy looking up obliquely at the clay-and-wattle frame
of the image of Durga and her family, worshiped annually, is a little off
Mr. Laha's usual beat.

A small-town boy or a rural boy, one cannot know. The photographer
seems to have caught his subject unawares. The boy gazes at the image.
The eyes in the absent, spectral head return his gaze. The knowledge of
the return of the image every year directs the boy's gaze; a cultural habit,
which also knows that the image will be destroyed, plunged in the river
with great pomp and circumstance at the end of the five days. It is the *dvaita*
habit institutionalized—to see in the obviously transient and ephemeral
the possibility of alterity—that conjures up the goddess's absent yet gazing,
living, head for the boy. It bears repetition: It is not just that the image is
not yet ready; it is that even when fully assembled and gorgeous, it will
carry its imminent death. The day of triumph—*bijoya*—is also the day of

Figure 9.1

the renouncing of the simulacrum—*protima bisharjon*—of floating—
bhashan—all words in grassroots vocabulary. And yet the gazes lock. In
fact if the image had been fully formed the picture would have signified
differently, for the goddess's fixed and stylized gaze (which I, like the boy,
can imagine) would be angled at the other corner of the photographic
space. The boy's expression does not lend itself to quick characterological analysis; in my reading there can be none. The *dvaitin* gaze is not
phenomenal.

   If we read the photo through Sigmund Freud's essay on "Fetishism,"
we would expect a fascinated gaze, and we would expect a doubled
anxiety of castration and decapitation.[55] But that is another culture, and
I hope I have demonstrated that I do not mean that word in some silly
Cultural Studies way. If our boy had looked between this humble unfinished great goddess's legs, as Freud's boy in "Fetishism" would, he would
"see" the absent gaze from the not-yet assembled human head of the
defeated buffalo, in a representation of the *dvaita*-moment caught in the
icon. Is this why polytheism (not a good word, but we will let it pass) is
scary, because of such powerful females, improbably limbed? Does it
"mean" that this representation of this boy, at least (we must beware of

making a singular representation exemplary, although Freud sometimes forgets this lesson), will not prove the case for subject-constitution on an error about genitals? To pose the question is to make Freud real, an occupational hazard of psychoanalytic cultural criticism.[56] They changed their minds through varieties of cultural conservatism from which approaches such as mine are to be distinguished.

I will not open my usual Kleinian argument here, since that will divert this line of thought too far.[57] I will simply repeat that the *dvaitin* gaze is not phenomenal, that in every act of Hindu worship or presentification alterity must be instituted in the material—*prānpratisth*—and then let go at the end, and that the relative permanence of built space—which organizes so much Hindu nationalist violence in India today—is irrelevant. The nonpassage between (above? below? beyond? beside? Can there be a relational word here? The *dvaita* gaze forever trembles on that brink) the boy's actively *dvaita* gaze and the metropolitan museum will have remained negotiated without his cultural (not necessarily deliberate) participation; that gaze, locked perhaps in the spectral gaze of the great goddess, will have fallen short of the exhibition.

My take on Kali is different.

The Bengali *bhakta* visionary Ramakrishna (1836–1886) often experimented with cross-gendered *bhāva*s or affective essences. As a *bhakta*, however, he was turned chiefly toward Kali.

Because of family involvement with Ramakrishna, his wife, his disciples, and the movement in his name, over four generations, as well as because of the sect-orientation of my father's ancestors, I was born and raised in the verbality of the praise of Kali.

The genealogy of the great goddess renders the distinction between Aboriginal and Aryan indeterminate. But Kali seems to have preserved some especial aura of aboriginality. It is difficult to clothe that joyous, leaping, naked black body altogether. If the buffalo-killing (*mahisāsuramardini*) golden Durga is not the object of worship of the aboriginal Indian, Kali has remained so. At least in the aboriginal group—the Kharia Sabars of Manbhum—known to me nonfigurative design is a major part of decorative art. It is perhaps no surprise that Kali has lent herself to the greatest abstraction, in the nonfigurative mystical diagrams or *yantra*s of *tantric* practice. I lack the scholarship to say this with confidence. In this section I will consider one such *yantra* as represented by the twentieth-century artist Nirode Mazumdar (figure 9.2) and his coupling of it with a verbal text from the celebrated eighteenth-century religious poet Ramproshad. The text is, among other things, a humanization of the goddess, which has something like a relationship with the *dvaita* episteme in the *bhakti*

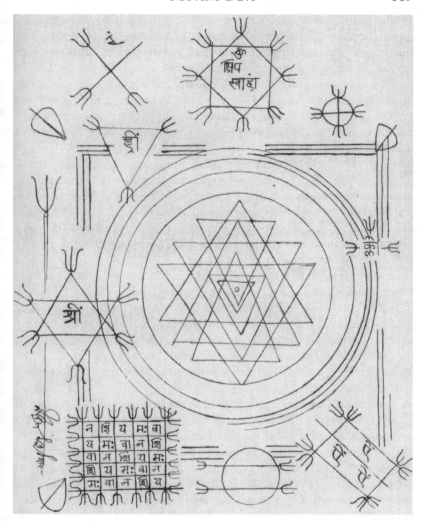

Figure 9.2

mode. (I hasten to add that Durga too is domesticated in Bengal. Her autumn festival is often coded as the married daughter visiting her parents' home and there is a wealth of songs welcoming her as such a daughter.)

In this hybridized representation of Kali by an Indian artist expatriate in France, well before the era when today's hybridist episteme had started to emerge—the exotic artist in Paris was an earlier stereotype—truth-in-painting discloses itself even as it misfires on its intention: To couple text and image.[58] The truth disclosed is that such a coupling would work only for the glance that would see India as a stable symbol of the promise of mystical liberation—the Herman Hesse mode—with tantalizing residues of an earlier, more Madame Blavatsky mode, which would hint at the esoteric-as-such. For the middle-class Bengali of *Shakta* (the sect loyal to *Shakti*—power in the feminine—generally understood as Kali) provenance, as perhaps Nirode Mazumdar was, the eighteenth-century verbal text looks forward to the dynamic of Bengali colonial modernity, constituting a female object of the *dvaita* gaze who could straddle the culture of the rural landowners (itself on the cusp of the "feudal"-residual—thus reaching out toward the culture of the tenants—and the "colonial"-dominant); as well as that of the devotional culture of the emerging urban, colonial middle-class, stratified along location-specific lines. The visual text, by contrast, looks back toward the "archaic."

Mazumdar's line drawing is a *yantra*—an instrument. *Yantras* are used to start inspiration in *tantra* practices. The line between the erotic *bhāva*s in *bhakti* and *tantra* is shifting and unclear. When, however, a *yantra* is used to focus ritual there is a clear distinction from the affect-centered practice of *bhakti*. A *yantra* is a calculus, a diagrammatic representation of the goddess and the god, female and male together, to help access the human body as itself a diagrammatic representation of the universe, not as a container of affects.

Tantra is the "reverse" method of appropriating the *dvaita* structure of feeling. Instead of emphasizing ascent or *arohana* by bracketing the *dvaita* event into "allegory" in a restricted sense, *tantra* attempts to arrest or capture by going *through* the descended flesh. Perhaps *tantra* longs to turn invagination inside out, by literalizing it?

To engage the affects would be, strictly speaking, contrary to the *tantra* endeavor. Theoretically the body that *tantra* wants to engage is a representation of the universe, not the text and instrument of affects. "The universe" is most often understood as a sexually differentiated force field.[59] The body engages in sex and comes to *jouissance* and has the skill to experience it (*mahāsukham*) as *advaita* transcendence. This skill is *tantra*.[60]

Nirode Mazumdar seems to have drawn a partial version of the most celebrated *yantra*—the *Shrichakra*: "There are nine *yoni*s or female organs, five of which have their apex pointing downwards, and these represent Shakti. The remaining four with apex pointing upwards represent Shiva. The *vindu* [dot] is situated in the smallest triangle pointing downwards."[61] In one corner is a hexagram expressing respect for Shiva.

With this *yantra* the artist has coupled the following two lines by Ramproshad Sen (1718/20–1775/81): "See how the bitch plays, in her own way of acting the secret play / Setting the phenomenal at odds with the noumenal / Hitting stone on stone." If you knew the significance of the *yantra* it is conceivable that these lines could be an admiring monstrative description of it. But Mazumdar, like the museum, is reconstellating. The "felicitous" text accompanying a *yantra* would tell the aspirant how to use it. This is why Naren Bhattacharya writes, somewhat querulously: "The term tantric art is evidently a misnomer."[62] You do not celebrate a baseball game for its choreography. Why not? We ask. That would be reconstellation.

Ramproshad Sen, the eighteenth-century poet, is also reconstellating. Working first as a clerk for a new colonial-style urban merchant, and patronized subsequently by a semi-feudal landowner–"king," he can be read as living a nostalgic regression into a social discursivity that was soon to become residual. He writes when the active modes of *bhakti* and *tantra* have already receded from the mainstream. His poems are informed with the *desire* to taste the divine madness of the true *bhakta*. All his songs outline this desire within an enactment of the *bhaktibhāvas*.[63] He is no mendicant minstrel and certainly not a practicing tantric, although he uses the metaphorology of both. His lines are playful, tuned into the affect of sweetness (*mādhurya*) or filiality (*vātsalya*). The "bad language" signifies the familiarity of affection. For this poet-persona a *yantra* would be somewhere between a curiosity and an artifact to be revered. Certainly in his own famous line: "I *yantra* you *yantri*," the use of the word is Bengali colloquial—"I am the instrument you the player." It would make no specifically *tantric* sense to call the aspirant the *yantra*. All Sen's *tantric* imagery is filled with the accuracy of descriptive, not potentially performative, passion.

If Ramproshad had written practicing *tantric* texts, they would have been *vāmāchāri* (focused on sinister- or woman-practice), since he invariably used the coupling of Shiva and Shakti as his vehicle. Let us therefore look not at a learned discussion of the *tantric* heritage, but at a text of grassroots *vāmāchāri tantra*, written in Bengali, on sale at that rural fair in West Bengal.

Here is the beginning of the text accompanying a *yantra* altogether less complex than the one we are looking at:

Penance must be continued for seven days. No food or drink. Only milk. Drinking that milk you must think that I am sucking immortal nectar from the Devi's large firm breasts. You must prepare a

yantra according to the figure above, with white sandalwood paste.
Then worship the *yantra* with karabiflower and vermillion. Get to a
hilltop on the ninth night of the waxing moon and constantly recite
the *mahabija mantra*. Devi will appear toward the end of the night.
Devi strips and undresses the aspirant. To make the aspirant engage
in erotic play she kisses, licks and embraces the aspirant constantly.
She gives him great wealth. The pure body of the Devi is the
aspirant's heaven. The aspirant enjoys this unearthly body for a
long time.[64]

The book is full of such injunctions, often very graphic, about how to
deal with the different erogenous zones of the female body. The passion-
less didactic tone is about as far from Ramproshad's funky affective use of
tantric imagery as can be. It is interesting that, in the opening chapter
("Devi Bagala's manifestation"), the oneness of the great goddess is
asserted: "In addition, it is this Devi who is also worshipped as Kali, Tara,
Shodashi, Tripura, Bhairavi, Rama, Bagala, Matangi, Tripurasundari,
Kamakshi, Jambhini, Mohini, Chhinnamasta, and Guhyakali" (p. 10).
    Who uses these pamphlets? Are there practicing *tantrics* in the rural
areas, or among the floating urban sub-proletariat? Here again we are
looking at a long delegitimized sector of what culturally defines India.
What word would Raymond Williams use for this?
    I cannot think that *tantra* ever allowed for women's sexual agency.
Although in the supernatural the Devi is dominant, in the *yantra*-inspired
activities the actual women representing her are the affectless receivers of
foreplay. In the act itself the goal is to arrest male ejaculation, so that
orgasmic pleasure can lead to a transcendental rather than merely organic
fulfillment. An actual event of this type, described by an ecstatic participant from the orthodox Bengali middle class, is rather horrible in the
implications of what actually happened to the passive young woman
involved.[65] If the evidence of this book is to be believed, the woman-
advisers within the system feel no hesitation in acting as procuresses.[66]
    Better I think to be the agent of the theater of the domestic in little
mother rituals than to be the victim or organizer of this curious reverse
figuration of the transcendent, upon the woman's body. And better to
join the chain-link of reconstellated desire for a cultural "lost object":
Ramproshad Sen, Nirode Mazumdar, and the negotiable figure of the
New Immigrant Model Minority lady-viewer. A politics is involved in
how we will represent that desire, how we will try to make the images mis-
speak, and who gets to represent; by the structures of social empowerment,
guaranteed by sexual difference, the lowest-level of institutionalization

that we can reach: The multicultural relative autonomy of gendering. Perhaps the chain-link should include the *tantra*-impulse itself, appropriating, for a specific practice, the general word for technè as weaving the base thread (*tantu*); resisting the strict theological dominant with the flesh.[67] We are all like the little boy in Laha's photo, looking up at an angle at the absent head of a not-yet-there Devi, making eye-contact with what is not yet there. When *vāmāchāra* in *tantra* needed to set a practical course, suspending affect to go through the flesh to transcendence became equated with learning to withhold male ejaculation on the bodies of doped or brainwashed girls or sexworkers.[68] We must keep on attempting to reconstellate, but we must not forget this fact and its corollary: The relative autonomy of gendering, everywhere.

Mazumdar makes a lovely experiment. Yet whatever the continuities or discontinuities of his visual–verbal couplings, a simulacrum ("citation without literal referent"), at best, of the condition–effect effect, there is no necessarily "female" component in the focalization of their two parts.

I did not engage in little mother practices in childhood and adolescence; although here and there women in my extended family performed them with the required regularity and they did not seem odd. If "I" am representative of the shift from *ethnos* to *ethnikos*, am I then deprived of the possibility of occupying designated womanspace in the praise of goddesses? Am I confined, at best, to the cultural reconstellations of the radical sector of the expatriate middle class, such as the experiments of Nirode Mazumdar? Before I ask this question again, let us look at the class-mobile rhythms (disclosed and effaced by the imperialisms that have nurtured our viewer) in *Chandimangal* by Mukunda Chakrabarti, a Bengali poet during the middle of the sixteenth century.[69] I am observing what Williams would call the "pre-emergent."[70]

This is the best of a series of *mangalkavyas* or rhymed romances of earthly good fortune, celebrating these minor goddesses. *Chandimangal* celebrates our major goddess—*Chandi*—as if she were a minor one.

Only two of the fourteen sections of the long poem are located in the world of the gods. There is an account of the ill-fated festival of Daksha, but no continuation into dismemberment. The fixing of the sacred geography of the subcontinent is not important here either. This poet steers by a real map. This poem, like others of this genre, is also an account of sea trade.

Barter—what Marx would call the relative value-form—is the medium of trade. An extraordinary passage of exchange valuation or *badol* occurs, for example, in Day Six, section 338 of the poem.[71] And the reader can almost feel the value-form straining toward some version of the general equivalent—the money-form—in sea trade. In 50-odd years the East India Company will come upon these shores. One of the gradual and necessary achievements of the East India Company was to standardize the many silver currencies in 1833. A uniform paper currency was established by the Negotiable Instruments Act of 1881. Thus with the straining of the value-form in *Kabikankonchandi* we are on the way, however remotely, to globalization—which is the establishment of a uniform electronic exchange system globally.[72]

K. N. Chaudhuri proposes a non-continental "Asia" constituted by unifying trade activities upon the Indian Ocean rim.[73] In my schooldays the Sri Lanka trade on the Bay of Bengal rim was incanted to establish in our volatile hearts a pan-Bengali culture stretching from Lanka to Indonesia: "Our son Bijoysingha, conquering Lanka, left a signal of his valor in the name 'Singhal.' "[74] Kabikankon Mukunda Chakrabarti's Chandi is also the patron goddess of trade.

She is conceived as a competitive woman: "Where will I get the best-quality worship?" is the question that motivates the entire romance.

If relative value trembles on the brink of the general equivalent in the details of the representation of trade, the *dvaita* form of appearance of the actant trembles here on the brink of what Roland Barthes would call "the 'character-person.' "[75]

The recognizably European form of the picaro is not available here. A new style of Comparative Studies would, however, catch this traveling Devi by the representation of her dynamic use of the shape-changing already available in the narrative impulse of the Puranas—as opposed to the rhapsodic or legiferant impulses of Sruti and Smriti.[76]

In order to compete for the best quality human allegiance this Devi literally manufactures curses so that the inhabitants of the supernatural world can descend (*avatarana* in the general sense) and play in the real world. The *dvaita* has become fully instrumental. We can perceive the realization of that remote structure—the Devi as competitive loyalty-buyer in the context of trade—as the corporate PIO of gender sidles into the museum, looking around her to make the right moves.[77] Every rupture is also a repetition.

If this suits her fancy our PIO might save the residual as it emerges into the emergent from the depredations of the dominant. For Kabikankon's Devi is split between two conjunctures. In the first phase of her descent she is the forest.[78] In this age of biopiracy and the export of hunger the viewer can perhaps cross identity a bit—go from U.S. PIO to a gendered citizen of the world—and realize in herself the Devi of the hunters and gatherers, who wished to establish peace in the animal kingdom.[79]

This gives a partial answer to the question of our access to woman-space. The secure *oikos* of the *broto*-bound woman has been delegitimized by the green revolution and its consequences. Our way in is unavoidably with the dominant—our ally is the elite of the forest as picara—looking for the better bid. (I do not think of it as necessarily a way forward. But that is another argument.)

Perhaps there is also an "aesthetic" answer to the question of our access to this particular womanspace.

I have described earlier the peculiar positioning of the disciplinary historian of South Asian art who happens also to be South Asian. To be an expatriate feminist literary Europeanist who happens to understand the easier Sanskrit of the ritual practices is also a peculiar designation. In the last forty-two years I have been present at two or three great goddess rituals among expatriates; sanitized yet not without a certain poignancy in the framed observance of a deliberately distanced unacknowledged *dvaita* mindset. On these upwardly mobile model-minority subcultural occasions the general nostalgic gender structure is preserved. Women who might otherwise hold corporate posts (not invariably, of course, and it was different until the mid–1970s) dress in costume and make elaborate preparations of food and flower; some men join, under their guidance, in the more masculine chores of fetching and carrying, the male priest(-for-a-day in this simulation) intones, the congregation repeats, the words are lost, the feast is the best, saved for last.

My stereotype of "myself," knowing the minimum Sanskrit required for comprehension of the service, combined with an altogether fierce training in "the willing suspension of disbelief" in 46 years in departments of English literature as a nonnative speaker, as student and teacher, moving through culturally fractured changing classrooms, is separated from the festive gender division described earlier.[80] I "read" the text of the service and address myself as reader to the image as figure, and animate the ritual as an act of "poetic faith" (Coleridge) in the broadest possible way. If anyone notices, which is unlikely, the most generous explanation would be: Bluestocking, and I choose the colonial word advisedly.

I should like to think that "suspension" in that description of poetic faith means both "*hanging on* and *hanging between, dependent* and *independent*, an 'assumption' both assumed and suspended."[81] And this quivering subject-fix, without its protective gender-skin, can perhaps be donated to the formation of one hyphenated (as in American) agent among many as subcultural practices become an increasingly inflexible, class-differentiated, special semiotic, to be performed (or not) like a dance routine, under special circumstances.

I think it is best, in view of such a hope, to put the historical distance of a great museum between the icons and the multicultural beholder. If multicultural mulch begins to affect museal practice it will have happened in the middle voice, neither active nor passive,—an expressive instrument we have lost in modern grammars. It will have happened—varieties of the future anterior is the closest we can get to that voice in modern Indian languages—only when the new museal discursive formation—internalized, becomes part of the migrant episteme; as it no doubt will with much *Sturm und Drang*, as Hinduism becomes one of the minor religions of the United States.

On my wall hangs M. F. Hussein's "Laxmi," which I acquired at the Sotheby's auction in January 1996, where the NRI (the nonresident Indian, an important category within the problematic I am discussing) entered the auction room to invest in contemporary Indian art. That lovely image of the dismembered Maha-Laxmi reminds me daily that I have not made the epistemic shift to the great goddess in hyphenated America. It is the museums, great and small, that will have led us in.

Paradoxically it is in this aesthetic challenge that I turn once again to the *broto*-bound rural women. The repetitive theatricality of the priestless *broto*-rituals was not necessarily connected, for these women, with a directed goal other than their performance. This can be put two ways: On the Indic register we can say that a *naimittic karma* (purposeful act) became formalized in daily practice as a *nitya karma* (routine act); on the European register, although both sides will object to this transgressive and scandalous reconstellation, we can call these repeated rituals a *Zweckmäßigkeit ohne Zweck*—an aimless purposiveness or, in the conventional translation, "a purposiveness without purpose."[82]

Coleridge was wrong, of course. The habit of art appreciation is a cultural *reflex* translated differently in different subjects, not a *willing* (or unwilling) suspension of disbelief.[83] It seems to me more and more, as I go further and further into the rural past and present of my corner of South Asia, that the everyday *dvaita* habit of mind is just such an unacknowledged cultural reflex. The *broto*-bound women can be imagined as bound to this reflex as well. They are not asked to *face* the great goddess in festival. Their theater is the restricted sylvan enclosures in and around their home. We cannot, therefore, substantively share their space, even as it shrinks into the archaic. But I can at least acknowledge the possibility that I am concatenated with them upon a chain of displacements when I animate "ritual" as "poetry"; if not, like them, as the theater that makes the everyday.

Unless one grants the possibility of such aesthetic judgment, one cannot account for the critical edge of the widows' talk, precisely at Vrindaban, the fabled loving-ground of Krishna and Radha, where they are paid in food and a pittance to pass their days in singing *bhakti*-ful adoration of Krishna, in the *dāsya-bhāva* (assigned by Lalan to the 11 post-Islamic wives of Muhammad) as also in *sakhi-bhāva*, girl-talk with Radha, the chief girlfriend.

Pankaj Butalia's documentary *Moksha* is here my text. It is too easy to have a politically correct interpretation of these widows, although the denunciation of the predatory male establishment of moneylenders and petty religion-mongers is altogether apt. Except for the one case of absolute depression where the subjecting script of *bhakti* has failed, the women are in the theater. These women, who would seem decrepit to the merely sophisticated eye, speak with grace, confidence, and authority, not as victims.[84] Their views on marriage, as expressed to these alien questioners, are poignant and innocent. They have come to Vrindaban for freedom, such as it is. The quality of their performance of improvisatory *palakirtan* (an antiphonal and choral narrative song of praise in the Eastern *bhakti*-tradition) is often excellent, the songs in *dāsya-* and *sakhi-bhāva* full of longing and humor. As old-age homes for a female parent, or orphanages for widowed female relatives, these dormitories are harsh indeed. But they are transformed into a space of choice and performance by the gift for theater of these near-destitute widows, ready to inhabit the *bhakti*-scripts that are thrust upon them. There is everything to denounce in a socioeconomic sex-gender system, which will permit this. But the women cannot be seen as victims, and the theater of *bhakti* cannot be seen as orthodoxy pure and simple. The contrast between the sentimental voiceover of the documentary and the dry power of the women is itself an interpretable text. Butalia has done well to begin and end with a song where the cracked tuneful strong voice of the female *kirtaniya* sings as god: "These cowgirls have tied me down, brother . . ."

Again subaltern women in theater. Again no great goddess to offer an improbable role for women. The invaginated *dvaita* habit is nowhere near a "naturally" feminist narrative of identification with great goddesses. No room for She-god essentialization here. Adoration legitimizes hostility by reversal. The many representations of the great goddess look stunning on the wall. Real women are distanced from her. She is no role model unless, by the cruelty of the *dvaita*, one of us is thrust into that space. I shiver with the icy detachment of words meant and spoken by one who had been so thrust.

I am thinking of Saradamani Devi (1853–1920),[85] the wife of Ramakrishna, whom I have mentioned earlier—an ecumenical visionary (he reminds me of William Blake), playing with gaiety as position without identity, who addressed himself chiefly, though not exclusively, to Kali, in the *bhakti* mode.

Sarada Devi was a village girl who could read some but not write. She was married at five, joined her husband at eighteen, and then was drawn into celibacy and the circuit of a tremendous assembly of male colonial subjects who gave her reverence and worshiped her often *avataric* husband. In her own life's detail, in the everyday detail of her marriage, she needed self-consciously to call upon the resources of the *dvaita* episteme in the most concentrated way. We have bits and pieces of her exquisite utterances as testimony.

This remarkable woman outlived her husband by 34 years. In the course of time his 12 young male disciples established her as the advisory head of an organization that became a monastic order devoted to social work. She performed her role with tact and wisdom, always remaining in the background. Here was a *broto*-bound girl transmogrified into an *avatarin*. Her husband had worshiped her ritually, officiating as his own priest.

It is one of her ice-cold sayings that haunts me, a questioning of the right to possessing the other and of self-determined identity at once: "[action] befitting the situation, [consequences] befitting the person, [gifts] befitting the recipient. Noone is anyone's, dear, noone is anyone's."[86] Paradoxically this admonition without an imperative describes without moralism the passing of the *dvaita* habit of seeing—into the museum. Perhaps it is the female as honorary male who can say this best.

Vivekananda, Ramakrishna's chief disciple, wrote a Sanskrit hymn to her. The addressers, in the plural, are grammatically in the masculine gender. My female cousin and I, when we sang the hymn together in Calcutta in the 1950s, quietly changed the gender of the collective singers to feminine, perhaps simply because we were two women incanting. A couple of years ago in New Delhi the female religious order founded in her name sang the hymn on her birthday. They had not disturbed Vivekananda's grammar. The collectivity of nuns spoke in male gendering. Sarada Devi had become a Devi—a goddess, the *dvaita* gaze frozen in the artifice of a forever present, standing in for eternity.

For me whatever she was remains afflicted by mortality. She could not have known what an art gallery was. Is it appropriate to dedicate these pages to her? You will judge.

Notes

1. The very first sentence encourages us to think of the possibility of counterfeit and perjury: "No doubt *like* . . .," and continues to present the essay as a representation of reader participation in

a contradiction of the body of thought "Derrida." This is also a reference to an undermining of his relationship to Rousseau ("*like* a profession . . . traitor to his habitual practice"), who, in turn, places his (?) "profession of faith" in a doubly fictive episode, in the name of another, of "the truth" of which he gives a fictive "guarantee," in a novel where he engages the question of an education that repudiates the institution: "We can be men without being scholars. Dispensed from consuming our life in the study of morality [la morale], we have at less expense a more certain guide in this immense maze of human opinions." (Jean-Jacques Rousseau [1979]. *Emile, or On Education*. Translated by Allan Bloom [New York: Basic Books], p. 290). Derrida's "habitual practice" with *Emile* is elaborated in *Of Grammatology* (Translated by Spivak [1976]. Baltimore: Johns Hopkins University Press). His traffic with Rousseau continues through his recent work on Paul de Man. How is Derrida asking us to permit him to be unfaithful to such habitual practice? Would that be professing with or against? Without venturing up to that perilous necessity, I ask if it is legitimate to (mis-)quote the profession of faith of the vicar of savoy: "One must begin by learning how to resist [nature] in order to know when one can give in without its being a crime." (*Emile*, p. 267). As recently as "Faith and Knowledge," (in Gil Anidjar [ed.], *Acts of Religion* [New York: Routledge, 2002], pp. 42–101) Derrida has tangled with Kant's "Religion within the Boundaries of Mere Reason" (*Religion and Rational Theology* [Cambridge, UK: Cambridge University Press, 1996]. And there we read: "any such profession of faith can well be hypocritically feigned" (p. 177). In a final passage, having connected professions of faith with the grounding principle of dishonesty or *Unredlichkeit*, Kant outlines the safe position regarding professions of faith. Of course Kant speaks of religion and Derrida of university. Yet for Kant Christ as model for reason is invariably and repeatedly a teacher. The connection may be a little stronger than a simple *mutatis mutandis*: "The genuine maxim of safety, alone consistent with religion, is exactly turned around (*umgekehrt*): what, as means and conditions of blessedness, can be known [*bekannt*]not through my own reason but only through revelation, and can be received [*aufgenommen*]into my profession [*Bekenntniss*]solely through the intermediary of a historical faith, does not contradict pure moral principles—this I cannot indeed believe and assert as certain, but just as little can I reject it as certainly false" (p. 205; translation modified). This proto-deconstructive position is what I hope Derrida guards in his "profession of faith," rather than the European competition with the United States in the name of a Kant I do not recognize, which is a later manifestation. (The phrase in the first Kantian passage I cite is translated "*confession de foi*," in the most commonly used French edition; in the second passage the translation is "*profession de foi*," Kant [1986]. *Oeuvres completes* [Paris: Gallimard], vol. 3, pp. 183, 227.)

2. I have discussed this in "Schmitt and post-structuralism: A response." *Cardozo Law Review*, 21.5–6 (May 2000), 1723–1737.
3. I have discussed these passing interventions in "Deconstruction and cultural studies: Arguments for a deconstructive cultural studies," in Nicholas Royle (ed.), *Deconstructions* (Oxford: Blackwell, 2000), pp. 14–43 and *Death of a Discipline* (New York: Columbia University Press, 2003), pp. 5–6.
4. My vulgarized analogy is with Emmanuel Levinas (1997). *Otherwise than Being: or Beyond Essence*. Translated by Alphonso Lingis (Pittsburgh: Duquesne University Press), pp. 59, 72–73.
5. "Moving Devi," in Vidya Dehejia (ed.), *Devi: The Great Goddess* (Washington: Smithsonian Institute, 1999), pp. 181–200.
6. Michael Hardt and Antonio Negri (2000). *Empire* (Cambridge: Harvard University Press), pp. 105–109.
7. I thank Jean Franco and Val Daniel for reading early versions of this essay; Maitreyi Chandra for her understanding and her help with library work; Jessica Forbes and Blythe Frank for their support; and Henry Staten for reading the version revised for this collection.
8. I have discussed the relationship between *ethnos* and *ethnikos* in "Acting bits/identity talk," in Dennis Crow (ed.). *Geography and Identity: Living and Exploring Geopolitics of Identity* (Washington: Maisonnneuve, 1996), pp. 41–72.
9. C. Mackenzie Brown (1990). *The Triumph of the Goddess: The Canonical Models and Theological Visions of Devi-Bhāgavata Purāna* (Albany: State University of New York Press), p. ix. It is still

appropriate to make such statements in a disciplinary textbook. For a somewhat more scholarly register, see Thomas B. Coburn (1984). *Devi-Māhātmya:The Crystallization of the Goddess Tradition* (Delhi: Motilal Banarsidass). No academic could be against disciplinarization. We are interested in what is left out when the discipline consolidates. These remains cannot become disciplinary authority as "experience." They can only interrupt knowledge to indicate its vulnerability and to signal pathways for the imagination, as dangerous as they are challenging. An inventory without traces.

10. In 1999 I read "[w]hat thus turns out to be interrupted, . . . in the first moment of hospitality is nothing less than the figure . . . of truth as revelation" (Jacques Derrida [1999]. *Adieu: To Emmanuel Levinas*. Translated by Pascale-Anne Brault and Michael Naas [Stanford: Stanford University Press], pp. 52–53). Is there something like a relationship between the interruption of the production of disciplinary knowledge by "cultural responsibility"—to each goddess as guest, if you like—and that more austere, messianic insistence? Can the ethical subtend such quotidian common sense?

11. This story is repeated in all histories of Hinduism, often between the lines. For a sober and learned account, see Sukumari Bhattacharji (1988). *The Indian Theogony: A Comparative Study of Indian Mythology From the Vedas to the Puranas* (London: Cambridge University Press, American Edition).

12. Biju Matthew et al., "Vasudhaiva Kutumbakam:The Internet Hindu." *Diasporas* (forthcoming).

13. Raymond Williams (1977). *Marxism and Literature* (New York: Oxford University Press), pp. 128–135.

14. The argument about Marx is in Derrida (1994). *Specters of Marx:The State of the Debt, the Work of Mourning, and the New International*. Translated by Peggy Kamuf (New York: Routledge), pp. 95–176. In making this move Derrida draws upon Kierkegaardian–Levinasian thought, which is best explained in Derrida, pp. 70–78. In what follows in my text the reader is asked to keep in mind that the two-ness of the Peoples of the Book is not the two-ness of the *dvaita*, although there is something like a relationship between them, perhaps. Derrida's work here relates, willy-nilly, to Jewish particularism and its vicissitudes, Levinas and Heidegger, if you like, and as such can take on board the figure of "a structure of feeling," not necessarily connected to an intending subject, although, as Levinas at least would argue, it is indistinguishable from intentionality as such:"Hospitality opens as intentionality" (Derrida, *Adieu*, p. 48).

15. This is how I think of Derrida and Williams together. Some think this is inappropriate because Williams thinks only in terms of an intending subject. I think "structure of feeling" can be thought of as a tiny narrateme without violence to Williams' system of thinking. It is of course (im)possible to think anything without the trace of an intending subject.That argument would take us too far afield. In so far, however, as structure of feeling is thought as a structure, it need not entail the *philosophical* presupposition of an intending subject, although the contamination of the philosophical by the trace of the empirical cannot be to strenuously disavowed. It seems to me, therefore, altogether possible to use Williams' bold methodological suggestion in a deconstructive way. I speak of feeling in thinking as a way of knowing. *Pouvoir-savoir*—the ability to know—is delivered by means of that structure, perhaps.

16. This is the first line of Rainer Maria Rilke's *Duino Elegies* (1923). It means "every angel is terrible." Literally "each one angel is terrible."

17. Mahasweta Devi (1999). "Statue," in Gayatri Chakravorty Spivak (trans.), *Old Women* (Calcutta: Seagull).

18. Jacques Derrida (1980). "The law of genre." *Glyph*, 7, 206.

19. Paul de Man (1979). *Allegories of Reading: Figural Language in Rousseau, Nietzsche, Rilke, and Proust* (New Haven:Yale University Press), p. 301. I have altered two words. I invite the reader to ponder the changes.

20. Sigmund Freud (1961–) "Moses and Monotheism," in James Strachey et al. (trans.), *The Standard Edition of the Complete Psychological Works* (New York: Norton), vol. 23, pp. 83, 93.

21. This is not necessarily "feminist." It can even be a limit to feminism within permissible narratives. Indeed this is the problem with Levinas's apparent privileging of the feminine.The best treatment

of the question of woman in Levinas is Luce Irigaray (1991). "Questions to Emmanuel Levinas: On the divinity of love," in Robert Bernasconi and Simon Critchley (eds), *Re-Reading Levinas* (Bloomington: Indiana University Press), pp. 109–118. The general insight about permissible narratives is part of Melanie Klein's legacy, not necessarily connected to feminism.

22. The task here is to transfer Gauri Viswanathan's extraordinary argument about "the resistances of converts to the erasure of their subjectivity" (*Outside the Fold: Conversion, Modernity, and Belief* [Princeton: Princeton University Press, 1998], p. 17), *mutatis mutandis*, to a precolonial setting.

23. For the sheer multiplicity of the *rasas*, see Venkatarama Raghavan (1975). *The Number of Rasa-s* (Madras: Adyar Library).

24. In "From Haverstock Hill flat to U.S. classroom, what's left of theory?," for instance, I have suggested this as a description of actually existing counter-globalist struggles in the Southern hemisphere (forthcoming in Judith Butler and Kendall Thomas [eds], *What's Left of Theory?* [New York: Columbia University Press]).

25. Parita Mukta (1994). *Upholding the Common Life: The Community of Mirabai* (Delhi: Oxford University Press) is indispensable for an understanding of women's *bhakti* in India today.

26. Achintya Kumar Deb (1984). *The Bhakti Movement in Orissa: A Comprehensive History* (Calcutta: Kalyani Devi), pp. 122–200.

27. *Ibid.*, p. 199. "Gora" (= golden) is also a sobriquet of Chaitanya. Fault of karma could also mean just simply "fault." Edward C. Dimock (1989). *The Place of the Hidden Moon: Erotic Mysticism in the Vaisnava-Sahajiya Cult of Bengal* (Chicago: University of Chicago Press) 2nd ed. is deservedly the text most consulted internationally. I have mostly consulted "Hindu" scholarship for the problem of negotiating the *dvaita* structure of feeling–thinking for uneven scholarly recoding, always negotiating with that unreliable autobiographical element, that "structure of feeling," which spells responsibility.

28. I say "emphasis" rather than "shift" because most of the members of the museum-going group also participate in an academic–institutional acculturation since childhood; which comes to the fore in the United States.

29. Georg Wilhelm Friedrich Hegel (1975). *Aesthetics: Lectures on Fine Arts.* Translated by T. M. Knox (Oxford: Clarendon Press), vol. 1, p. 340.

30. For the distinction between "story" and "fabula," see Mieke Bal (1985). *Narratology: Introduction to the Theory of Narrative.* Translated by Christine van Boheemen (Toronto: University Of Toronto Press), p. 5.

31. Bhattacharji, *Theogony*, p. 158.

32. Virginia Woolf (1929). *A Room of One's Own* (New York: Harcourt), pp. 4–5.

33. Sukumari Bhattacharji (1996). *Legends of Devi* (Calcutta: Orient Longmans), pp. 46–47.

34. *Kālikāpurāna* 17.16, in B. N. Shastri (ed.), *The Kālikāpurāna* (Delhi: Nag Publishers, 1991), Pt. I, p. 179.

35. *Devibhāgavatapurāna* 7.30.37, in Panchanan Tarkaratna (ed.), *Devibhāgavatam* (Calcutta: Nabobharat, 1981), p. 696.

36. *Devi* 7.30.45–46 (p. 696); *Kālikā* 18.41–43 (p. 194).

37. There is a large body of female-authored collective oral tradition and some written work that remains peripheral to the authoritative voice of these Puranas. Navaneeta Dev Sen has written two ethereal texts around this fact for the reader of Bengali. (*Sita Theke Shuru*, [Calcutta: Ananda Publishers, 1996], pp. 13–78; and *Bama-Bodhini* [Calcutta: Deb Sahitya Kutir, 1997]).

38. *Devi* 7.30.85 (p. 698).

39. For "poetic function," see Roman Jakobson (1960). "Closing statement: Linguistics and poetics," in Thomas A. Sebeok (ed.), *Style in Language* (Cambridge: MIT Press), p. 358.

40. For "archaic," see Williams, *Marxism*, p. 122.

41. For a stateside account of this "passing off," see Matthew *et al.*, "*Vasudhaiva.*"

42. The list is available in Thomas B. Coburn's good translation, *Encountering the Goddess: A Translation of the Devi-Māhātmya and a Study of its Interpretation* (Albany: SUNY Press, 1991), pp. 53–54.

43. Alexander Garcia Düttmann (Fall/Winter 1994). "On translatability." *qui parle*, 8.i, 36.
44. Sigmund Freud, "The uncanny." *Standard Edition*, 17, 244–245.
45. On "focalization," see Bal, *Narratology*, pp. 100–114, and Shlomith Rimmon-Kenan (1983). *Narrative Fiction: Contemporary Poetics* (New York: Routledge), pp. 71–85.
46. Subroto Kumar Mukhopadhyay (1994). *Cult of Goddess Sitala in Bengal* (Calcutta: KLM), p. 50.
47. Jacques Derrida (1997). *Politics of Friendship.* Translated by George Collins (New York: Verso), p. 69; translation modified. It is not a good idea to describe a phenomenon as an unmediated example of deconstructive discourse. But this old settler colony—India—requires from me a bolder and more "mistaken" descriptive gesture than the more visibly violent examples of Australia or South Africa.
48. Shambhunath Gangopadhyay (1994). *Madhyayuger Dharmabhavana o Bangla Sahitya* (Calcutta: Sanskrita Pustak), p. 27; translation mine. I have tried to keep to the sense of *tal* in "error" as mistake and wandering. I have also tried to keep to the polysemous relationship between teacher and student—whether the teacher can only speak to students who are deaf, whether when the teacher says this the student is deaf, and the like.
49. Prankrishna Pal and Bijoykumar Pal, eds. (n.d.). *Meyeder Brotokatha* (Calcutta: Annapurna Library).
50. Jacques Lacan (1992). "The splendor of Antigone," in Dennis Potter (trans.), *The Ethics of Psychoanalysis* (New York: Norton), pp. 243–283.
51. Sanat Kumar Mitra (1981). *Folk Life and Lore in Bengal* (Calcutta: G.A.E. Publisher), p. 9.
52. Brown, *Triumph*, p. ix.
53. I have put together two popular reference sources here. One is of course the dictionary. The other is Bimla Churn Law (1976). *Historical Geography of Ancient India* (Delhi: Ess Ess Publications).
54. Bhattacharji, *Theogony*, p. 159.
55. Freud, *Standard Edition*, vol. 21, pp. 152–157.
56. Both the earlier Sudhir Kakar and the earlier V. S. Naipaul, coming from quite different politics but applying a "real" Freudian standard, had concluded that Indian men do not pass Narcissus (Sudhir Kakar [1981]. *The Inner World: A Psycho-analytic Study of Childhood and Society in India* [New York: Oxford University Press], esp. pp. 154–211; and V. S. Naipaul [1978] *India: A Wounded Civilization* [New York: Vintage Books]).
57. Lacan's geometrics of the gaze pre-comprehend the Oedipus and cannot be significantly helpful here.
58. Gayatri Chakravorty Spivak, *Kali Calling* (text accompanying Nirode Mazumdar retrospective; Calcutta: Seagull, forthcoming).
59. N. N. Bhattacharya (1982). *History of the Tantric Religion* (New Delhi: Manohar), p. 283.
60. Not all *tantra* is *vāmāchāri* or sex-practicing *tantra*. See Swami Lokeswarananda, ed. (1989). *Studies on the Tantras* (Calcutta: Ramakrishna Mission Inst. of Culture). Nirode Mazumdar's use of the *yantra* points toward *vamachar*.
61. Ibid., p. 333.
62. Ibid., p. 370.
63. In *Devoted to the Goddess: The Life and Work of Ramprasad* (Albany: SUNY Press, 1998), Malcolm McLean confuses the limning of desire and the use of metaphorology with the author's practice. It is like calling someone a psychoanalyst because s/he uses psychoanalytic imagery with conviction. In my estimation Ramproshad's use of the available topos of the rhetorical question is somewhat overemphasized by McLean as genuine characterological astonishment at the contradictory "personality" of Kali.
64. Surendramohan Bhattacharya (n. d.). *Brihat Adi o Asal Bagalamukhi Tantram* (Calcutta: Benimadhab Seal's Library), p. 81.
65. B. Bhattacharya (1988). *The World of Tantra* (New Delhi: Munshiram Manoharlal), pp. 357–370.
66. Parita Mukta gives a fine account of these practices in *Upholding*, pp. 41–42.

67. The possibility of this resistance is already inscribed in the socius. The opening lines of the second chapter of *Manusmriti* (the laws of Manu) are one famous engagement of it: "[now] understand intrinsically [*nibādhata*] the constant [*nitya*] sustaining principles or code [*dharma*], assent to which is [already] a knowing-tendency of the heart [*hridayena abhi-anu-jn ta*]. Although it is not commendable to be predicated by desire alone [*kāmātma*], there is no such thing as being desireless. To accede to (knowledgeability or) the *vedas* and to act (knowledgeably, or) according to the *vedas* [I put the alternative there because Manusmriti invariably inserts that heart-tendency clause] is desirable [*kāmya*]" (Panchanan Tarkaratna, ed. [1993]. *Manusamhit* [Calcutta: Samskrita Pustaka Bhandar], p. 19; translation mine). Commentators have worried about the heart-tendency clause, which would seemingly make the distinction between the proper name *Veda* (the ancient texts of knowledge) and the simple verb form "know(s)" as in the *Brāhmanas* (*ya evam veda* = "who knows thus") (Monier Monier-Williams [1993]. *A Sanskrit–English Dictionary* [Delhi: Motilal Banarsidass], p. 963) or *ved hametat* = "I know this." Perhaps *Manusmriti* attempts what all lawgivers do: To equate desire with law. The commentators close this off. Kullukabhatta (fl. mid-fourteenth century), arguably the best-known commentator on the laws, glosses the invagination of desire (access to vedas contained in human desire) by breaking it into a binary opposition: *srutisca dvibidha—vaidiki* tāntriki ca (*Manusmriti*, p. 19). Heard or orally transmitted wisdom (the most sacred kind) are of two kinds (as in dispositions)—*vedic* and *tāntric*. Since *sruti* could literally also take the meaning of hearing or rumor, there is the possibility that Kulluka, using Sanskrit as an active language, is also making a distinction between sacred knowledge (*veda*) and profane oral dissemination (*tantra*). It is only by reversing this already available distinction and then displacing it that *tantra* in the narrow sense discloses the possibility of resistance and begins to efface it by institutionalizing it, at one go. And the instrument of effacement is the relative autonomy of the baseline institution: Gendering. The Devi is caught in it. Michel Foucault lays out the possibility of describing this sort of thing in *History of Sexuality*. Translated by Robert Hurley (New York: Vintage Books, 1980), vol. 1, pp. 94–97. There is no guarantee, of course, that that is how it "really happens."

68. Jacques Derrida represents comparable (though not identical) masculine contortion effects on his own part in order to accede to his dying mother, in "Circumfessions," in Geoffrey Bennington (1993). *Jacques Derrida* (Chicago: University of Chicago Press). In the more "vedic" mode it is also Derrida who warns us that if we set a practical course on intractable "new philosophies," we risk falling into the opposite of the new. Yet one cannot quite ignore the call to *sapere aude* (dare to know). This see-saw is, I believe, the dynamic of Derrida, *Politics*, pp. 75–77.

69. Mukundaram Chakrabarti (1986). *Chandimangal*. Edited by Sukumar Sen (Calcutta: Sahitya Akademi).

70. Williams, *Marxism*, p. 127.

71. Ibid., pp. 195–196. For a fuller list, see Somnath Mukhopadhyay (1984). *Candi in Art and Iconography* (Delhi: Agam Kala), pp. 102–104.

72. See Sanjay Subrahmanyam, ed. (1994). *Money & the Market in India 1100–1700* (Delhi: Oxford University Press), for a sense of the turbulence of the scene.

73. K. N. Chaudhuri (1990). *Asia before Europe: Economy and Civilisation of the Indian Ocean from the Rise of Islam to 1750* (New York: Cambridge University Press).

74. Satyendranath Datta (n. d.). "Amra," in *Kabbo-Sanchayan* (Calcutta: M.C.Sarkar & Sons), p. 32.

75. Roland Barthes (1977). "The structural analysis of narrative," in Stephen Heath (ed.), *Image/Music/Text* (New York: Hill & Wang), p. 104.

76. Or indeed the parabolic impulse of the 10 principal Upanisads, an altogether separate stream in the service of the *advaita* as such. Romila Thapar has connected this to the movement in India from lineage to state.

77. PIO (Person of Indian Origin) is a category devised by the new budget of the government of India for granting visa privileges.

78. See Sen, "Introduction," *Chandimangal*, pp. 20–24.

79. See Sen, "Introduction," *Chandimangal*. For the immediately contemporary situation vis-à-vis the global "rural," see George Monbiot June 4, 1998). "The African gene," *The Guardian* (London), 22; and Bob Herbert (June 7, 1998). "At what cost?," *New York Times*.

80. The phrase "willing suspension of disbelief" is from one of the great texts of English literary criticism, which generations of disciplinary students of English are invited to internalize (Samuel Taylor Coleridge [1960]. *Biographia Literaria* [New York: Dutton], pp. 168–169).

81. Jacques Derrida (1992). " 'This strange institution called literature'," in Derek Attridge (ed.), *Acts of Literature* (New York: Routledge), p. 49.

82. Immanuel Kant (1951). *Critique of Judgment*. Translated by J. H. Bernard (New York: Collier), p. 55.

83. Wordsworth does speak of producing good cultural *habits* in *Lyrical Ballads and Other Poems*. Edited by James Butler and Karen Green (Ithaca: Cornell University Press, 1992), p. 745.

84. One of the women interviewed is not conventionally "decrepit." I hope to comment on her extraordinary remarks about her chosen life in a more appropriate context.

85. I am thinking also of Sivani Chakravorty (1913–2003) who, a month before her death, in a shaking hand, cites in her journal a poem of Radha addressing Death as the image of her dark lover. What is it to cite in extremis? That, I have argued, is the essence of *bhakti*, divided-toward-the-other. Ms. Chakravorty, institutionally educated in Bengali literature, quotes a modern version of the subaltern song by Rabindranath Tagore; and she keeps her distance: "For me now it is as if dear Death you're like my Shyam." I have argued elsewhere that her generation of women was the implied reader of a significant section of Tagore's fiction and poetry ("Burden of English," in Carol Breckenridge and Peter van der Veer [eds]. *Orientalism and the Postcolonial Predicament: Perspectives on South Asia* [Philadelphia: University of Pennsylvania Press, 1993], pp. 137–138).

86. I have not been able to grasp the simple poetry of the Bengali where the abstract nouns are implied rather than stated.

CHAPTER TEN

Ourselves as Another: Cosmopolitical Humanities

PETER PERICLES TRIFONAS

Now, more than ever, there is an obligation to recognize the presence of the infinite possibilities and multiple horizons of alterity, which destabilize the grounding of subjectivity and our knowledge about what it means to be human. This responsibility highlights the problem of exposing or creating locations for otherness within communitarian-based institutions such as the university, which still occupy the colonized space of traditional knowledge archives and are at the same time alterior to the logic of the status quo simply by producing new forms of knowledge and blazing trails of discovery that change the disciplines.[1] If so, how and where are gestures toward the spaces of these new locations enacted within the human sciences by which we define the difference of ourselves as another?

The inside and outside borders of any cultural spaces we define according to the age old concepts of community and humanity open up the material locations within which theory and praxis are renewed. The syncretic nature of subjectivity is symptomatic of the impossibility of pinning down the essence of being and the gist of what it means to be human. *On the one hand* the demise of the autotelic subject—a subject defined *in, of,* and *by* itself—is fueled by a global vision of a shared community running rampant today. *On the other hand* the idea of global citizenship as the seat of human hybridity nurtures the impetus toward a communal proclivity of the autotelic Subject as a shared identity, and produces the call for a leveling of difference, quite ironically, through what Jacques Derrida has called the cosmopolitical point of view. The world vision of a new humanity privileges both particularity and therefore uniqueness while at the same time creating the conditions for essentialism and the universalization of difference, which effaces differences in a mass sharing of an amorphous "global culture." The productive effect of alterity marks itself on subjectivity as a reflectivity characterized by alienation and growth in relation to the articulation of differences across the signs of culture, language, and the archives of knowledge manipulated and guarded by communications technologies. But the rapid proliferation of new systems, *technes*, and means of representation have hastened the call for a new humanities that is cosmopolitically friendly, whereby communities of difference are conjoined in new affiliations that render their uniqueness in the difference of themselves as a common feature of a world picture molded by the forces of globalization. Otherness is present yes, but with a debt and duty to the historicity of what has gone before. The concept of the cosmopolitical defines human heterogeneity and similarity via the necessity of marking the interior and exterior limits of culture through language and the rise of other technologies of representation, which seek to transfix the world picture of the socioeconomic and ethico-political future of global citizens. The logic of the cosmopolitical within the notion of a global subjectivity broaches the question of human rights and education. It asks us to rethink the certainty of knowledge as a philosophical project of genealogical excavation in relation to social justice and educational equity. The ethical problem of who *can, should be*, or *is* capable of determining the propriety of the formal location of inquiry regarding the "human sciences" characterizing the Humanities and Cultural Studies—the space and place of the cultural–institutional indexicality marking the public paths of difference, its entrances and exits—is a flash point of conflict. Pedagogical institutions put in motion the academic machinery of the cultural reproduction of knowledge and are always already implicated in the perennial question of democracy and discipline, of knowledge, difference, otherness, social justice, and the right to education for each and every subject and citizen.

In "The future of the profession or the unconditional university," Jacques Derrida engages in a moment of questioning regarding the nature of academic community and its "profession of faith" to knowledge within the university. It invokes the urgency of the need to recognize new tasks for the humanities after the cosmopolitical orientations of globalization, which directly address the academic responsibility of educational institutions and, by extension, those who teach, work, and live *in* and, perhaps, *for* them, as the teaching body *(le corps eneignant),*[2] to value difference. What does this mean exactly to the future of the "professor" of knowledge? To say that a pedagogical institution, and those who are a part of it, are it, possess total and unabiding and hence *irresponsible and unaccountable* control of the intellectual domain they survey is to surmise a legacy of exclusion. There is no space left to welcome other possibilities and conditions of knowledge, *impossible conditions.* It becomes a question of unconditional affinity and openness toward embracing the difference of the Other without giving way to hesitance or reservation, empirical qualification and moral judgment, let alone indignation.

The question of a "proper domain" of the question of rights, of institutions, of community and difference, of humanity and what is proper to the study of humanity—of propriety and domination, appropriation, expropriation, of property, participation, ownership and fairness, and therefore of law, ethics, and, ultimately, of social justice—brings us back to the connections between culture and knowledge within the university. It extends the problem of democracy and *democraticity,* governance and governmentality, of the responsibilities and principles relating to the formation and formativity of a system of public education on an international scale. Derrida alludes to this unconditional responsibility toward otherness via the cosmpolitical as "mondialization" or "worldwide-ization" within the disciplines of the Humanities rooted in the enigmas of subjective experience that inflect knowledge. It is a matter of locating the axiomatic difference of these terms, the difference of their axiomaticity, and their inter-relatability, within a hospitable space and place that only an open concept of community and education can entreat them to because there is difference. The university and its academic community must welcome the production of different knowledges and efface the traditional boundaries of research, which build walls around the disciplines. The concept excavation that deconstruction enables, essentially exposes a genealogy of difference within formations of thought constructed as logical and rational. It eventually leads to a productive recognition of alterity, which breaks down what is thought to be common sense without self-interest; that is, deconstruction enables an ethical expansion of thought and thinking without limitations or borders, or conditional limits within knowledge protected by the ideological beacon of the discourse of "enlightened thinking." Academic responsibility within the "unconditional university" would safeguard freedom of thought: "The principle right to say everything, whether it be under the heading of fiction and the experimentation of knowledge, and the right to say it publicly."

The principle of reason "as principle of grounding, foundation or institution"[3] has tended to guide the science of research toward techno-practical ends within the university.[4] It has put conditions on inquiry that have limited the possibilities for knowledge creation. From this epistemic superintendence of the terms of knowledge and inquiry, there has arisen the traditional notion of academic responsibility, which is tied to the pursuit of truth via a conception of science based on the teleological orientation of intellectual labor toward the production of tangible outcomes achieved according to a method of procedural objectivity.[5]

For Jacques Derrida this is not an insignificant historicity because its effects determine the nature of the epistemic subjectivity of the researcher. The ethics and politics of research—and the role "the ['modern'] university may play"[6] in helping to construct the dimensions of a scholastic arena for paideai impelled toward the quest for the pragmatic application of results, or the "pay off" (p. 12) of pre-directed outcomes of inquiry—is fed more and more by competing interests situated outside of the rationale of the institution itself. Most certainly, academic work "programmed, focused, organized" (p. 11) solely on the future expectation of its profitable utilization does not and cannot take into account the democratic ideals protecting the welfare of the nation-state, especially when the quest for knowledge becomes driven by particularized and exclusionary agendas arbitrarily guiding the course of inquiry for political or economic reasons. A myopic orientation to research as an instrumental process of usable outcomes limits intellectual freedom and responsibility because it is, Derrida has contended, "centered instead on [the desires of] multinational military–industrial complexes of techno-economic networks, or rather international technomilitary networks that are apparently multi-or trans-national in form"(p. 11).[7] Indeed such regulatory forces wielding the power of "in-vest-ment"—not necessarily monetary—are always wanting to control the mechanisms of creative production to commodify knowledge so as to make it a useful product of preordained and preconceived epistemological directives and scientific outcomes not necessarily for the sake of science, truth, or knowledge. These "external" influences affecting and reflecting the purposes of the university are to be found more and more in not so obvious, but covertly strategic, areas within the architectonical confines of the traditional institutional structure. This is possible thanks to the "channel of private foundations"(p. 14) that have penetrated the sphere of the modern research university and are therefore indispensable to the logic of its goals and operation. In fact the direction and scope of research within and throughout the university institution are guided by the irresistible lure of funding and other personal and professional incentives arising thereof (e.g., power, status, career advancement, etc.).

And yet to intimate, as I have, that the "pragmatic" (utilitarian) interests of an "applied science" are in opposition to the relative disinterestedness of "fundamental" (basic) inquiry is to create a binary distinction. A qualitative and evaluative division of research along these lines is, without a doubt, problematic. The ethics of its logic is something that can and should consistently be worked against as deconstruction has shown. Derrida reminds us however, that such a metaphysical conceit separating theory and practice is of "real but limited relevance"(p. 12): Given that the deferred dividends of the "detours, delays and relays of 'orientation,' its more random aspects"(p. 12), are either incalculable or go unrecognized until a suitable situation of the advantageous use of research presents itself. The use-value of research cannot be an unimportant consideration because the ethics of science and its endeavors quickly occupies the foreground of analysis as the purpose of knowledge discovery comes into question. For Derrida it is naive to believe there are some "basic disciplines ['philosophy,' 'theoretical physics,' and 'pure mathematics' are the examples he gives] shielded from power, inaccessible to programming by the pressures of the State or, under cover of the State, by civil society or capital interests"(p. 12). That thought has now been unthinkable for some time, especially since the monstrous dawning of the "post-critical" age of nuclear politics and in the wake of the informatizing function of science as research "[a]t the service of war"(p. 13). In this sense what has been at stake with respect to the purpose of research in all of its manifestations as a mode of conquering the symbiotic field of the human and nonhuman Other, concerns the "control" of knowledge and the industry or commodification of its results as intellectual by-products to be used by the State apparatus. This desire to command the path and ethics of science has and will pivot around the "higher priority" issue of protecting "national and international security"(p. 13) interests, however heterogeneous the calculation of a plan of insurance or the lack of it is to the logic of "peace" or "democracy."

The differentiation of the aims of research is not that discreet an indicator of its "use-value" so as to clearly distinguish between the profitability of application and the destructive effects of misappropriation, despite the usual factoring-in of "reasonable" margins of error. Derrida comments,

Research programs have to [in the sense of, *are made to*] encompass the entire field of information, the stockpiling of knowledge, the workings and thus also the essence of language and of all semiotic systems, translation, coding and decoding, the play of presence and absence, hermeneutics, semantics, structural and generative linguistics, pragmatics, rhetoric. I am accumulating all these disciplines in a haphazard way, on purpose, but I shall end with literature, poetry, the arts, fiction in general: The theory that has all these discipline as its object may be just as useful in ideological warfare as it is in experimentation with variables in all-too-familiar perversions of the referential function. Such a theory may always be put to work in communications strategy, the theory of commands, the most refined military pragmatics of jussive utterances (by what token, for example, will it be clear that an utterance is to be taken as a command in the new technology of telecommunications? How are the new resources of simulation and simulacrum to be controlled? Furthermore, when certain random consequences of research are taken into account, it is always possible to have in view some eventual benefit that may ensue from an apparently useless research project (in philosophy or the humanities, for example). The history of the sciences encourages researchers to integrate that margin of randomness into their centralized calculation. They then proceed to adjust the means at their disposal, the available financial support, and the distribution of credits. A State power or forces that it represents no longer need to prohibit research or to censor discourse, especially in the West. It is enough that they can limit the means, can regulate support for production, transmission, diffusion (p. 13).

Within the "concept of information or informatization" (p. 14), the ethics and the politics of research take shape essentially as the conservative ideal of "Science" the university itself stands on is overtaken. The transformation of research goals and purposes consumes the institution because the autonomy of its own self-regulating measures of knowledge advancement is sacrificed to the real-world pressures of simply securing a sustainable future for itself as an economically and politically viable institution of culture. And that is understandable, although it may not be ethically defensible or acceptable. Not even to those unquestioning defenders of the dominant (or onto-teleological) interpretation of the principle of reason and science the university is grounded on: Essentially by its logic of "integrat[ing] the basic to the oriented, the purely rational to the technical, thus bearing witness to that original intermingling of the metaphysical and the technical"(p. 14) within the disciplinary corpus of the institution.

The academic responsibility Derrida has wished to "awaken or resituate" (p. 14) is "in the university or before *(devant)* the university, whether one belongs to it or not" (p. 14). *Its double gesture bridges the ungrounded space of the conditions of possibility over which positions on ethics and responsibility, reason and rationality are thought-out and taken.* The difficulty of this "new academic responsibility" is elaborated, according to Derrida, by actively opposing the "prohibiting limitations" (p. 13) that "presses, [public and private] foundations, mass media" (p. 13) and other "interest groups" place on the act of research within the institution: "The unacceptability of a discourse, the non-certification of a research project, the illegitimacy of a course offering are declared by evaluative actions: Studying such evaluations is, it seems to me [he emphasizes], one of the tasks most indispensable to the exercize of academic responsibility, most urgent for the maintenance of its dignity" (p. 13). To intervene decisively in the business of the university is to appeal (to) reason, to ask for the concession of reasons out of which to judge judgments made in the name of truth, and the imperative for gaining knowledge and teaching it as such.

The medium in question, which relates the obligation and responsibility of ethics to politics and the practices of the institution, is language and two ways of thinking about the *value of language.* Derrida defines these complementary modes of thought in relation to the principle of reason as "instrumental" (informative) and "poietic" (creative), essentially by associating their contrasting methods of semiological effect (e.g., representation/undecidability) with research-type, which is end-oriented and fundamental. On the basis of the difference of values of finitude, which must not proceed from knowledge but always head toward the possibility of its reinvention, is grounded the deconstructive attempt to define a new academic responsibility "in the face of the university's total subjection to the technologies of informatization" (p. 14). The cross-contamination between the instrumental and the *poietic* aims of research science is obvious "at the outer limits of the authority and power of the principle of reason" (p. 14), where the specificity of goals or purposes is blurred by the shared logic of *praxis.* Derrida situates this antinomic responsibility—of "the experience and experiment of the *aporia*,"[8] more or less—within the general domain a hypothetical "community of thought,"[9] a community that is committed to the "sounding [of] a call to practice it."[10] The *"group-at-large"* referred to is not one "of research, of science, of philosophy, since these values [of 'professionalism' and 'disciplinarity' no matter how 'radical'] are most often subjected to the unquestioned authority of the principle of reason"[11] and can be absorbed into the homogeneous magma of intra-institutional discourse (e.g., the standardization of Marxism and psychoanalysis). Derrida has named this loosely gathered consortium a "community of the question"[12] after the death of philosophy, a chance for safekeeping the possibility of the question of the *violence of metaphysics,* onto-theo-logical and proto-ethical. How would it function? Derrida explains as follows:

> Such a community would interrogate the essence of reason and of the principle of reason, the values of the basic, of the principial, of radicality, of the *arkhe* in general, and it would attempt to draw out all the possible consequences of this questioning. It is not certain that such a thinking can bring together a community or found an institution in the traditional sense of these words. What is meant by community and institution must be rethought. This thinking must also unmask—an infinite task—all the ruses of end-orienting reason, the paths by which apparently disinterested research can find itself indirectly reappropriated, reinvested by programs of all sorts. That does not mean that "orientation" is bad in itself and that it must be combatted, far from it. Rather, I am defining the necessity for a new way of educating students that will prepare them to undertake new analyses in order to evaluate these ends and choose, when possible, among them all.[13]

For Derrida, the ordeal of decision is an instant of madness regarding action; it "always risks the worst,"[14] especially, as concerns us here, in relation to the ethics of research and the grounding of the preconditions of the violence of an existing foundation like the idea of the university's reason for being an institution for scientific innovation and cultural reproduction:

> It is not a matter simply of questions that one *formulates* while submitting oneself, as I am doing here [in the discourse], to the principle of reason, but also of preparing oneself thereby to transform the modes of writing, approaches to pedagogy, the procedures of academic exchange, the relation to languages, to other disciplines, to the institution in general, to its inside and its outside. Those who venture forth along this path, it seems to me, need not set themselves up in opposition to the principle of reason, nor give way to "irrationalism." They may continue to assume *within* the university, along with its memory and tradition, the imperative of professional rigour and competence.[15]

The meta-logic of deconstruction defines the site of the struggle for a new academic responsibility. The double-sided responsibility of its "to" and "for" peripatetic aims at a *Verwindung* of the principle of reason, which would rearticulate the ethics of science and/as research within the university. After the affirmative ethics of deconstruction this means a "going-beyond that is both an acceptance and a deepening"[16] of reflection on the concepts of ethics, science, and responsibility as Gianni Vattimo has argued, not to get over, overcome, or to distort the principle of these concepts by outbidding them into submission, but to resign the compliance of thought to a rethinking of them.[17] And thus to effectuate a change in the thinking of the being of the University and the academic responsibility of our roles in it as researchers, teachers, and intellectuals. To avoid reproducing the classical architectonic of the Kantian institution, thereby entrenching its effects still further, Derrida asserts that " 'Thought' requires *both* the principle of reason *and* what is beyond the principle of reason, the *arkhè* and an-archy."[18] With this I agree. The creation of a chance for the future occurs by keeping the memory of the past alive. There must be an archive, a body of knowledge, to work from, for, and against. It is at the interspaces of old and new knowledge constructions beyond the grasp of "meaning" or "reason" that risks are taken to move beyond what we already know by endeavoring to put the systematicity of what may appear to be grounded or static into motion, play, *kinesis*. The institutional meeting place of a deconstructive ethics and politics would engage the undecidability of interpretative links where a new academic responsibility could be forged between those faculties speaking a constative (theoretical) language of a Kantian type and others who make performative (interventive) statements of an Austinian type. Like a bridge across an abyss of reason.

For Derrida the heterogeneous scope of this impossible territory after the reason of "Enlightenment—*Aufklärung, Lumières, Illuminisimo*" is where the struggle over difference and human rights has to take place after Immanuel Kant. It "risks" reenvisioning the Humanities after the cosmopolitical condition: A hypothetical situation of geo-global interconnectivity or mondialization having an "inter-national or inter-state dimension"[19] and related to the question of the *emanation* and diaspora of the *polis* and *politeia as a way of life*. The idea of the cosmopolitical solidifies the problem of a universal history or "the link among the cities, the *poleis* of the world, as nations, as people, or as States."[20] However we cannot in good conscience subscribe to the constellations of a panoptic vision of an "abstract universalism,"[21] which strangles difference in the name of a general culture of homogeneous communities, permanent archives, and exclusionary institutions. Kant postulated the cosmopolitical as an organic global synthesis of cultures and subjects upon which a template for writing the blueprint of any and all institutions *to come* can be. In many ways the vision still guides us and the pedagogical imperatives of today's educational and social institutions. Interrogating the modality of this desire for sameness demands a rethinking of the future of thinking and works toward illuminating and transforming rather than dismissing or deriding the historicity of "philosophical acts and archives."[22] Questioning the ground of institutions and the reason of their institutionality with respect to the formation of subjectivity, engages the real-world effects produced by the performative force of epistemological discourses and their responsibility as instances of founding and therefore of foundation, which forces us to rethink the nature of what it means to be sovereign, to have rights, to be human. The notion of the cosmopolitical humanities arises from an anti-utopian thrust, contrary to the ideal of a natural universalism of thought and action uniting thinking and subjectivity in the image of the global citizen. It enables us to link the problem of human rights and difference with the Derridean conception of the Kantian cosmopolitical point of view in a positive rather than a negative way via the notion of mondialization. We must remember that knowledge and knowing are articulated by the continual reaggregation of the logic of the letter, the terms of its reading as production and reproduction, and the domain of its archive. The problem of how to go about securing both private and public "access to this language and culture, first and foremost by means of education,"[23] involves, more or less, the working-out of the problems of subjectivity, community, and difference central to answering the question of academic privilege (who has the right to knowledge?) and the power of location (how? and why?).

The pedagogical onus on an affable (simple, crude, vulgar) modality of cultural production and reproduction without the complexity of resistance or complications of difference fixes the parameters of an institutional ethic of response and responsibility on the conditional boundaries of knowledge, and limits the horizons of new forms of thinking and research. But this reduction of the frame of reference to categorical imperatives, which willfully ignore the limitations and boundaries of a project of repeating the historicity of Western education, occurs only if and when the cosmopolitical nature of difference as a source for new professions of faith is not taken into account. It would be wrong to ignore the diversity within the composition of what we call knowledges and to cull a universal thinking without a diversity of knowledge. The emanation of the cosmopolitical view is a gathering of multiplicity in knowledge communities that articulates the ethical terms of a responsibility to acknowledge the profundity of differences within the same archive of knowledge and thinking, the unimaginable manifestation of many it parts and partners, nations, states, and peoples whose materiality comprises and cannot but exceed the conceptual totality of its essence. These aspects are not unrelated insofar as such ethico-qualitative judgments require an identification of who would have the privilege and opportunity of participation regarding curricular decisions about the future of the right to education, and why. The global diaspora of subjectivity is the open ground of a *democracy-to-come*, with a *pedagogy-to-come*, and the potentially diverging paths of its filiations, friendships, what is held close, in affinity, to the spirit and the heart, not the mind.

Kant's ethical universalism, and its Eurocentric bias, can be used in a novel way by turning it toward the question of human rights, community, and difference to mobilize the cosmopolitical as a viewpoint *not only* for reconceptualizing the "eternal becoming"[24] of being-in-the-world, *but as a new approach to realizing the impossible futures of a "progressive institutionality" to come and the unforeseeability of its educational methods and apparatus.* This does not simply mean a securing of the opportunity for freedom in thinking and teaching; neither does it defer pedagogically, nor ethically, to the teaching of thinking without reference to the tradition of Western episteme, however, it may be defined in curricular terms. The notion of the cosmopolitical reawakens and resituates the Eurocentrism of the concept and its implications for reinscribing the "horizon of a new community"[25] of the question and the impossibility of the question that teaches the Other to question the sources of the Self and the Other through meditations on difference. This may sound strange to those who envision and portray deconstruction as a *destruction* of Western metaphysics, its institutions, and its teachings. All Western ideas about education *predict* a trajectory of thinking along a "teleological axis"[26] with respect to the epistemologico-cultural ideal of the "infinite progress" of Being, and the temporal procession of beings toward perfectability, achievable or not. Anything else "would be nothing but a novel"[27] given the inseparability of the European epistemological tradition from the notion of the universal, "a plan of nature that aims at the total, perfect political unification of the human species *(die vollkommen bürgerliche Vereinigung in der Menschengattung)."*[28] Any social or cultural institution is founded on memory and the material conditions of its working out as a dynamic tradition of theory and practice, philosophy and action. Communities are predicated *on taking memory and it differences into account*: Accounting for the causality of its effects, its bias, its exclusions, rendering an account of what makes memory, disrupts it, constructs its limits, openings, how and why it favors. It mobilizes a thoroughly Western conceit and philosophical project directed toward the pragmatic rectification of Being as presence and the sending of itself forward in time toward the infinity of progressive becoming.

We have to accept the reality of the forces of globality and cosmopolitanism and yet safeguard the right to difference within thinking. A critique—coming down on one side or the other—of efficacy is not at all useful, but a misleading endeavor seeking an ethical refuge in the evaluative power of a binary form of metaphysical reasoning pitting "the good" against "the bad," "essentialism" against "antiessentialism," "Eurocentrism" against "anti-Eurocentrism," and so on. The end work of such a critical task, which freely places blame or adjudicates value for the sake of a castigation or rejection of worth, is performed too quickly and easily. Its decisions are rendered by an appeal to the dictates of a universalist conception of reason and its demotic (and not at all democratic) corollary of "common sense" to construct the ideologico-conceptual grounds of what is "good" and what is "bad." The judgmental edifice of its EITHER/OR rationale presumes a lack of interpretative complexity, a plainness of truth, which is totally transparent and obvious to everyone, a clear-cut and unarguable judgment made with no fathomable case to be made for the possibility of opposition or exemption to the rule of law. One life-world. One reality. One Truth. The metaphysical value of this ethic of perception and its monological model of representation determines the non-oppositional grounds of truth. Conditional and definitive limits thereby demarcate the freedom of what it is possible to know and to think and what it is possible to say without offending the much guarded sensibilities of reason and "good taste"—however their values might be constructed and articulated—as the ideals of commonly held responses to cultural institutions and practices. Difference is abdicated in favor of a community of shared interpretative responsibility and the unethical hegemony of its "majority rules" attitude, which bids one to erect barriers against diversity, "to see and talk about things only as they are or could be." The priority of clarity as an ethical prerequisite of a "responsible response" is, without a doubt, everything when the analytical imperative is NOTHING BUT an exercise of choosing sides. There is a more productive approach.

The ethical impetus of the "postcolonial," "anticolonial," or even the "neocolonial" moment as it is called by Gayatri Chakravorty Spivak begins with a philosophical nod to what is, for Derrida, the performative legacy of the institutions and models of "Greco-European memory."[29] Addressing the textual composition of this epistemic and cultural genealogy of Western knowledge, Kant's discourse on the cosmopolitical is only one example of a host of writings by philosophers who possess the temerity to have made such audacious and largely accurate statements about the dominance of "the guiding thread *(Leitfaden)* of Greek history *(griechische Geschichte)*"[30] with respect to explaining the unfolding of the Reason of Being within communities across space and over time. The axiomaticity of this logic directed at excluding an "Other" from the fundamental (pure) archive of its heritage would only be natural from a philosophical perspective of human historicity, which narcotizes the productive value of difference and thus denies the validity of allowing for the possibility of a heterogeneous opening to a world community from a cosmopolitical point of view. As Derrida says, "One encounters [its Eurocentric axiology] again and again, intact and invariable throughout variations as serious as those that distinguish Hegel, Husserl, Heidegger, and Valéry."[31] But of course there is a difference in what Kant proposes by way of a vision of the world from a cosmopolitical point of view and its universal enactment in the form of a "Society of Nations" despite the emphasis he places upon Greek philosophy and history, because it attempts to *sublate*, to synthesize, and, at the same time, keep the tensions of the values of cultural difference in an amicable and moral unification of humanity worked out, more or less, along with the trajectory of the "teleological axis of this discourse [that] has become the tradition of European modernity."[32] The concept of nature, and specifically the "unsociability *(Ungeselligkeit, Unvertragsamkeit)*"[33] of human being *by nature*, is actually the means to a salvation "through culture, art and artifice *(Kunst)*, and reason, to make the seeds of nature grow."[34] And Kant truly believes in the potentially unifying power of this "natural or originary state of war among men"[35] (in Kant's time there could literally only be a state of war *among men*). Because of the propensity of subjective (cultural) differences to force antagonisms, territoriality, and conflict, there is only one possible solution that "resembles a novel-like story yet isn't one, that which in truth is but the very historicity of history, is the ruse of nature."[36] And here we may be amazed (or not) by the implications of the Kantian vision.

For Kant violence—and its threat to the security of human *Dasein*—is the catalyst that allows nature "to aid reason and thereby put philosophy into operation through the society of nations"[37] we forge under the auspices of global security and nations united. This is a troubling thesis, holding together the logic of the cosmopolitical community of global proportions around the concept of alterity as productive tension. On the one hand peace achieved through the danger of violence is not really a peace made at all. It is a provisional state of human entropy with respect to the appeasement of the tensions of difference and the possible uprising of transgressions and aggressions against subjective alterity, which depends on the ethico-philosophical essence of the cosmopolitical covenant of being. The condition of peace represents the satiating of a reaction to nullify the difference of difference. On the other hand a peace compelled by the dark side of the human spirit is perhaps the only *possible and natural* peace that could be rendered effective or legislated under circumstances within which no other decision or action is acceptable, viable, or defensible, given the alternative of violence. This of course begs the question of the constitutive force of community—whatever that IDEAL may entail as an affective identification of a subjective sense of belonging, a *being-at-home-in-the-world WITH OTHERS*—and the responsibility of its opening-up of the Self unto the difference of the Other. When these two states or conditions of existence, peace (community) and violence (war), are placed in direct opposition to each other, the ethical choice is clearly delineated by the power of a humanistic appeal, which is made to a *universal* and hence *moral will* denying the propriety of any transgression of subjectivity at all costs, even if this means suppressing human rights and freedoms for "the greater good." Community, then, is a matter of instilling and practicing a homogeneous concept of culture, a *general* culture whose model of a collective intersubjectivity acts as a unified resistance to the threat of alterity. The promoting of common points of recognition and identification within the ideologico-philosophical consciousness of its constituents in order to defy or suppress the propensity for violence against the threat of difference— or at the very least to quell the performativity of the desire to do so— establishes the psychic and figural ground for the foundations of friendship and belonging. Playing by the determinative ethics of these rules of consensus in the name of community and commonality, and also of communication, reduces the Other to the Same and minimizes the potential of a subjective resistance to the inclusion of contrariety within the sphere of a closed system of shared associations. This illusion of unity masks the radical violence of alterity and softens the risk of its provisional acceptance by replacing the shock of its reality with the comforting image of a single, harmonious group, a majority without difference. *They is Us.* The correlation of subjectivity relieves the discord of diversity because one has to inhere and adhere to the fundamental agreements of a consensual state of abstract universalism to be part of the general yet specific culture of a community. *I am We.* An ethical and philosophical contrition of sorts must be achieved in this case by the subject to ensure the manifestation of a "responsible response" that is itself a coming to peace of the Self with the avowable laws of a community and its effacing of difference. If we consider the Eurocentrism of the reasoning put forward for pursuing a universal alliance of humanity from the cosmopolitical view, and its prefiguring of new models of global gathering and world institutions like the United Nations and UNESCO, we cannot avoid addressing the ethico-philosophical focus of such an idea aimed at rearticulating the notion of an academic community, citizenship, and the right to knowledge as unconditional possibilities of self-expression both within and without the university after recognizing the multiplicity of difference throughout the disciplines constituting the Humanities today.

Notes

1. Derrida, "Of the humanities and the philosophical discipline: The right to philosophy and the cosmopolitical point of view." *Surfaces*, 4, 1.1.
2. See Jacques Derrida, "Où commence et comment finit un corps enseignant," in *Du droit à la philosophie*, (1990), pp. 111–153.
3. Jacques Derrida (Fall 1983). "The principle of reason: The university in the eyes of its pupils." *Diacritics*, 11.
4. See Derrida, "The principle of reason."
5. Peter Trifonas (1996). "The ends of pedagogy: From the dialectic of memory to the deconstruction of the institution." *Educational Theory*, 46: 3, 303–333. Peter Trifonas (2000), *The Ethics of Writing: Deconstruction and Pedagogy*. (Lanham, Maryland: Rowman & Littlefield); Peter Trifonas (forthcoming), "Deconstructive psychographies: Ethical discourse and the institution of the university," in *Discourse: Studies in the Cultural Politics of Education*; Peter Trifonas (forthcoming), "Teaching the other II: The ethics of writing and the violence of difference," in Gert Biesta and Denise Égea-Kuehne (eds). *Derrida and Education* (New York and London: Routledge); Peter Trifonas (forthcoming), "Technologies of reason: The grounding of academic responsibility beyond the principle of reason as the metaphysical foundation of the university," In Peter Trifonas *Revolutionary Pedagogies: Cultural Politics and the Discourse of Theory* (ed.), (New York and Routledge: Routledge); Peter Trifonas (forthcoming), "Reason unbound: Toward a re-grounding of the metaphysical foundations of the university," *Educational Theory*.
6. Trifonas, "The ends of pedagogy," p. 11.
7. "The principle of reason" we must remember was written and presented in April of 1983. At the time—the peaking of the "Cold War," this is a fair description of the homogeneous "conditionality" of the Western 'nation-states'"—most conspicuously exemplified by America and Russia—that according to Derrida were spending in total upward of "two million dollars a minute" on the manufacture of armaments alone.
8. Jacques Derrida (1992). *The Other Heading: Reflections of Today's Europe*. Translated by Pascale-Anne Brault and Michael Naas (Bloomington: Indiana University Press), p. 41.
9. Derrida, "The principle of reason," p. 16.
10. Ibid., p. 16.
11. Ibid., p. 16.
12. Jacques Derrida (1978). "Violence and metaphysics: An essay on the thought of Emmanuel Levinas," in Alan Bass (trans.), *Writing and Difference* (Chicago: University of Chicago Press), p. 80.

13. Derrida, "The principle of reason," p. 16.
14. Derrida, "The principle of reason," p. 19.
15. Ibid., p. 17.
16. Gianni Vattimo (1988). *The End of Modernity: Nihilism and Hermeneutics in Postodern Culture.* Translated by Jon R. Snyder (Baltimore: Johns Hopkins University Press), p. 172.
17. See Rodolphe Gasché (1994). *Inventions of Difference: On Jacques Derrida* (Cambridge, MA: Harvard University Press).
18. Derrida, "The principle of reason," pp. 18–19.
19. Derrida, "Of the humanities and the philosophical discipline," p. 2.
20. Ibid.
21. Ibid.
22. Ibid.
23. Ibid.
24. The "Roundtable discussion" on Jacques Derrida's "Des humanités et de la discipline philosophiques"/"Of the humanities and philosophical disciplines" in *Surfaces* Vol. VI.108 (v.1.0A-16/08/1996), 5–40 involved Hazard Adams, Ernst Behler, Hendrick Birus, Jacques Derrida, Wolfgang Iser, Ludwig Pfeiffer, Bill Readings, Ching-hsien Wang, and Pauline Yu. All further quotations from this text are comments made by Derrida. The page references are from the website version of the text to found at http://tornade.ere.umontreal.ca/guedon/ Surfaces/vol6/derrida.html. This endnote refers to a quotation from page 3.
25. Ibid., p. 3.
26. Ibid., p. 3.
27. Derrida, "Of the Humanities and the Philosophical Discipline," p. 2.
28. Ibid., p. 2.
29. Ibid., p. 4.
30. Ibid., p. 3.
31. Ibid., p. 3.
32. Ibid., p. 3.
33. Immanuel Kant cited in Derrida, "Of the humanities and the philosophical discipline," p. 3.
34. Ibid., p. 3.
35. Ibid., p. 3.
36. Ibid., p. 3.
37. Ibid., p. 3.

INDEX